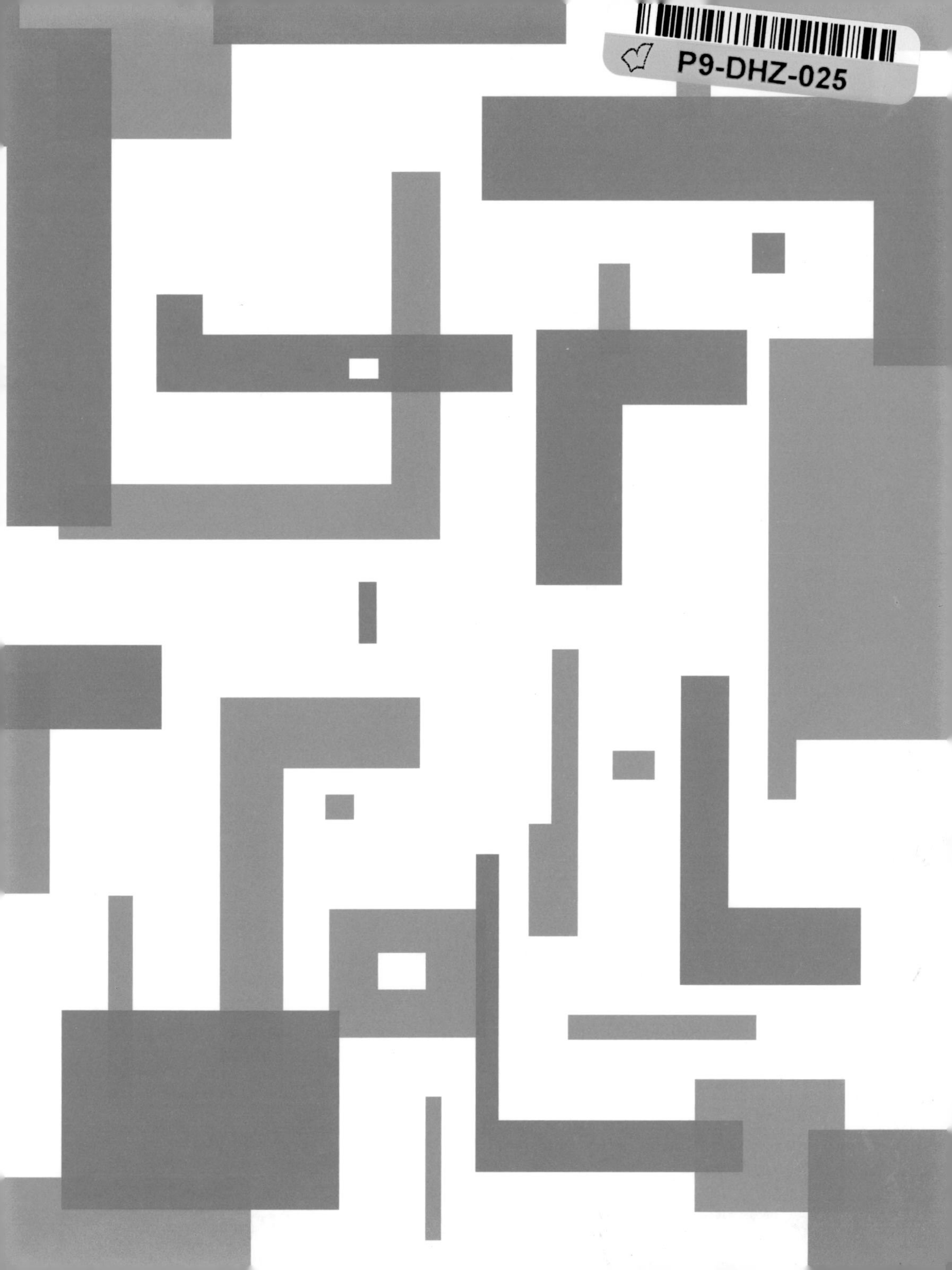

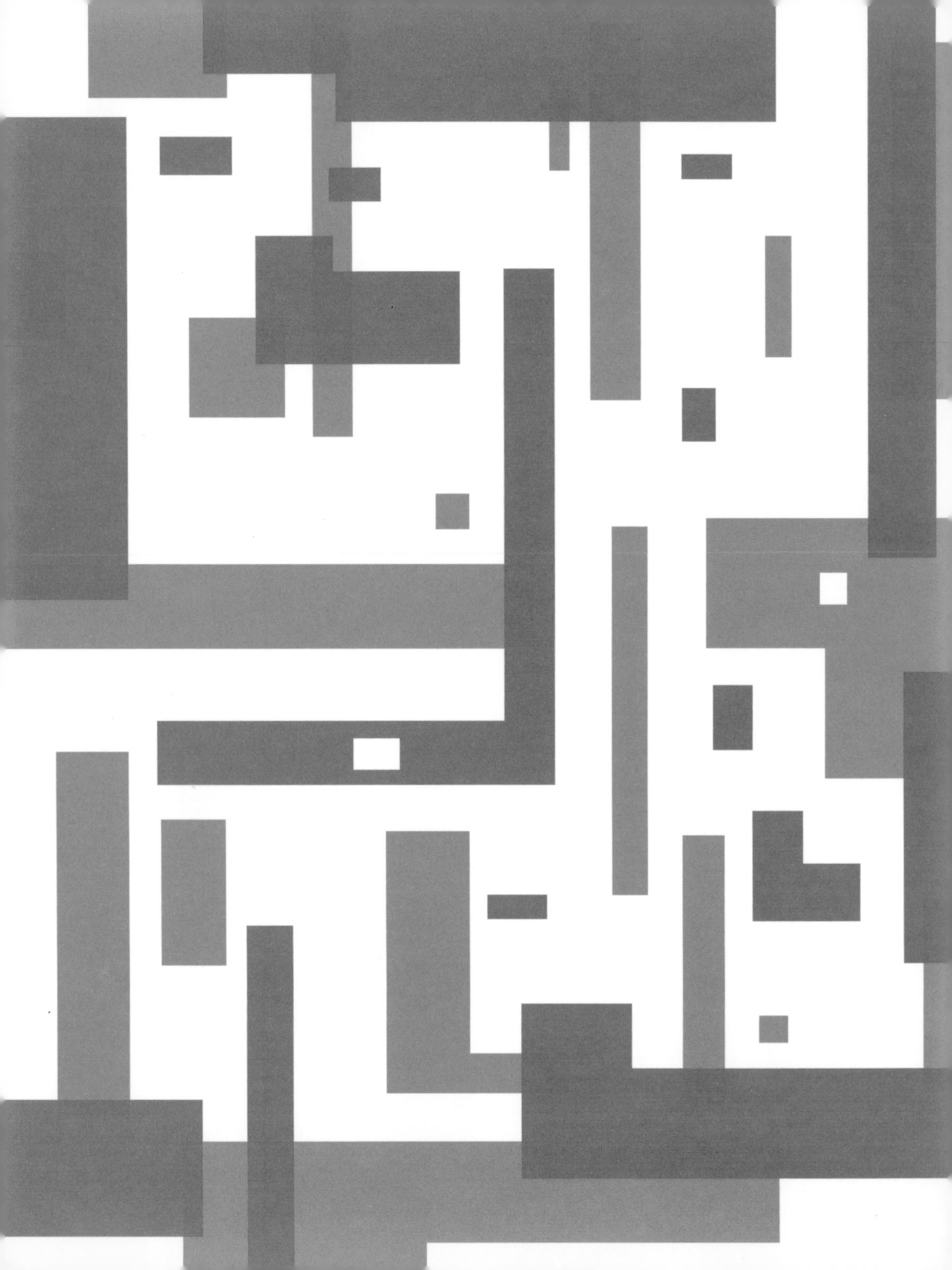

EMPIRE
STATE

Editor: Sheila Keenan
Design Manager: Neil Egan
Production Manager: Alison Gervais

Library of Congress Control Number: 2010934622

ISBN 978-0-8109-9747-9

Printed and bound in Singapore

10 9 8 7 6 5 4 3 2 1

Abrams ComicArts books are available at special discounts when purchased in quantity for premiums and promotions as well as fundraising or educational use. Special editions can also be created to specification. For details, contact specialmarkets@abramsbooks.com or the address below.

THE ART OF BOOKS SINCE 1949

115 West 18th Street
New York, NY 10011
www.abramsbooks.com

EMPIRE STATE

A LOVE STORY (OR NOT)

JASON SHIGA

COLORS BY JOHN PHAM

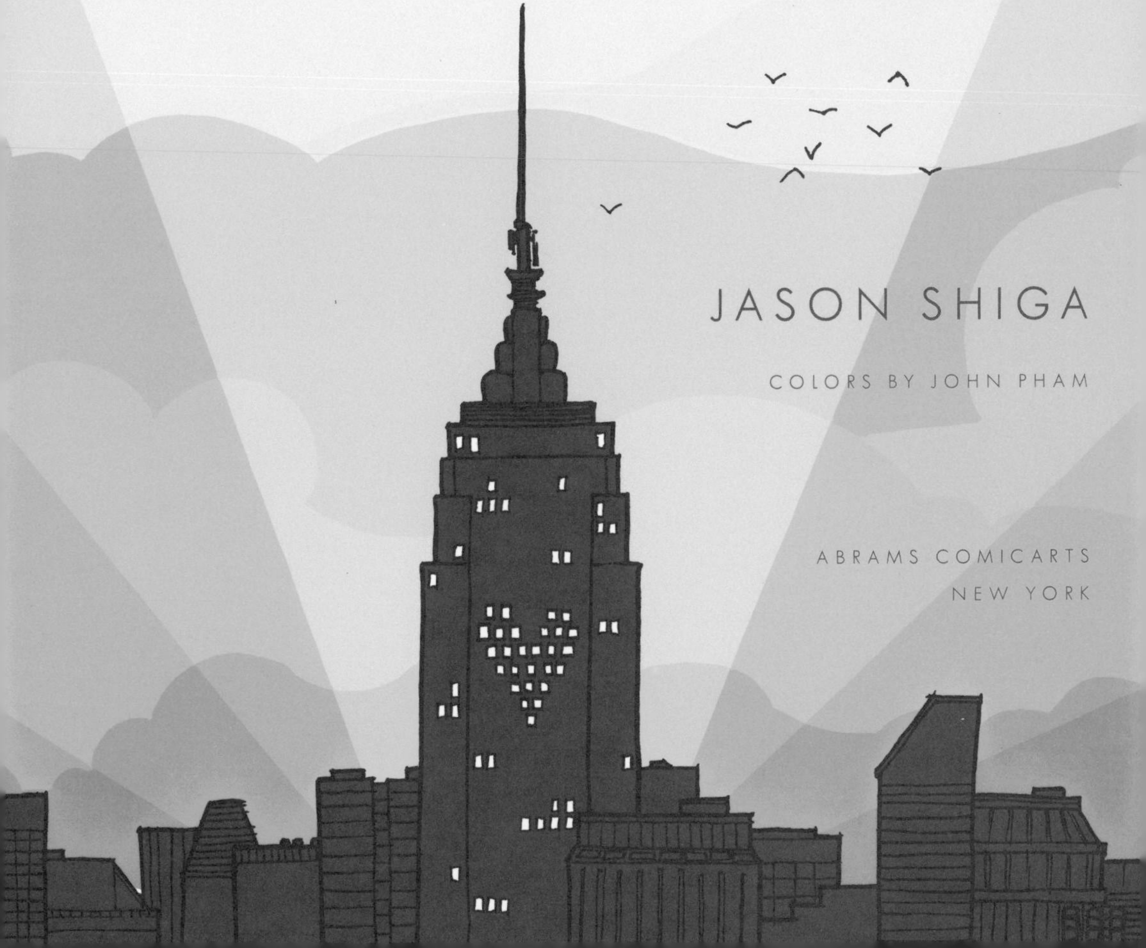

ABRAMS COMICARTS
NEW YORK

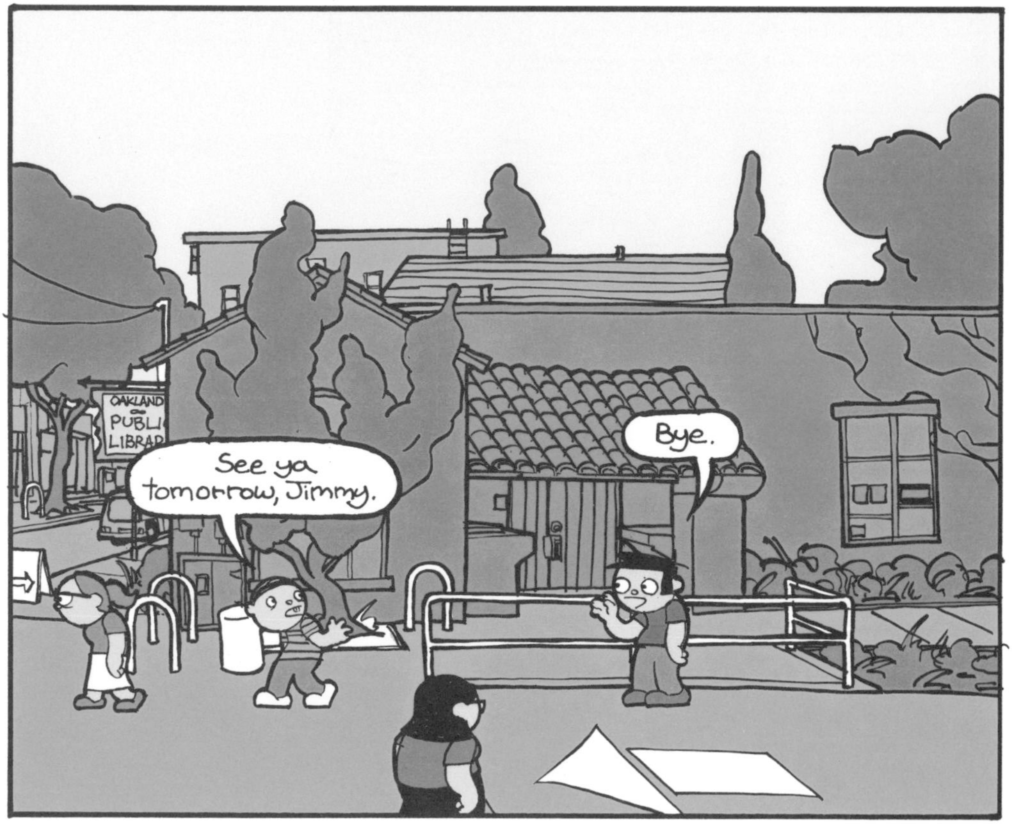
OAKLAND PUBLIC LIBRARY
See ya tomorrow, Jimmy.
Bye.

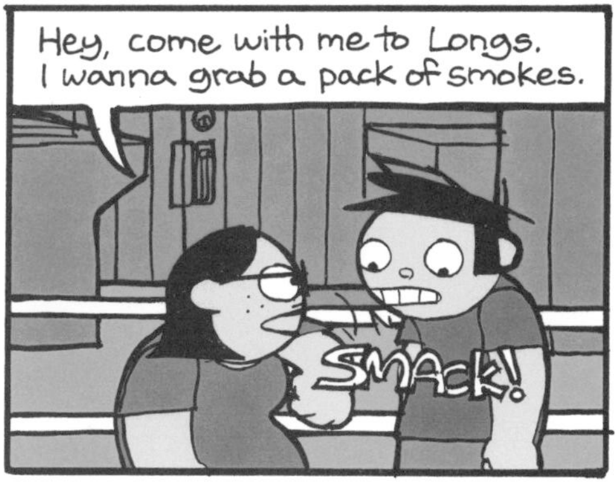
Hey, come with me to Longs. I wanna grab a pack of smokes.
SMACK!

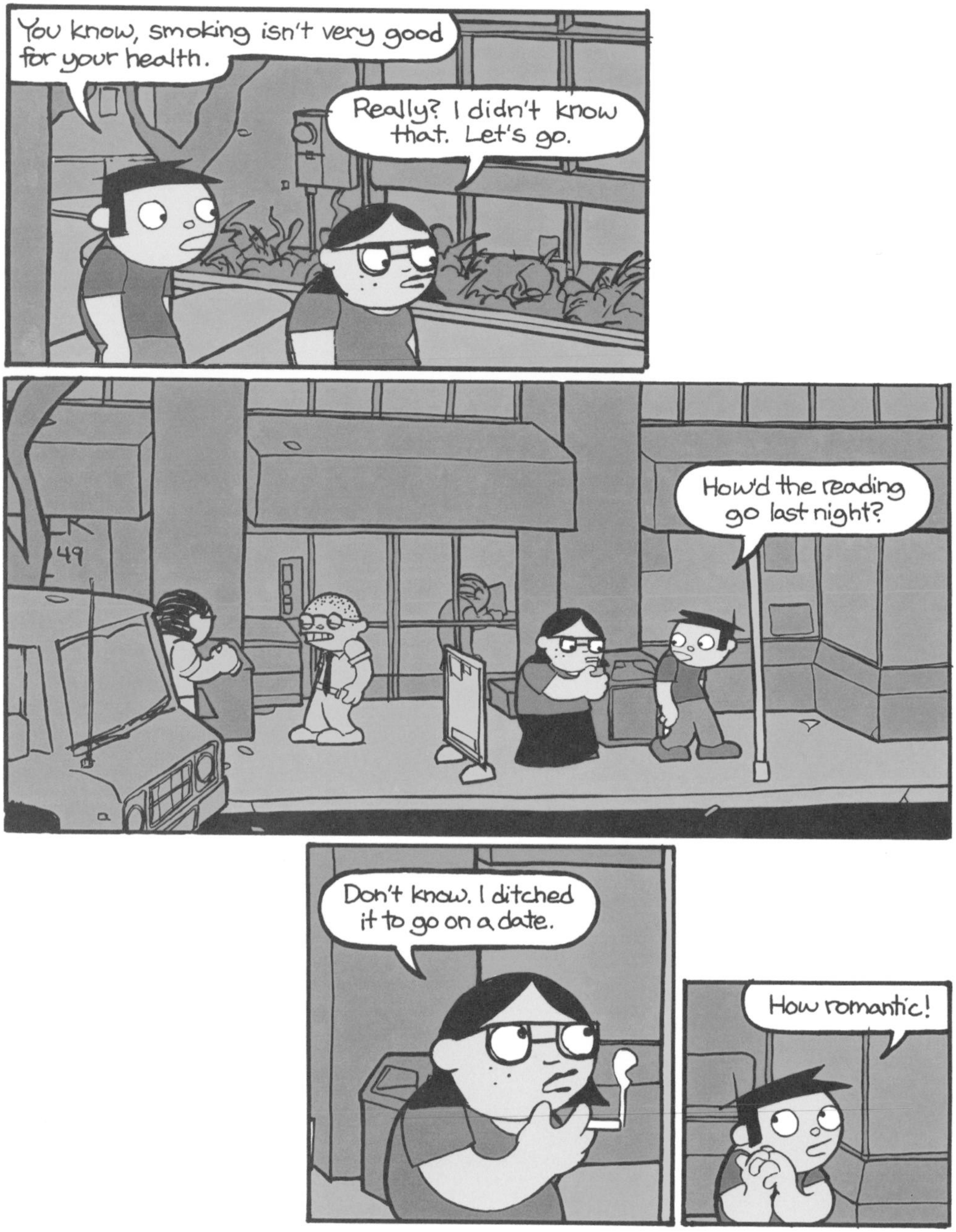
You know, smoking isn't very good for your health.
Really? I didn't know that. Let's go.
How'd the reading go last night?
Don't know. I ditched it to go on a date.
How romantic!

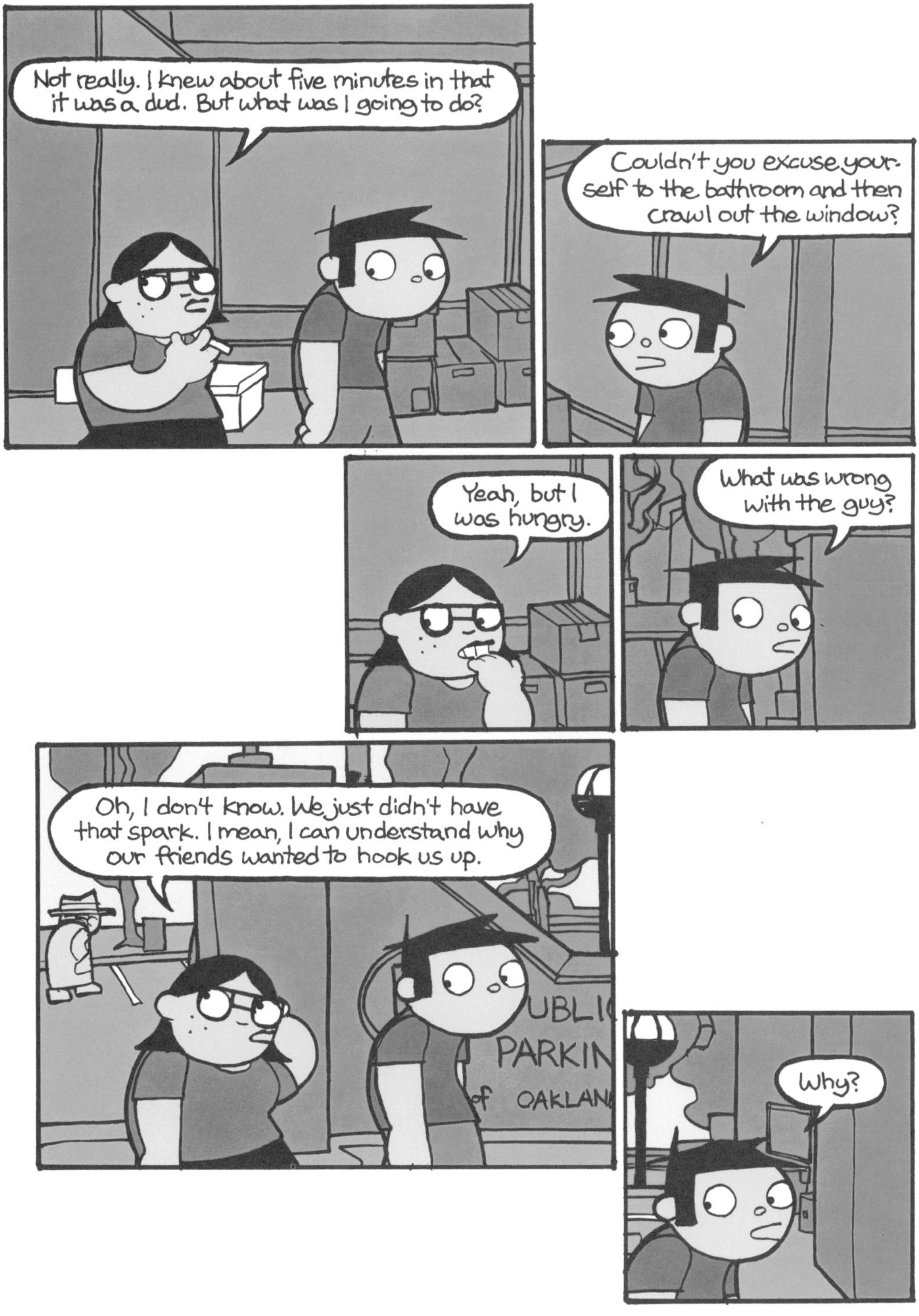
Not really. I knew about five minutes in that it was a dud. But what was I going to do?
Couldn't you excuse your-self to the bathroom and then crawl out the window?
Yeah, but I was hungry.
What was wrong with the guy?
Oh, I don't know. We just didn't have that spark. I mean, I can understand why our friends wanted to hook us up.
UBLI
PARKIN
of OAKLAN
Why?

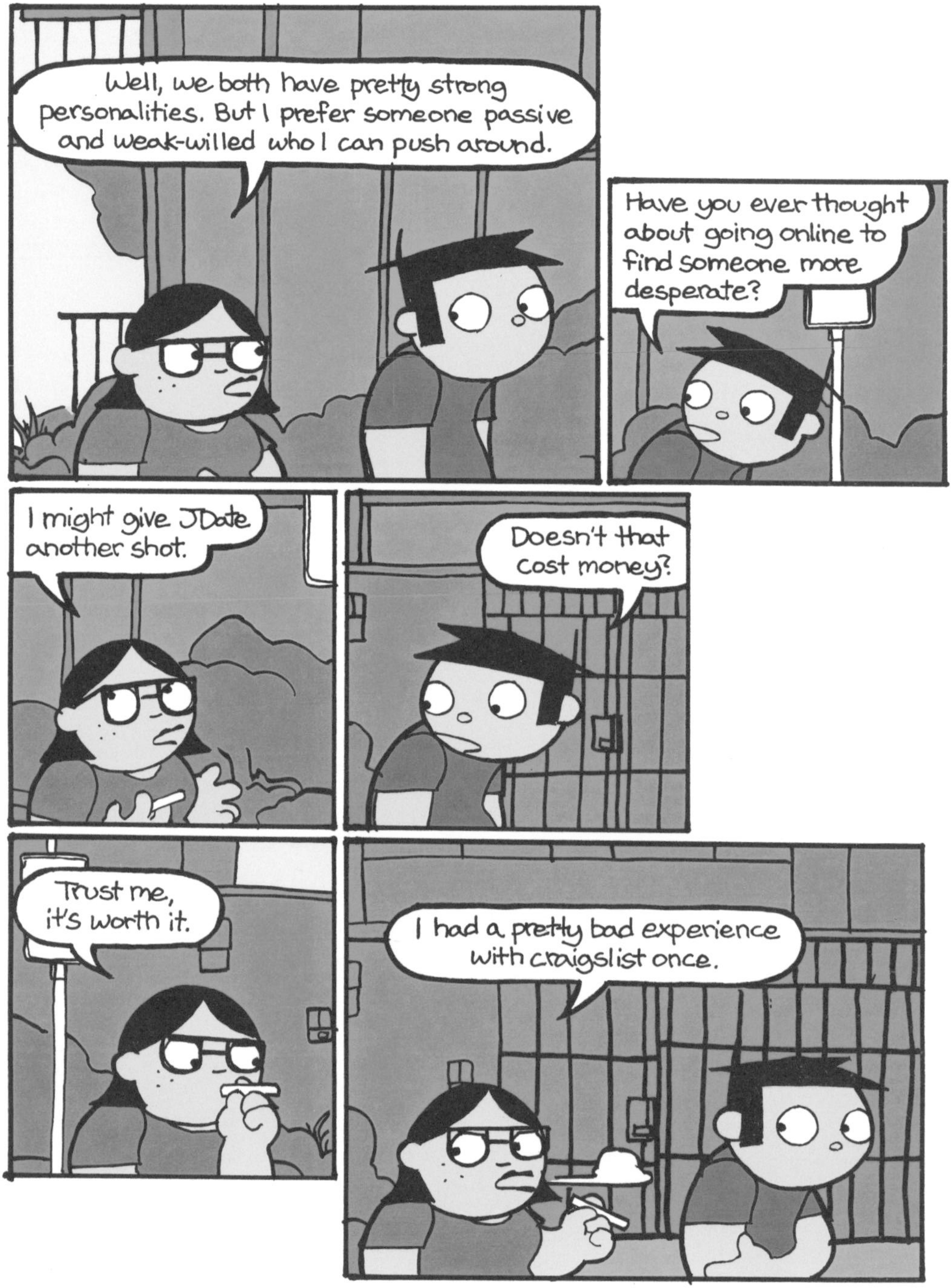
Well, we both have pretty strong personalities. But I prefer someone passive and weak-willed who I can push around.
Have you ever thought about going online to find someone more desperate?
I might give JDate another shot.
Doesn't that cost money?
Trust me, it's worth it.
I had a pretty bad experience with craigslist once.

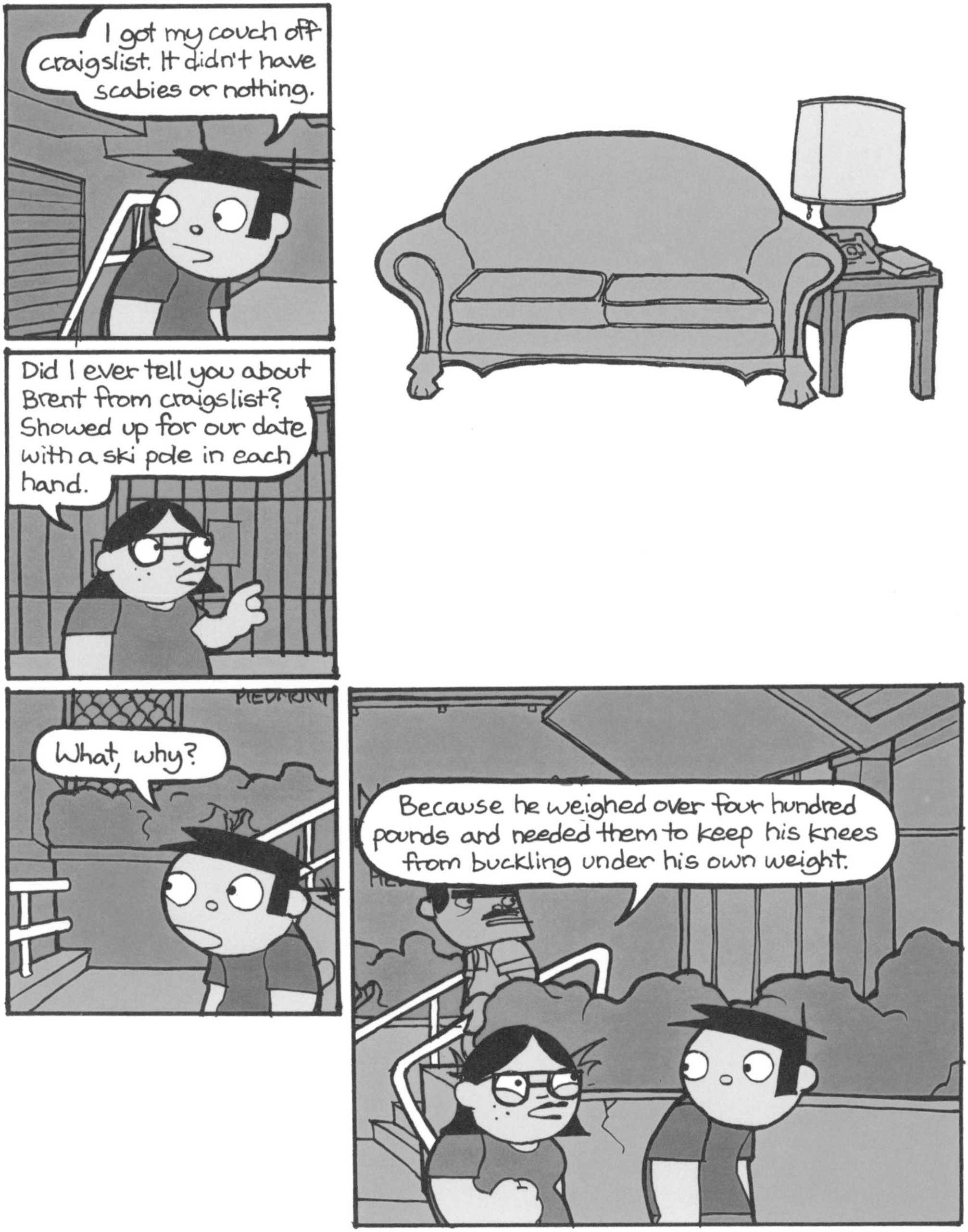
I got my couch off craigslist. It didn't have scabies or nothing.
Did I ever tell you about Brent from craigslist? Showed up for our date with a ski pole in each hand.
What, why?
Because he weighed over four hundred pounds and needed them to keep his knees from buckling under his own weight.

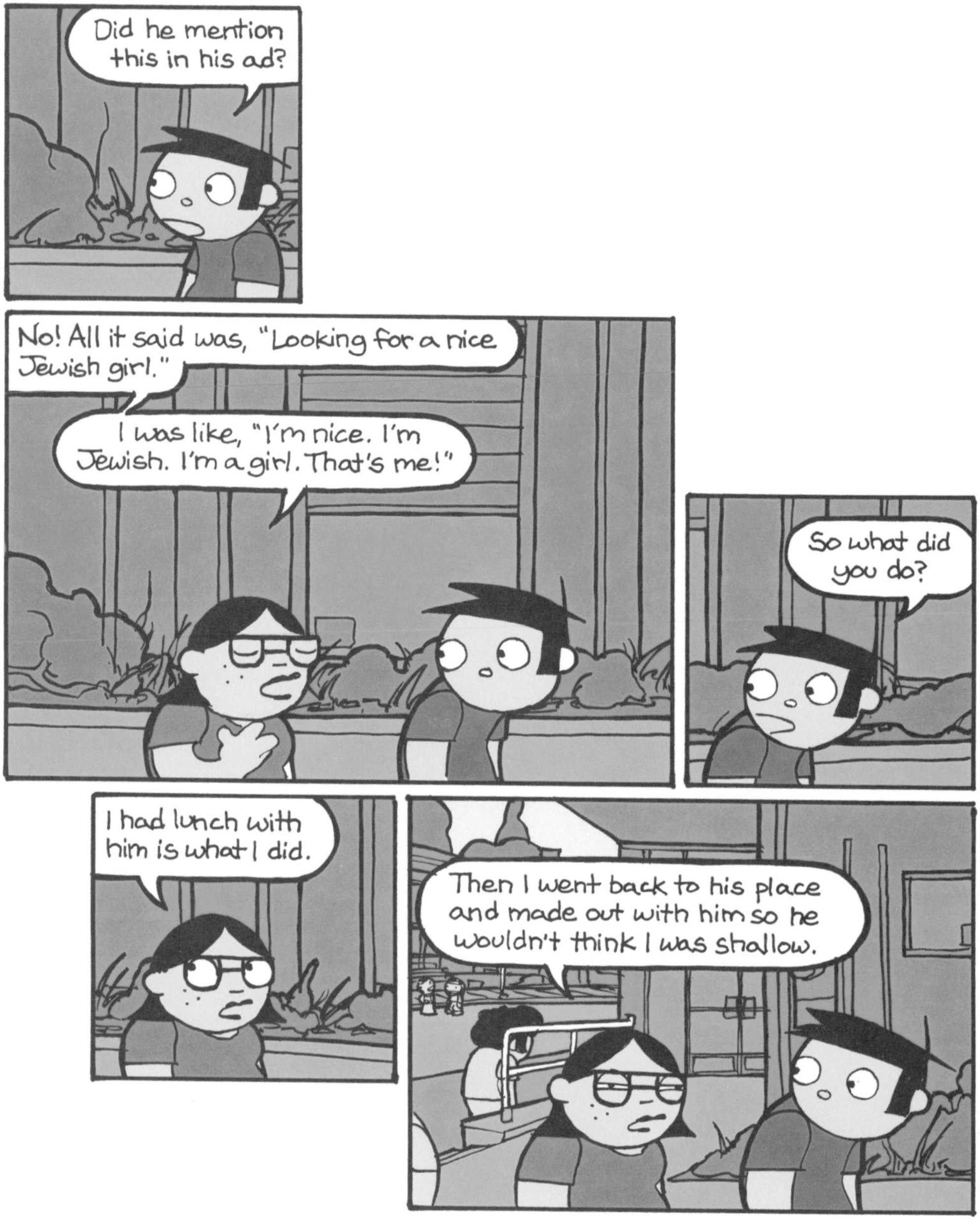
Did he mention this in his ad?
No! All it said was, "Looking for a nice Jewish girl."
I was like, "I'm nice. I'm Jewish. I'm a girl. That's me!"
So what did you do?
I had lunch with him is what I did.
Then I went back to his place and made out with him so he wouldn't think I was shallow.

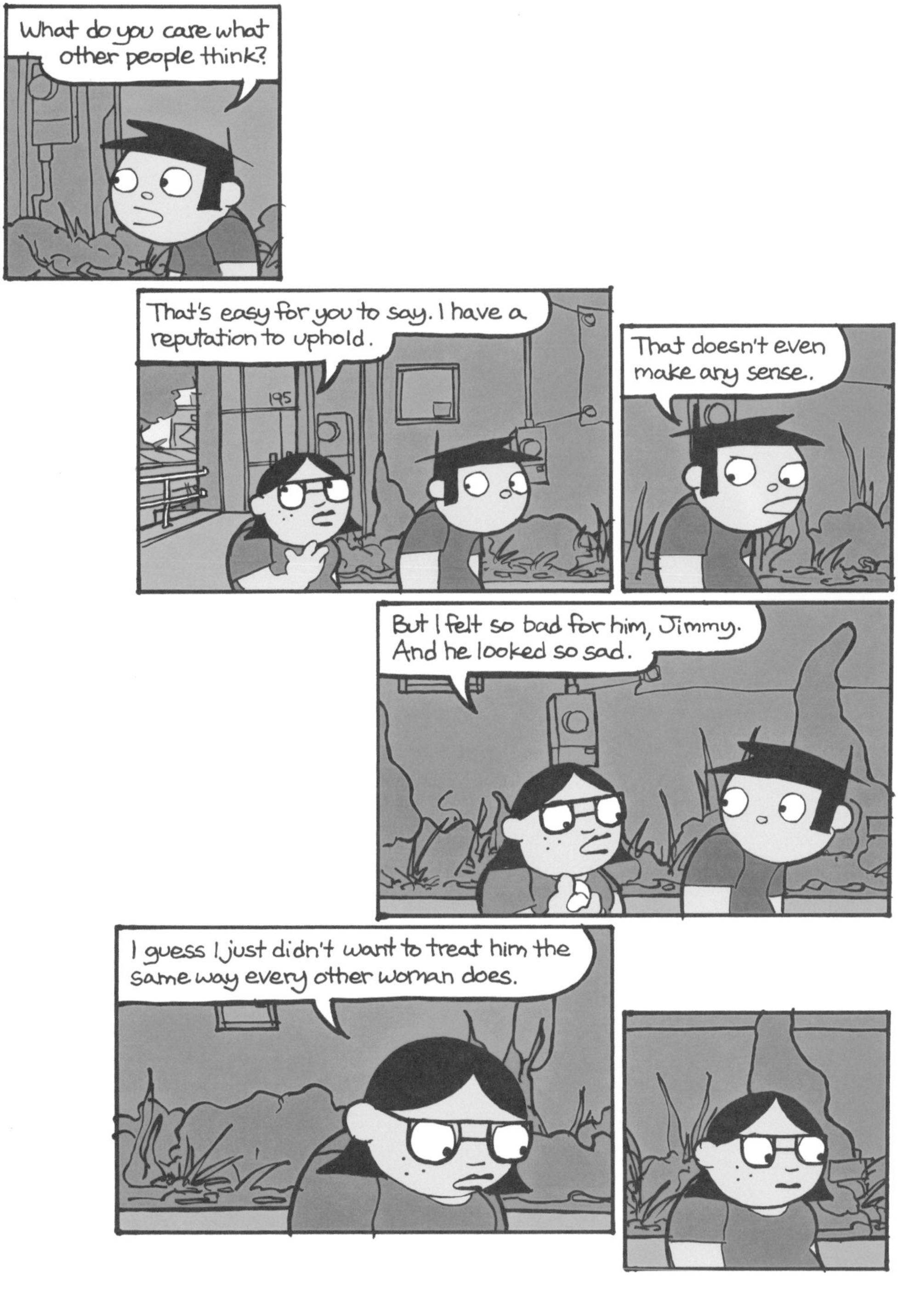
What do you care what other people think?
That's easy for you to say. I have a reputation to uphold.
195
That doesn't even make any sense.
But I felt so bad for him, Jimmy. And he looked so sad.
I guess I just didn't want to treat him the same way every other woman does.

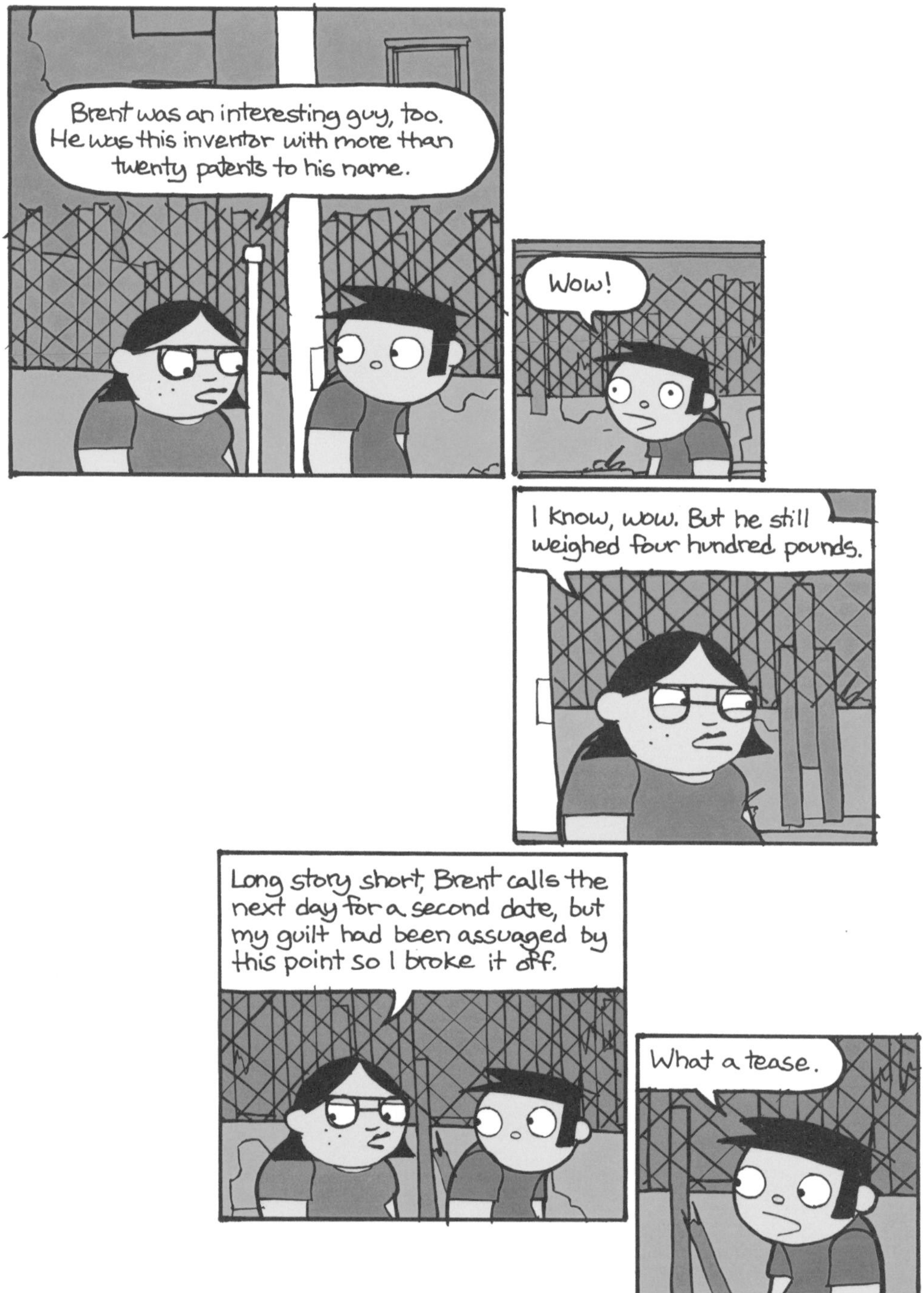
Brent was an interesting guy, too. He was this inventor with more than twenty patents to his name.
Wow!
I know, wow. But he still weighed four hundred pounds.
Long story short, Brent calls the next day for a second date, but my guilt had been assuaged by this point so I broke it off.
What a tease.

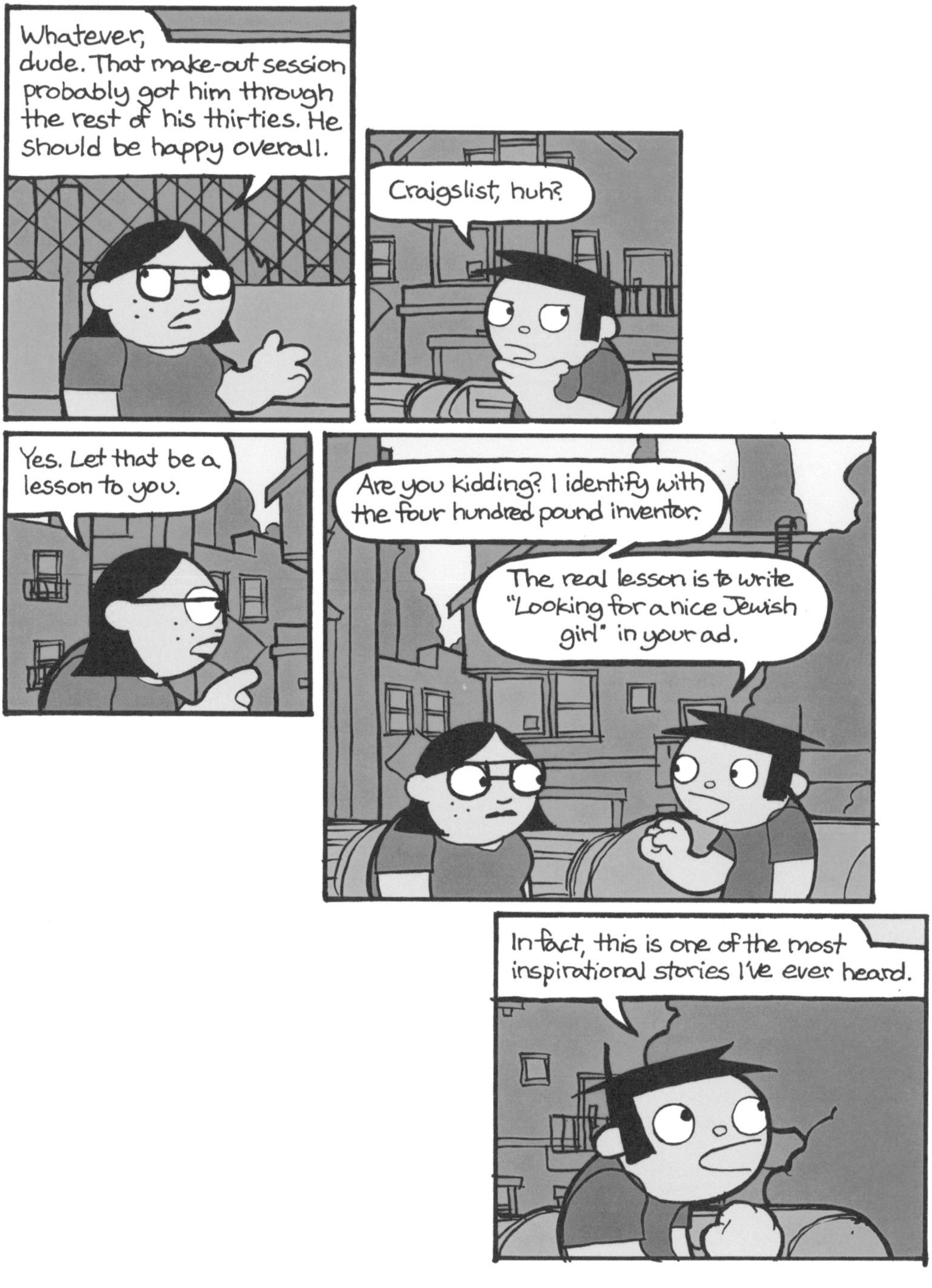
Whatever, dude. That make-out session probably got him through the rest of his thirties. He should be happy overall.
Craigslist, huh?
Yes. Let that be a lesson to you.
Are you kidding? I identify with the four hundred pound inventor.
The real lesson is to write "Looking for a nice Jewish girl" in your ad.
In fact, this is one of the most inspirational stories I've ever heard.

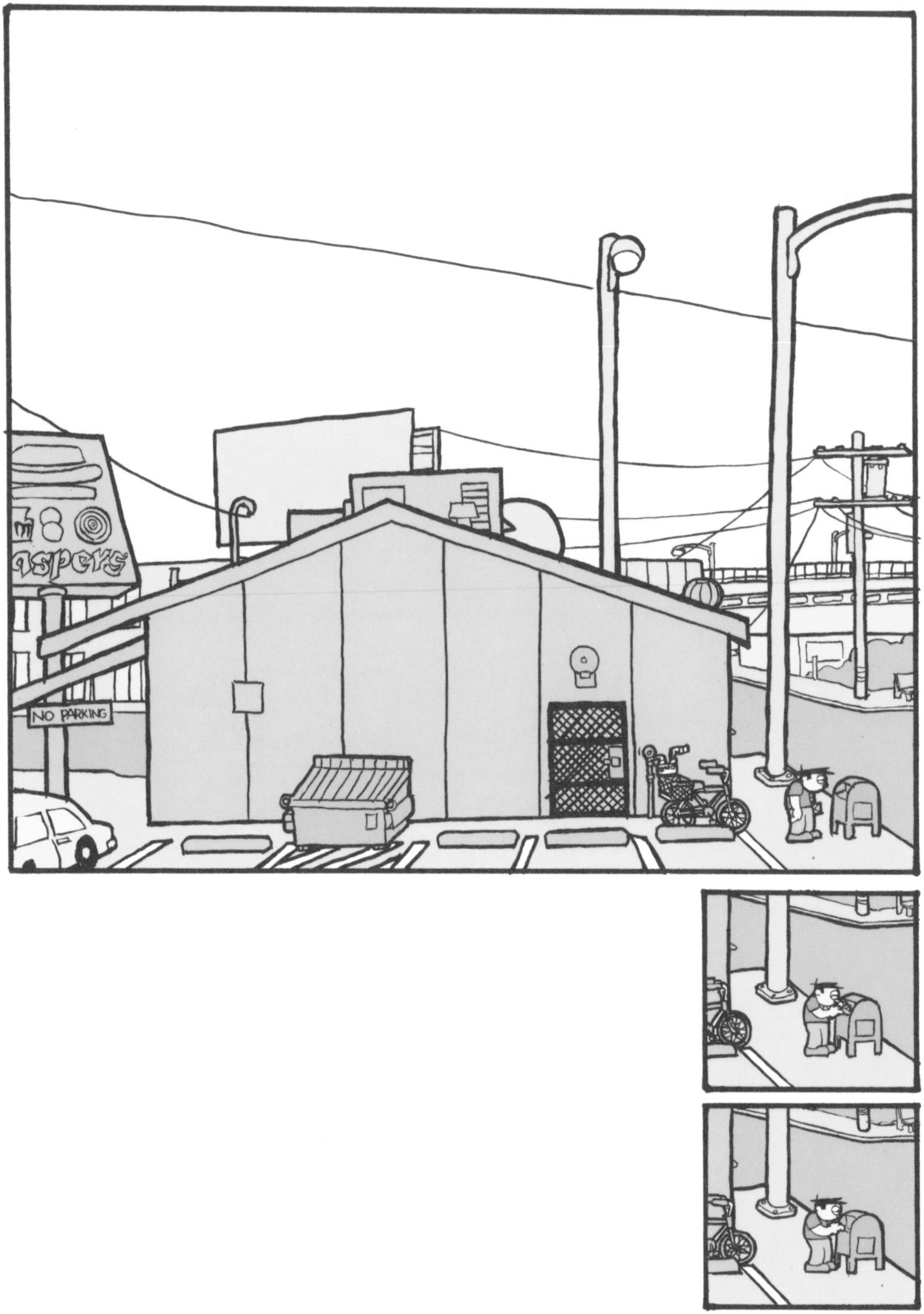
NO PARKING

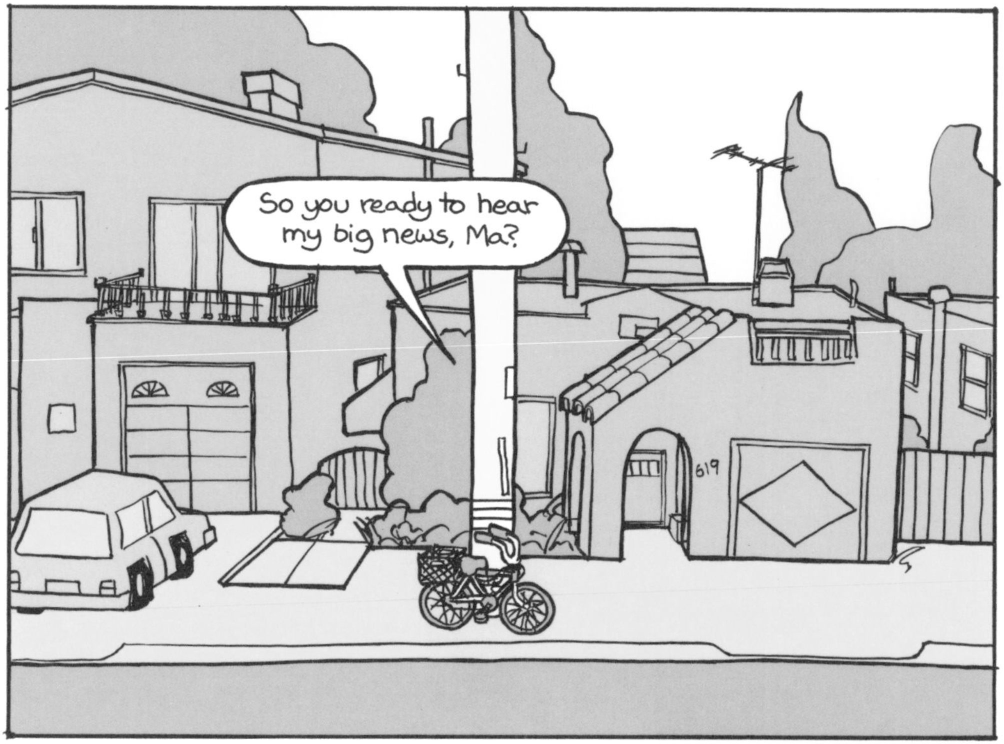
So you ready to hear my big news, Ma?
619

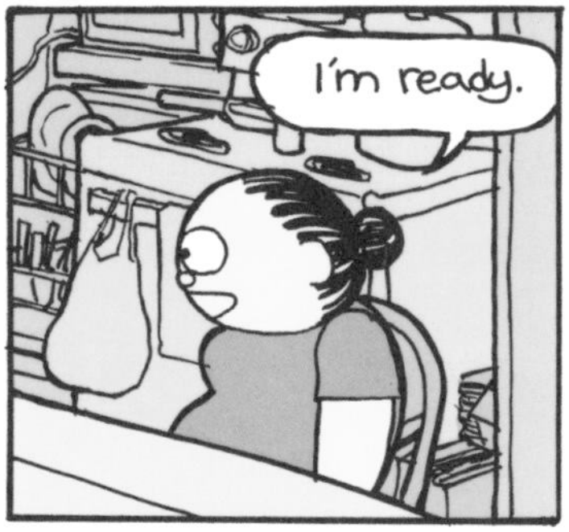
I'm ready.

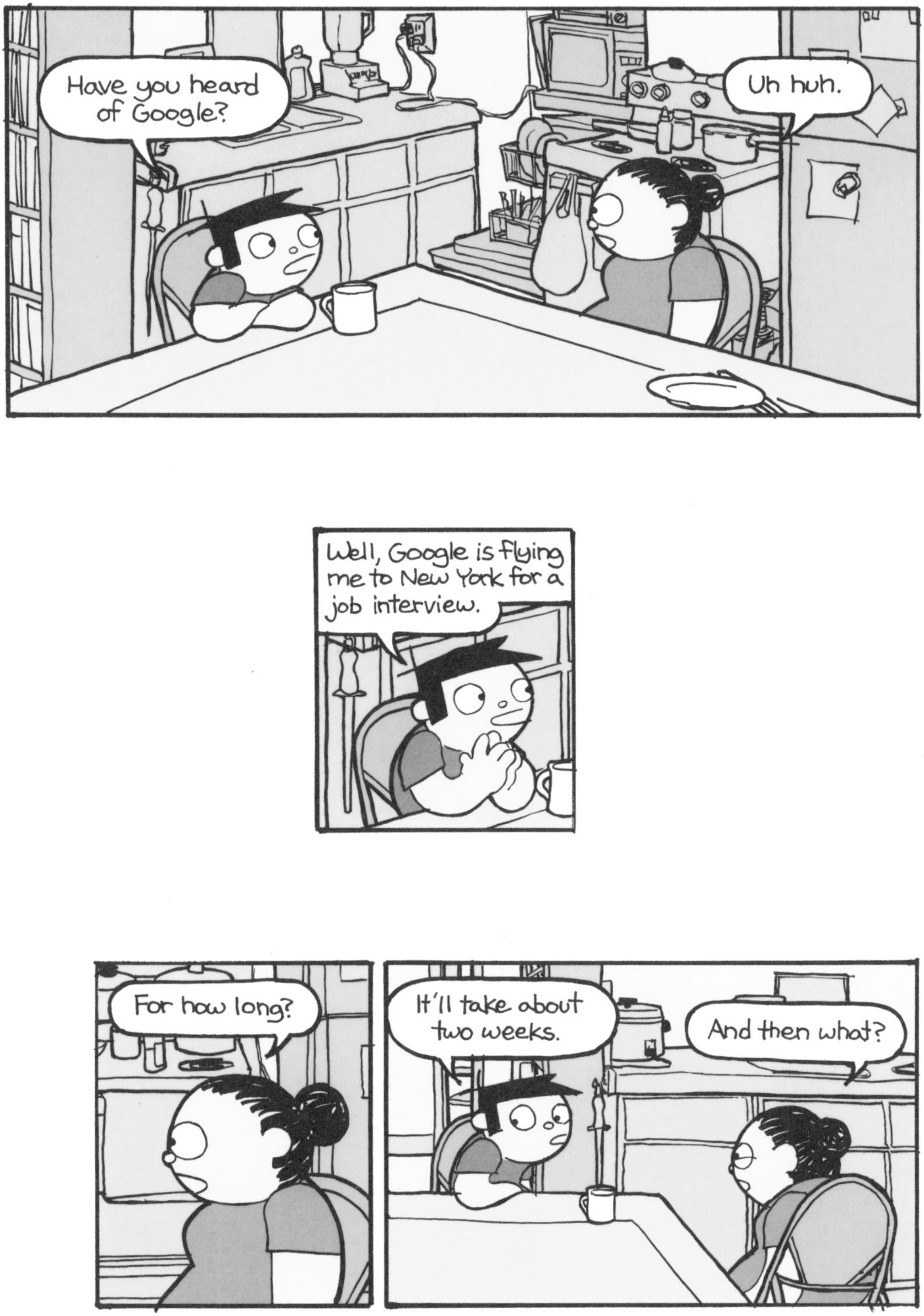
Have you heard of Google?
Uh huh.
Well, Google is flying me to New York for a job interview.
For how long?
It'll take about two weeks.
And then what?

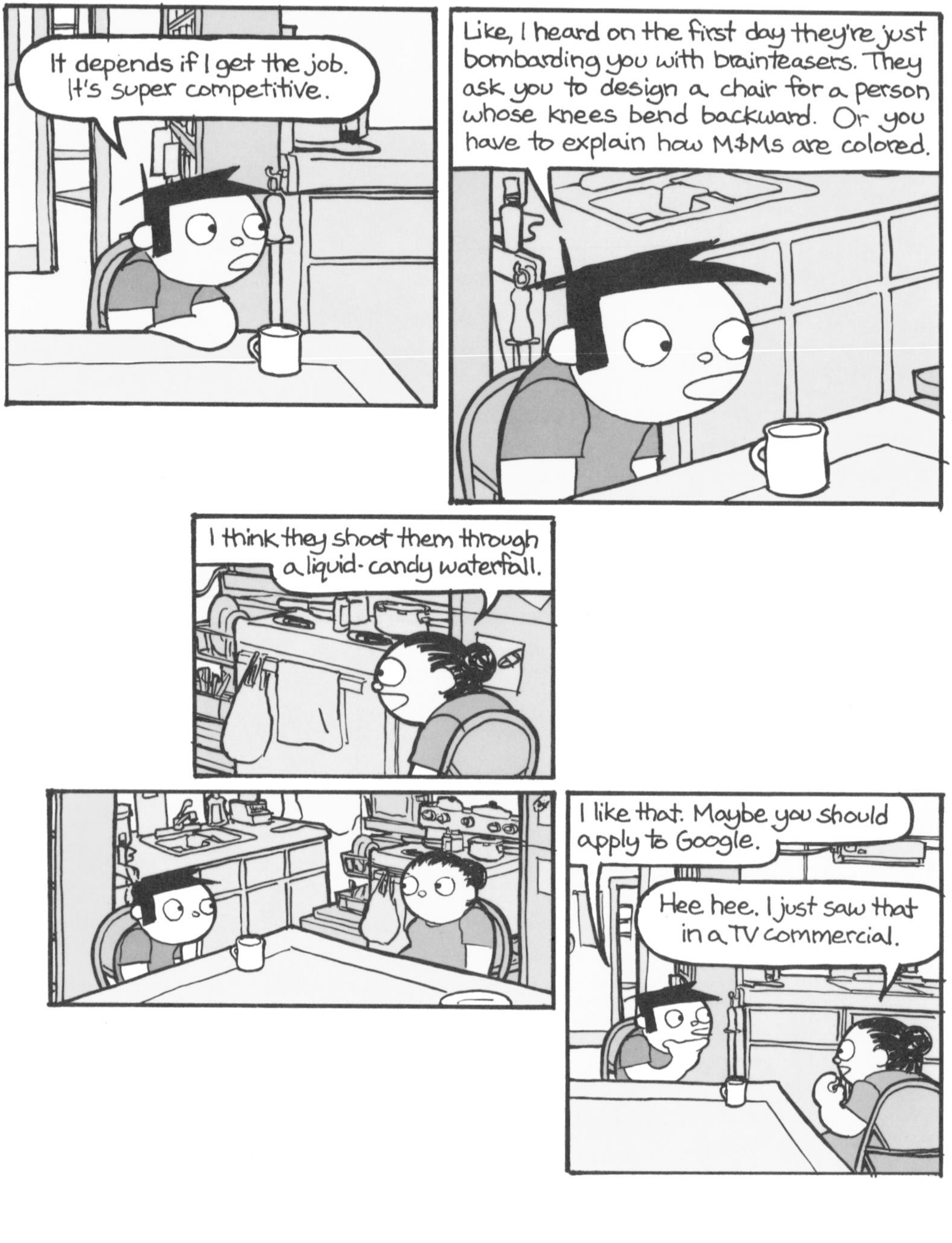
It depends if I get the job. It's super competitive.
Like, I heard on the first day they're just bombarding you with brainteasers. They ask you to design a chair for a person whose knees bend backward. Or you have to explain how M$Ms are colored.
I think they shoot them through a liquid-candy waterfall.
I like that. Maybe you should apply to Google.
Hee hee. I just saw that in a TV commercial.

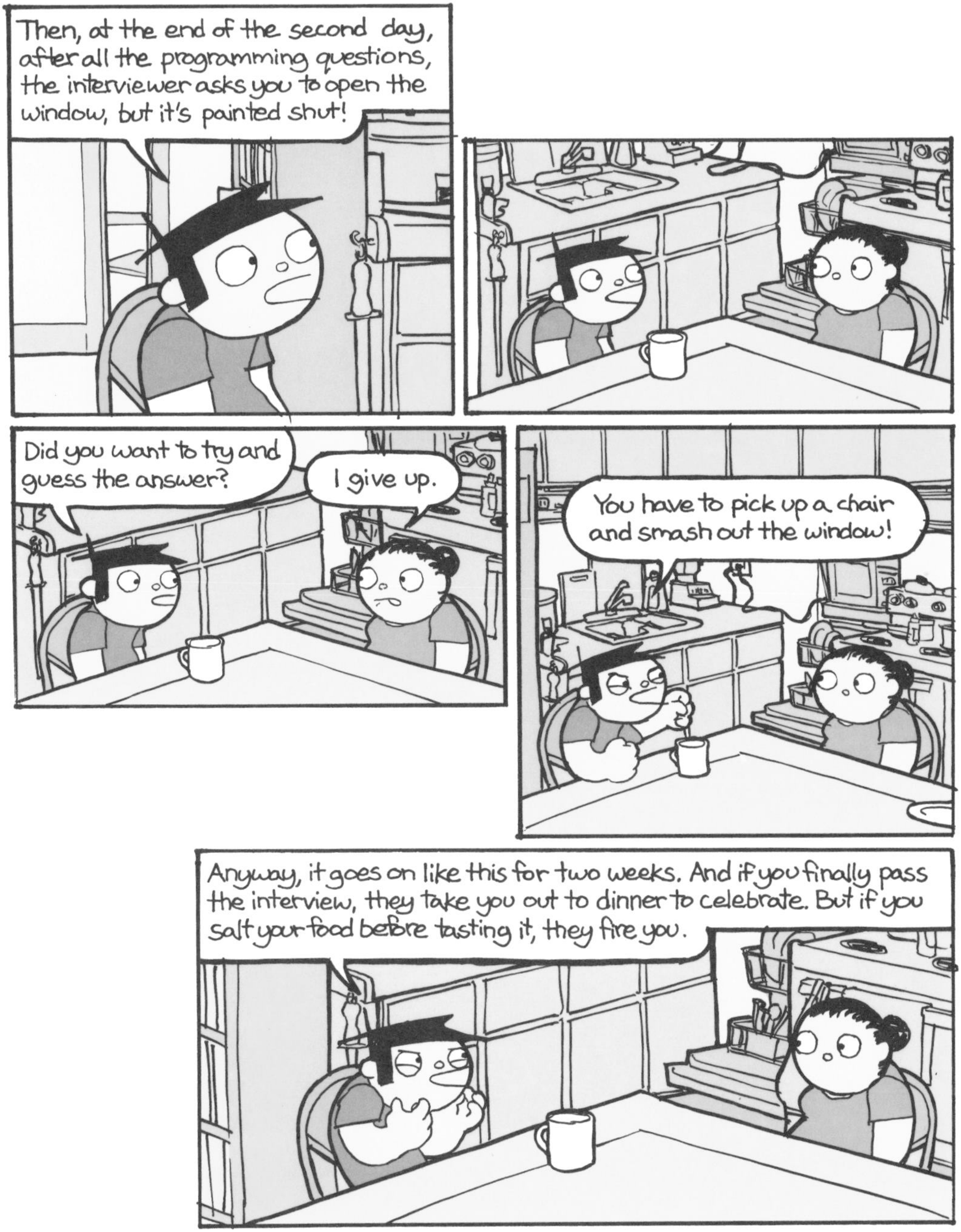
Then, at the end of the second day, after all the programming questions, the interviewer asks you to open the window, but it's painted shut!
Did you want to try and guess the answer?
I give up.
You have to pick up a chair and smash out the window!
Anyway, it goes on like this for two weeks. And if you finally pass the interview, they take you out to dinner to celebrate. But if you salt your food before tasting it, they fire you.

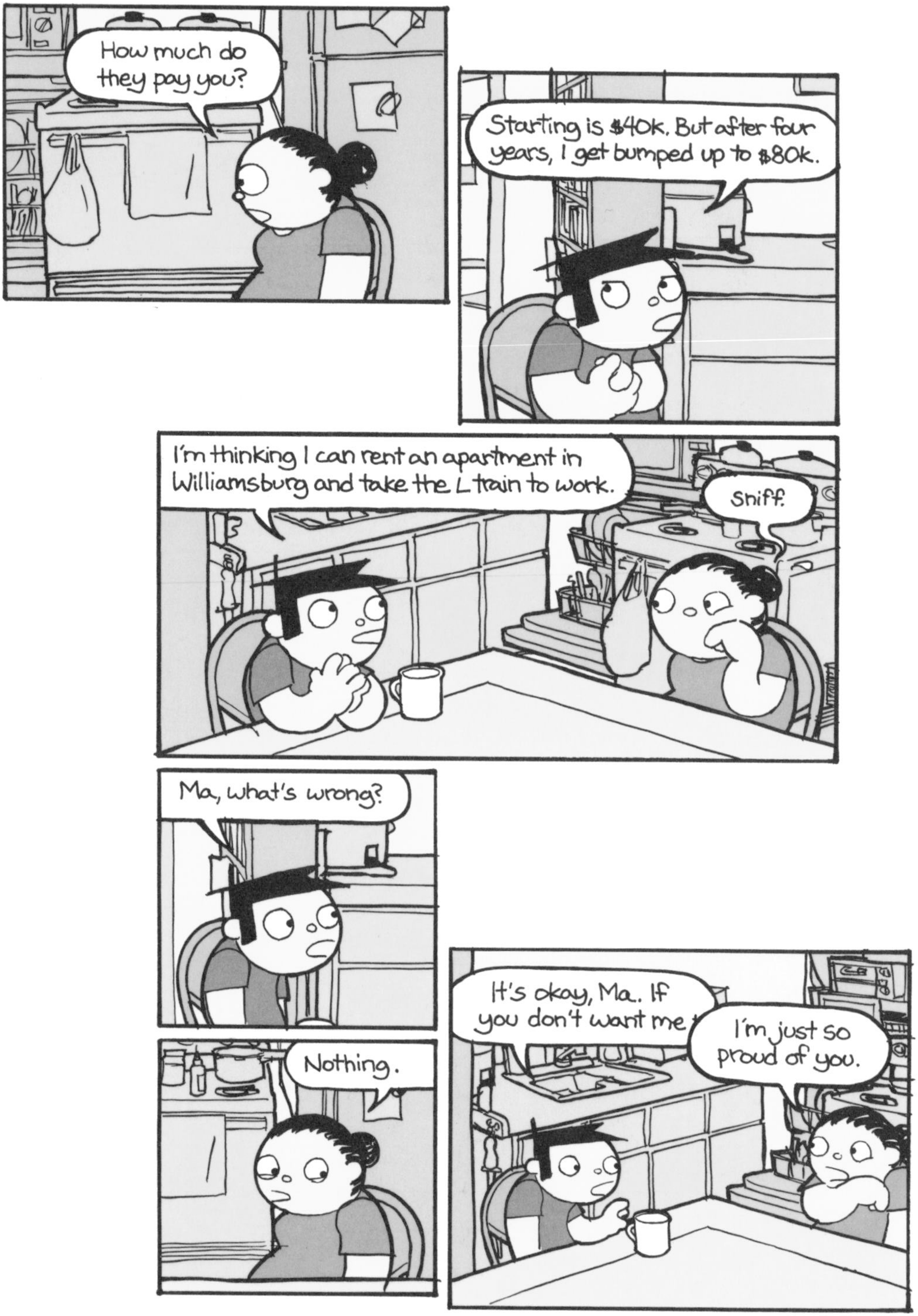
How much do they pay you?
Starting is $40k. But after four years, I get bumped up to $80k.
I'm thinking I can rent an apartment in Williamsburg and take the L train to work.
Sniff.
Ma, what's wrong?
Nothing.
It's okay, Ma.. If you don't want me
I'm just so proud of you.

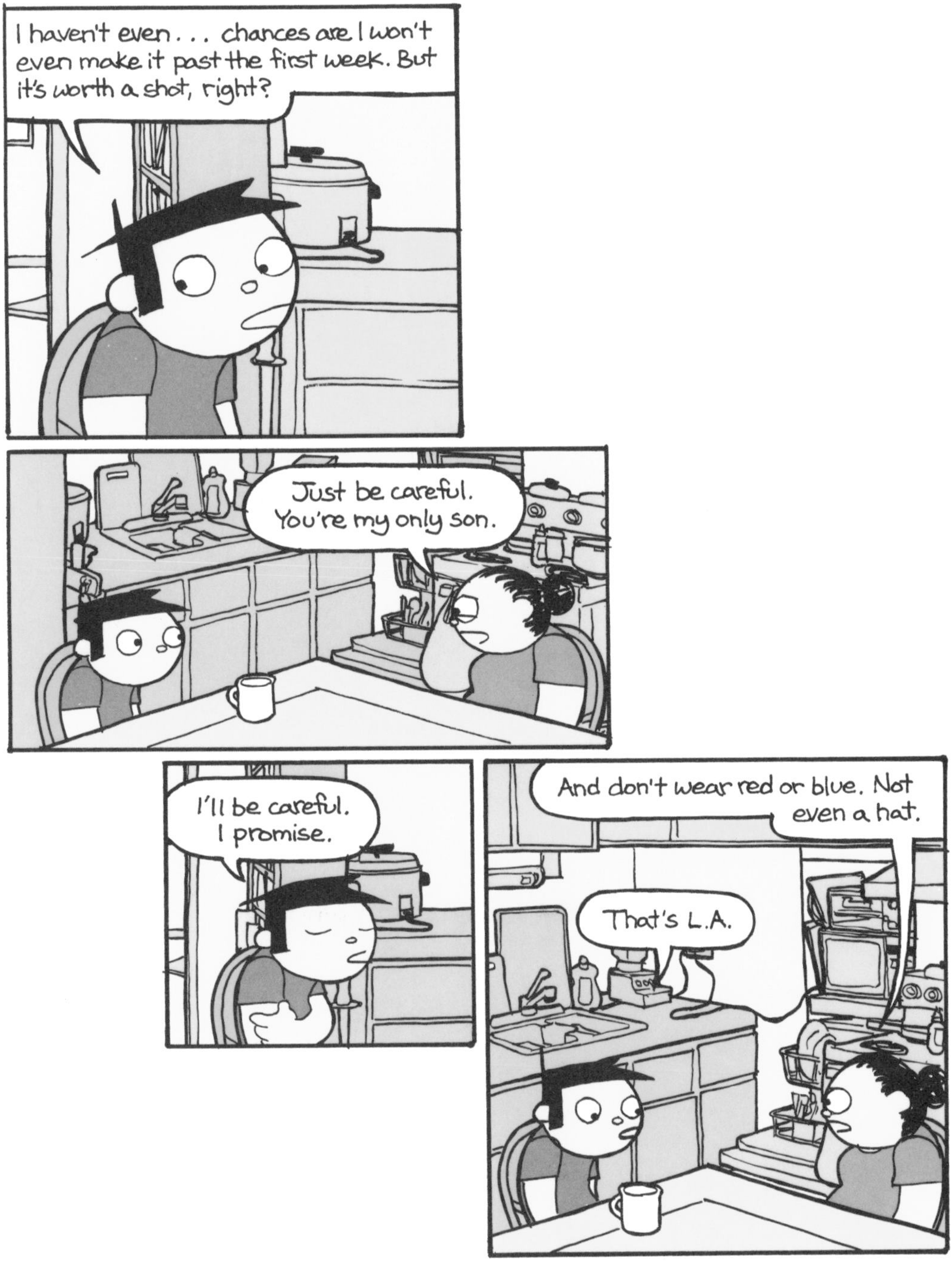
I haven't even . . . chances are I won't even make it past the first week. But it's worth a shot, right?
Just be careful. You're my only son.
I'll be careful. I promise.
And don't wear red or blue. Not even a hat.
That's L.A.

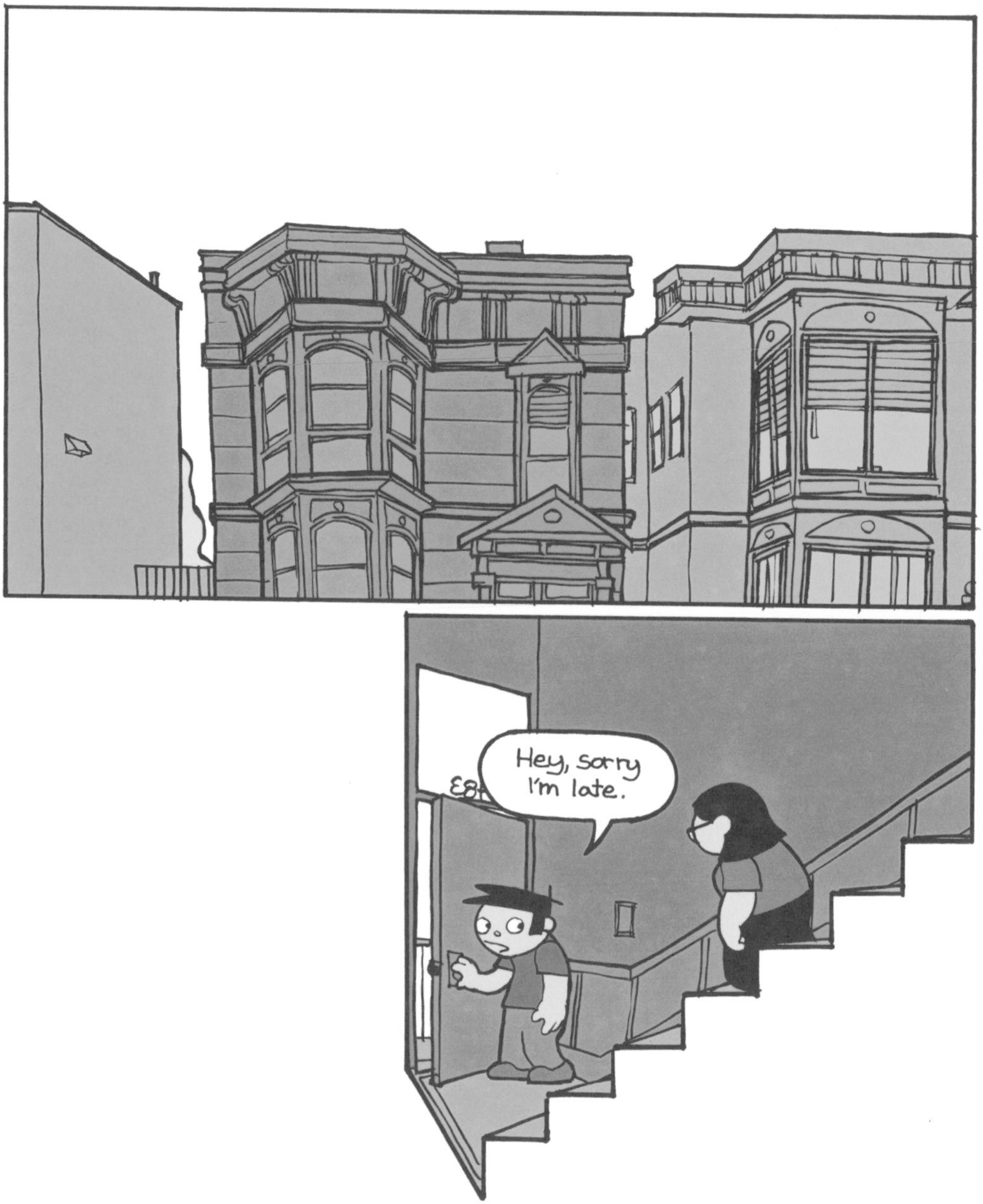
Hey, sorry I'm late.

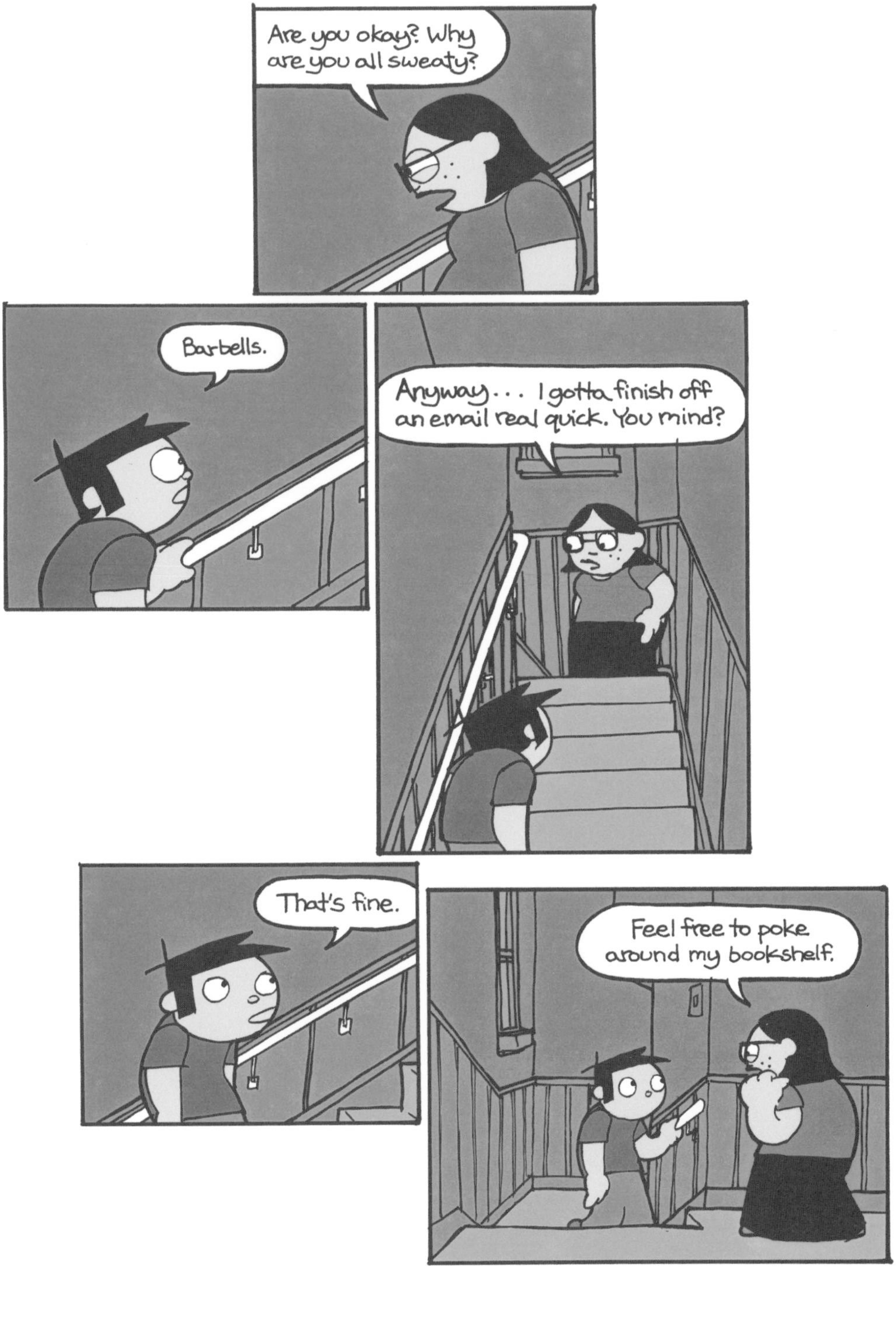
Are you okay? Why are you all sweaty?
Barbells.
Anyway... I gotta finish off an email real quick. You mind?
That's fine.
Feel free to poke around my bookshelf.

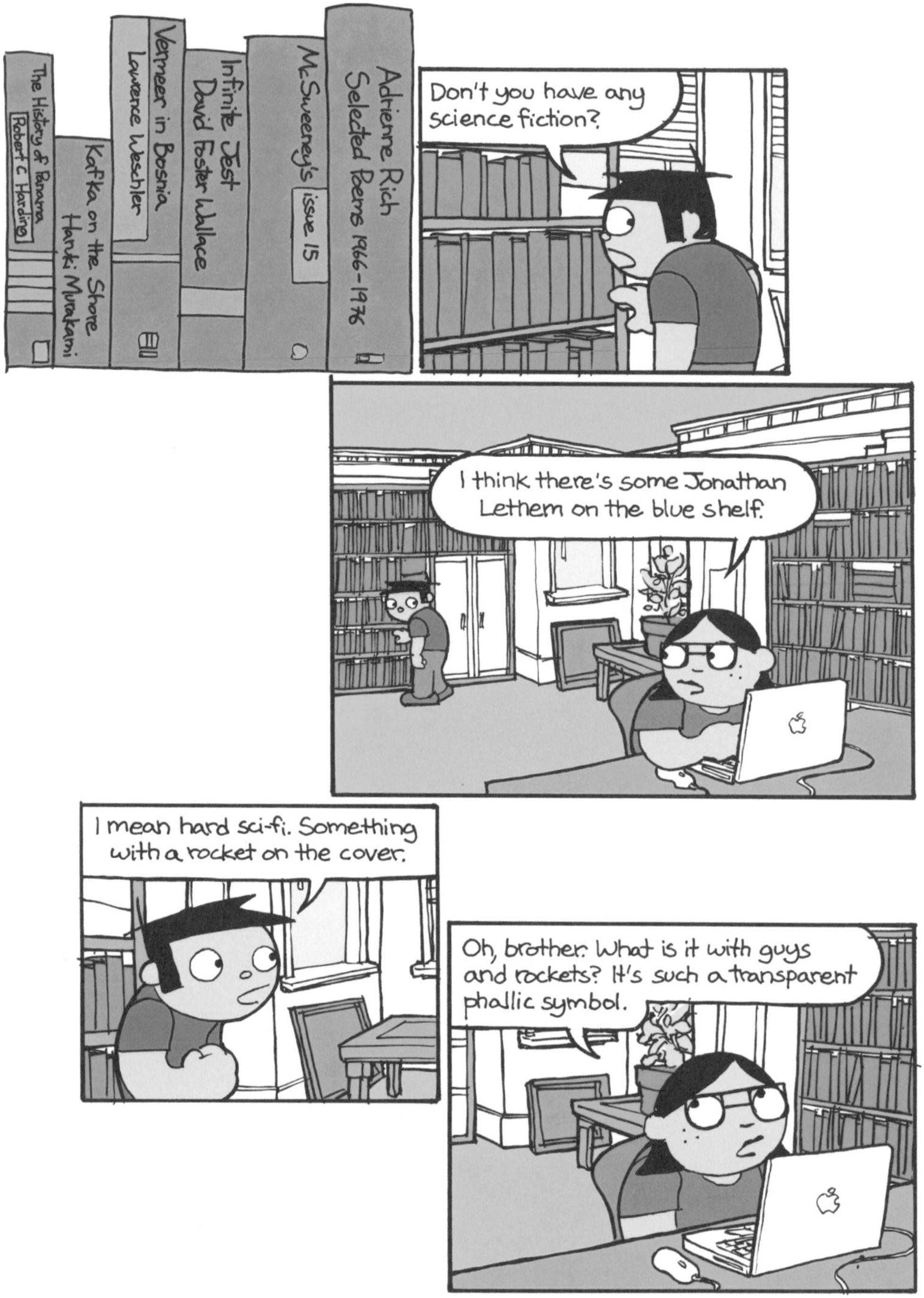

The History of Panama
Robert C Harding
Kafka on the Shore
Haruki Murakami
Vermeer in Bosnia
Lawrence Weschler
Infinite Jest
David Foster Wallace
McSweeney's
issue 15
Adrienne Rich
Selected Poems 1966-1976
Don't you have any science fiction?
I think there's some Jonathan Lethem on the blue shelf.
I mean hard sci-fi. Something with a rocket on the cover.
Oh, brother. What is it with guys and rockets? It's such a transparent phallic symbol.

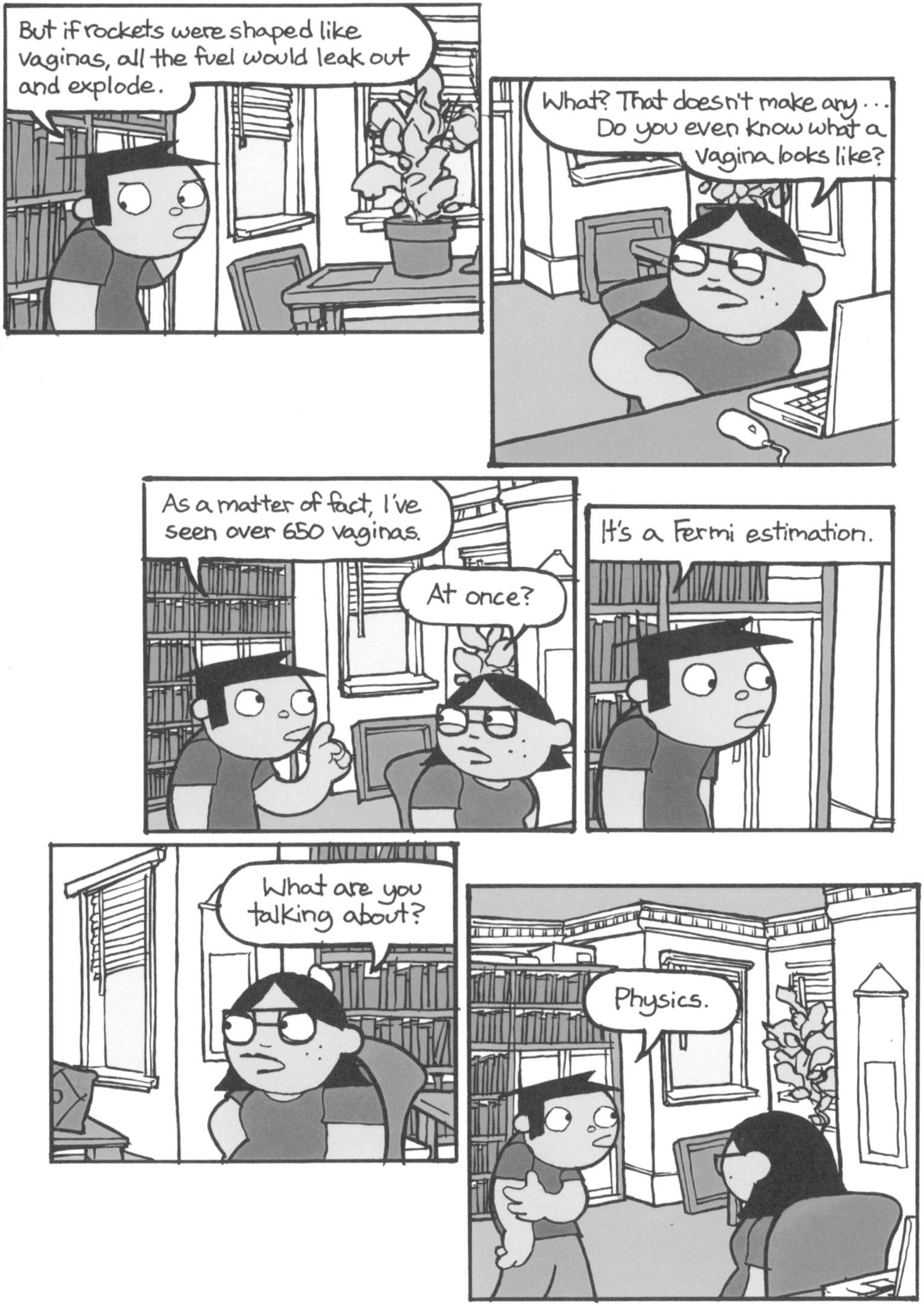

But if rockets were shaped like vaginas, all the fuel would leak out and explode.
What? That doesn't make any . . . Do you even know what a vagina looks like?
As a matter of fact, I've seen over 650 vaginas.
At once?
It's a Fermi estimation.
What are you talking about?
Physics.

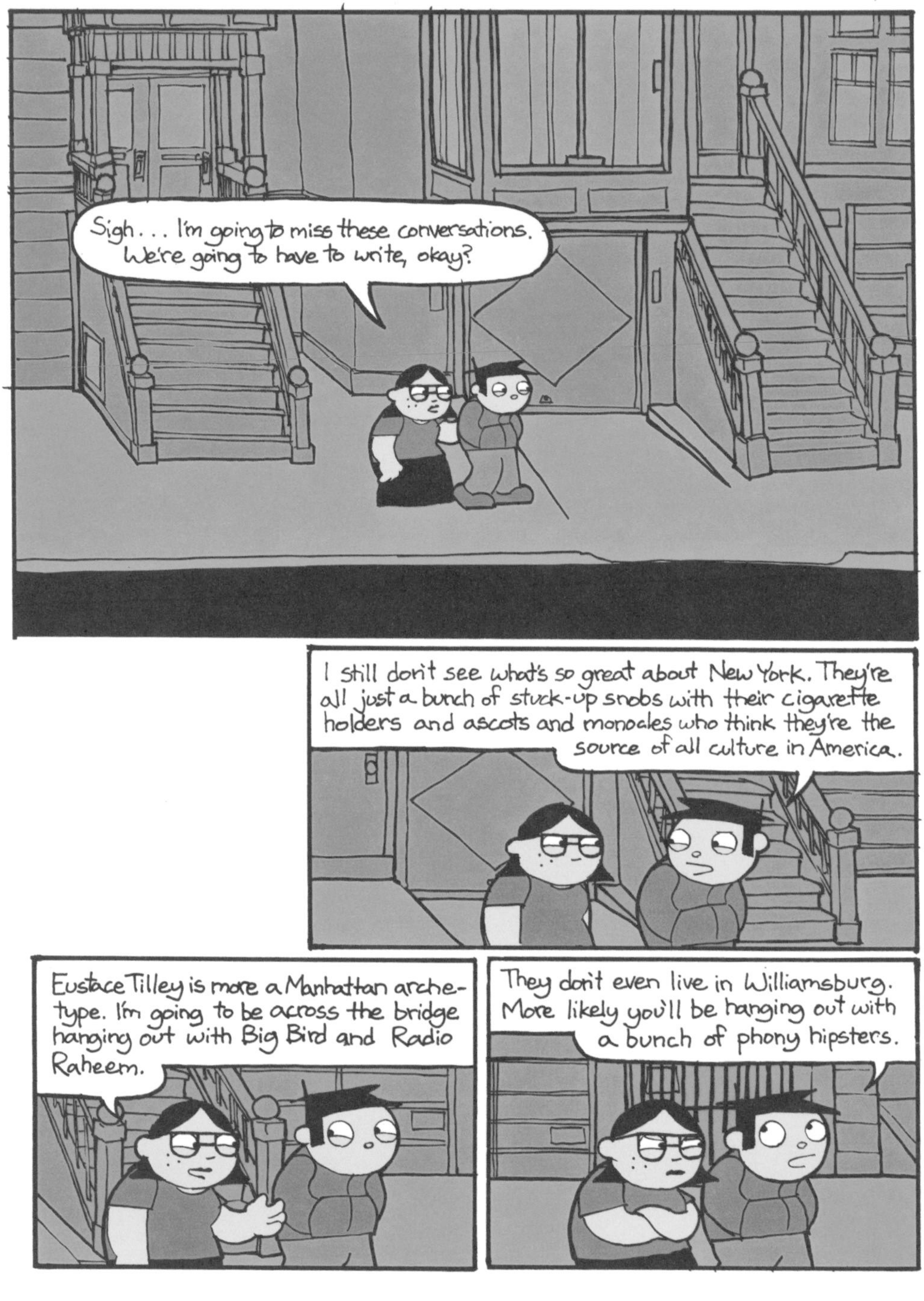
Sigh... I'm going to miss these conversations. We're going to have to write, okay?
I still don't see what's so great about New York. They're all just a bunch of stuck-up snobs with their cigarette holders and ascots and monocles who think they're the source of all culture in America.
Eustace Tilley is more a Manhattan arche-type. I'm going to be across the bridge hanging out with Big Bird and Radio Raheem.
They don't even live in Williamsburg. More likely you'll be hanging out with a bunch of phony hipsters.

And what's so great about Oakland? It's like a giant suburb of San Francisco.

What!!??

Heh heh.

Seriously, I've been here for more than three years now. I've pretty much exhausted everything interesting there is to do here.

But you haven't even been to the Laney Flea Market.

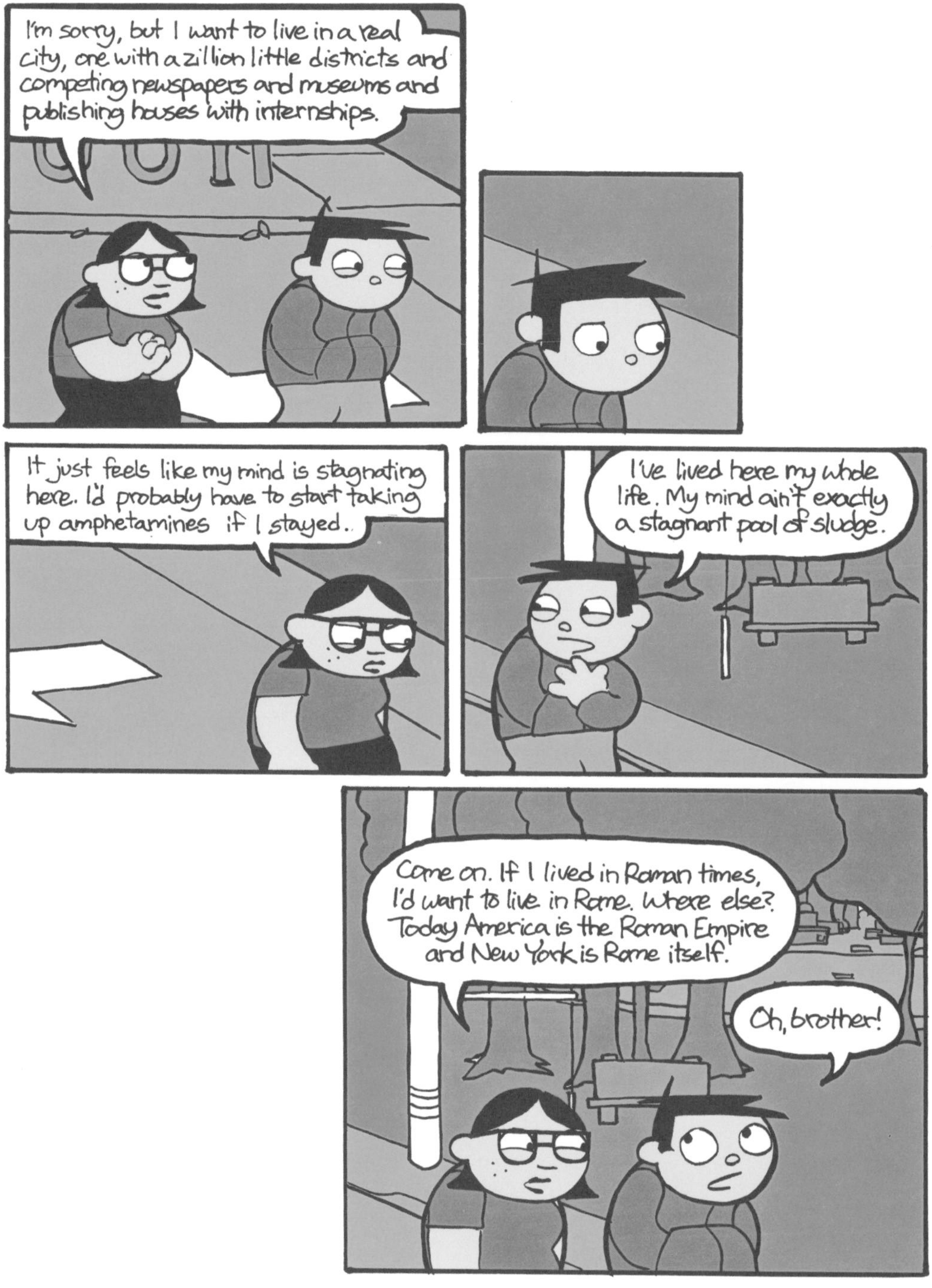
I'm sorry, but I want to live in a real city, one with a zillion little districts and competing newspapers and museums and publishing houses with internships.
It just feels like my mind is stagnating here. I'd probably have to start taking up amphetamines if I stayed..
I've lived here my whole life. My mind ain't exactly a stagnant pool of sludge.
Come on. If I lived in Roman times, I'd want to live in Rome. Where else? Today America is the Roman Empire and New York is Rome itself.
Oh, brother!

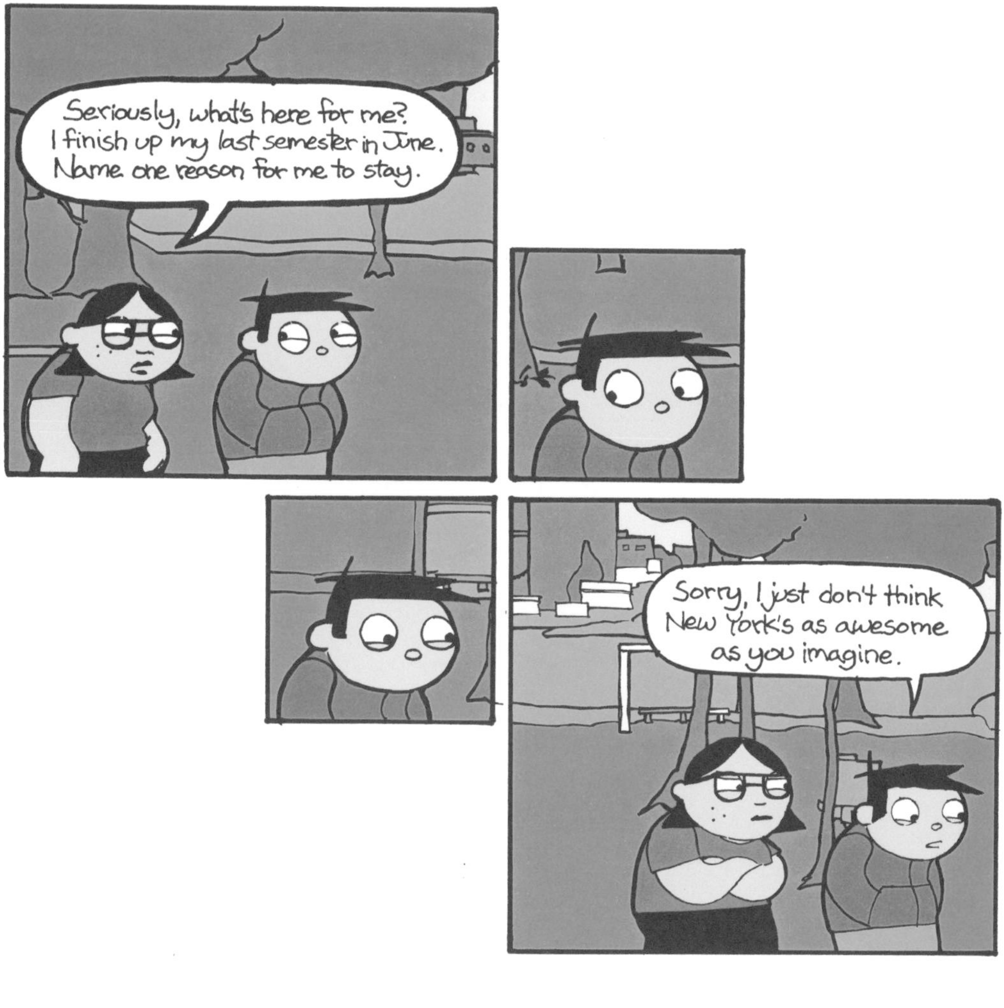
Seriously, what's here for me? I finish up my last semester in June. Name one reason for me to stay.
Sorry, I just don't think New York's as awesome as you imagine.

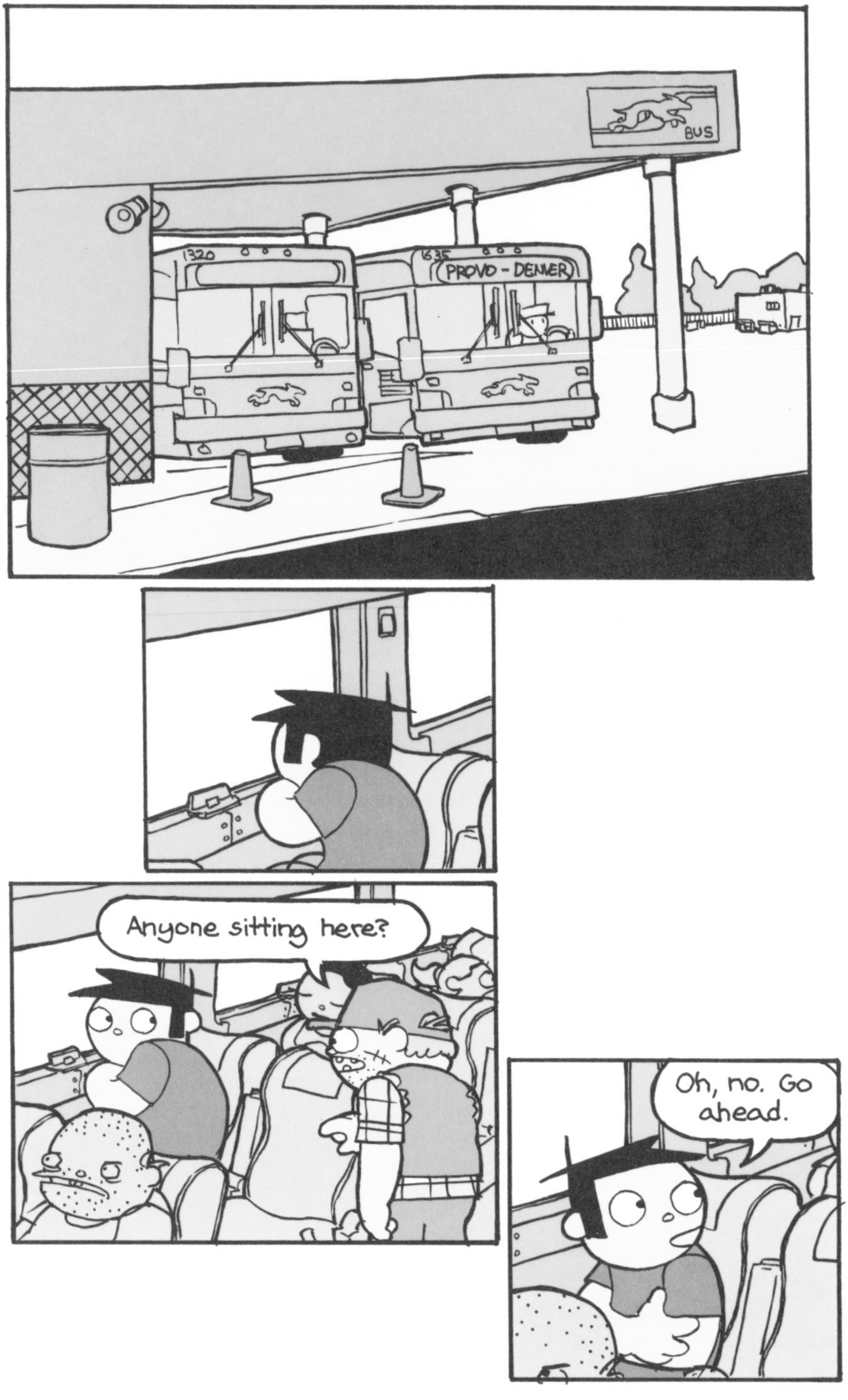
BUS
1320
1635
PROVO - DENVER
Anyone sitting here?
Oh, no. Go ahead.

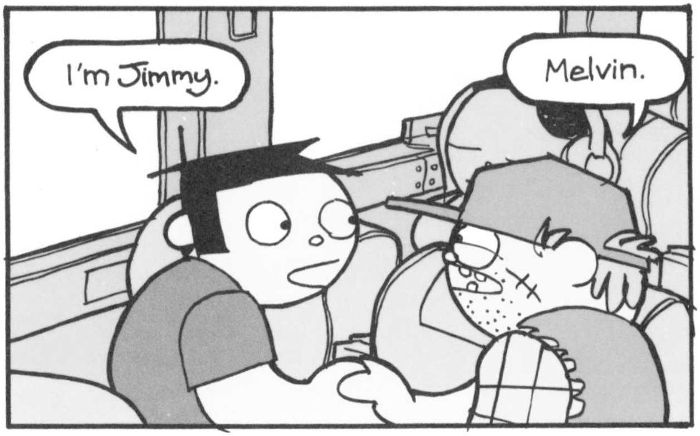
I'm Jimmy.
Melvin.

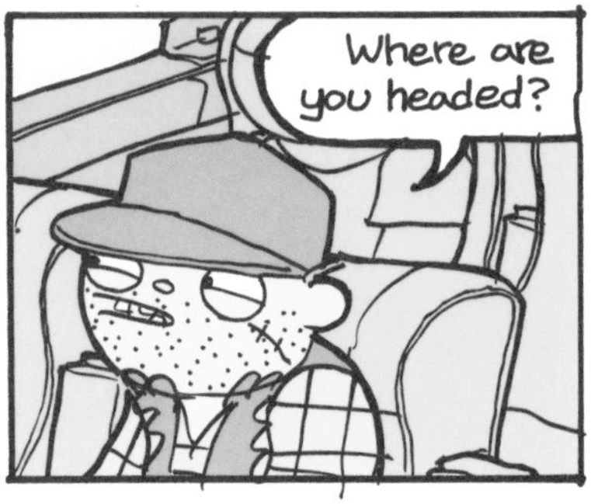
Where are you headed?

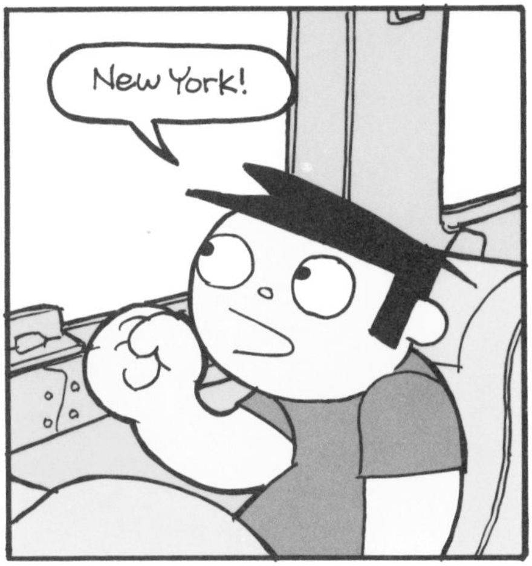
New York!

Why the hell didn't you fly, kid? Are you nuts?

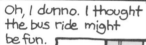

Oh, I dunno. I thought the bus ride might be fun.

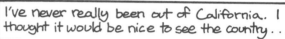

I've never really been out of California. I thought it would be nice to see the country...

...traveling from town to town, solving mysteries like Lou Ferrigno in "The Incredible Hulk."

Haw haw! That ain't how it is, kid!

SLAP!

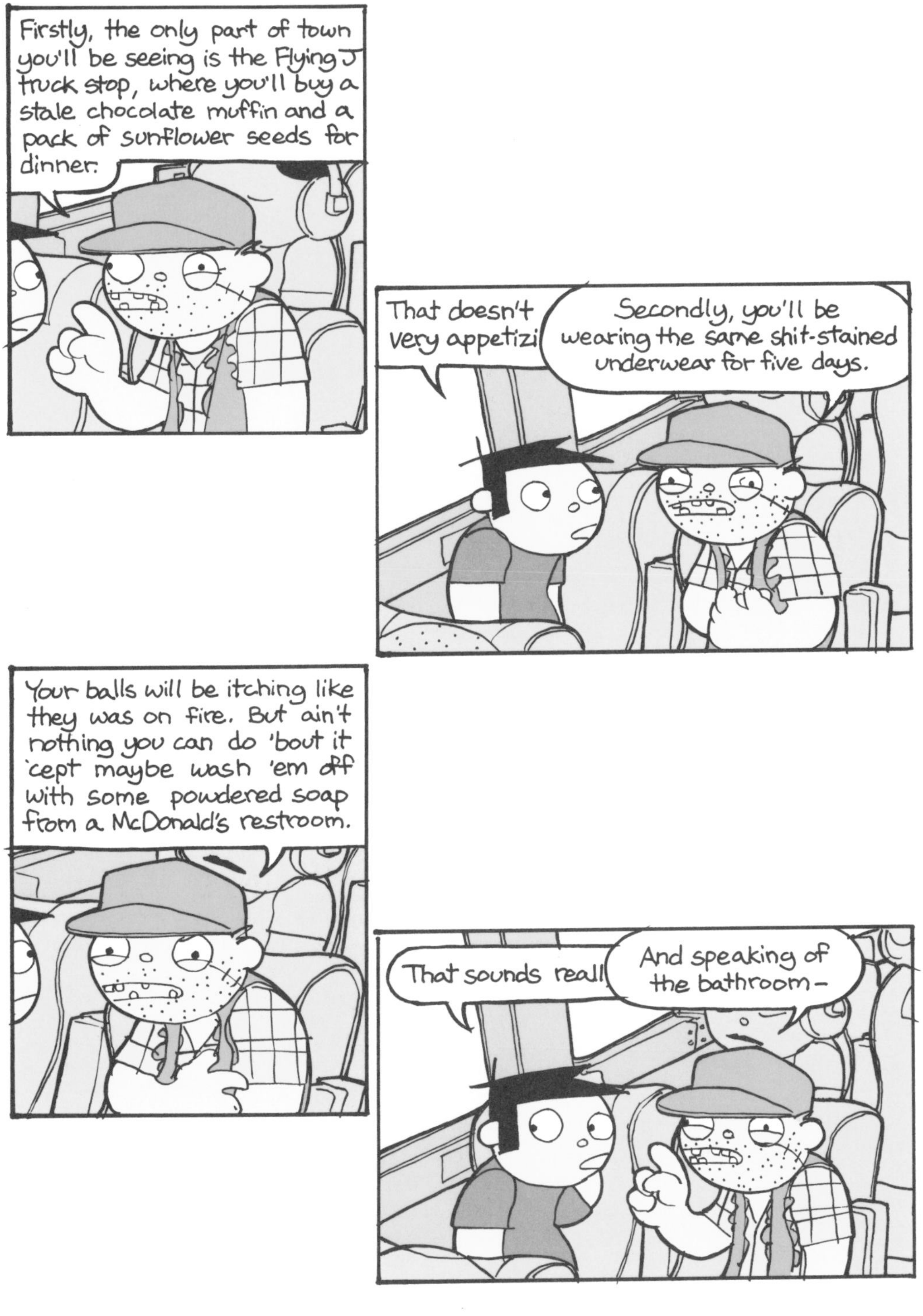
Firstly, the only part of town you'll be seeing is the Flying J truck stop, where you'll buy a stale chocolate muffin and a pack of sunflower seeds for dinner.
That doesn't very appetizi
Secondly, you'll be wearing the same shit-stained underwear for five days.
Your balls will be itching like they was on fire. But ain't nothing you can do 'bout it 'cept maybe wash 'em off with some powdered soap from a McDonald's restroom.
That sounds reall
And speaking of the bathroom –

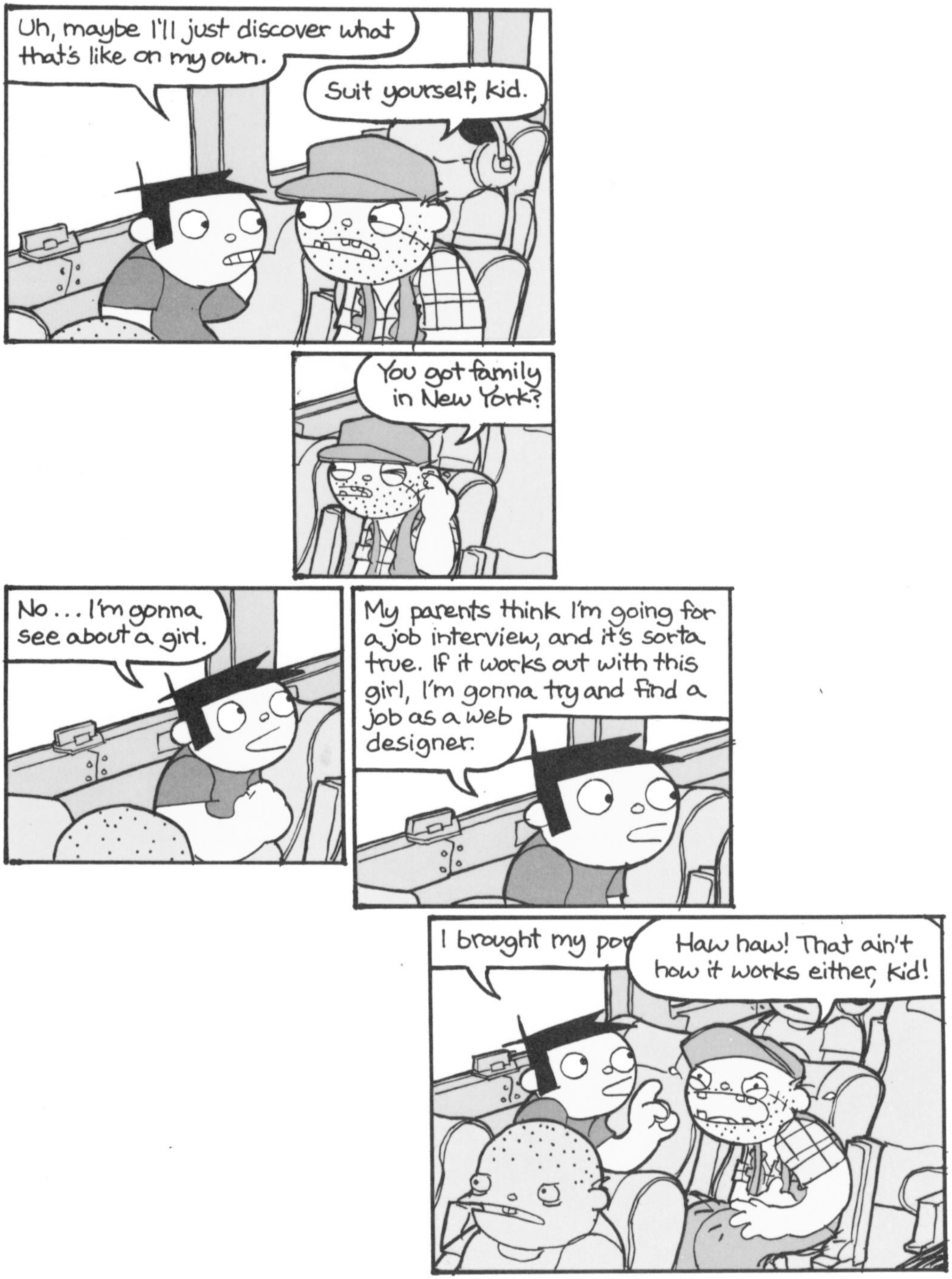
Uh, maybe I'll just discover what that's like on my own.
Suit yourself, kid.
You got family in New York?
No . . . I'm gonna see about a girl.
My parents think I'm going for a job interview, and it's sorta true. If it works out with this girl, I'm gonna try and find a job as a web designer.
I brought my por
Haw haw! That ain't how it works either, kid!

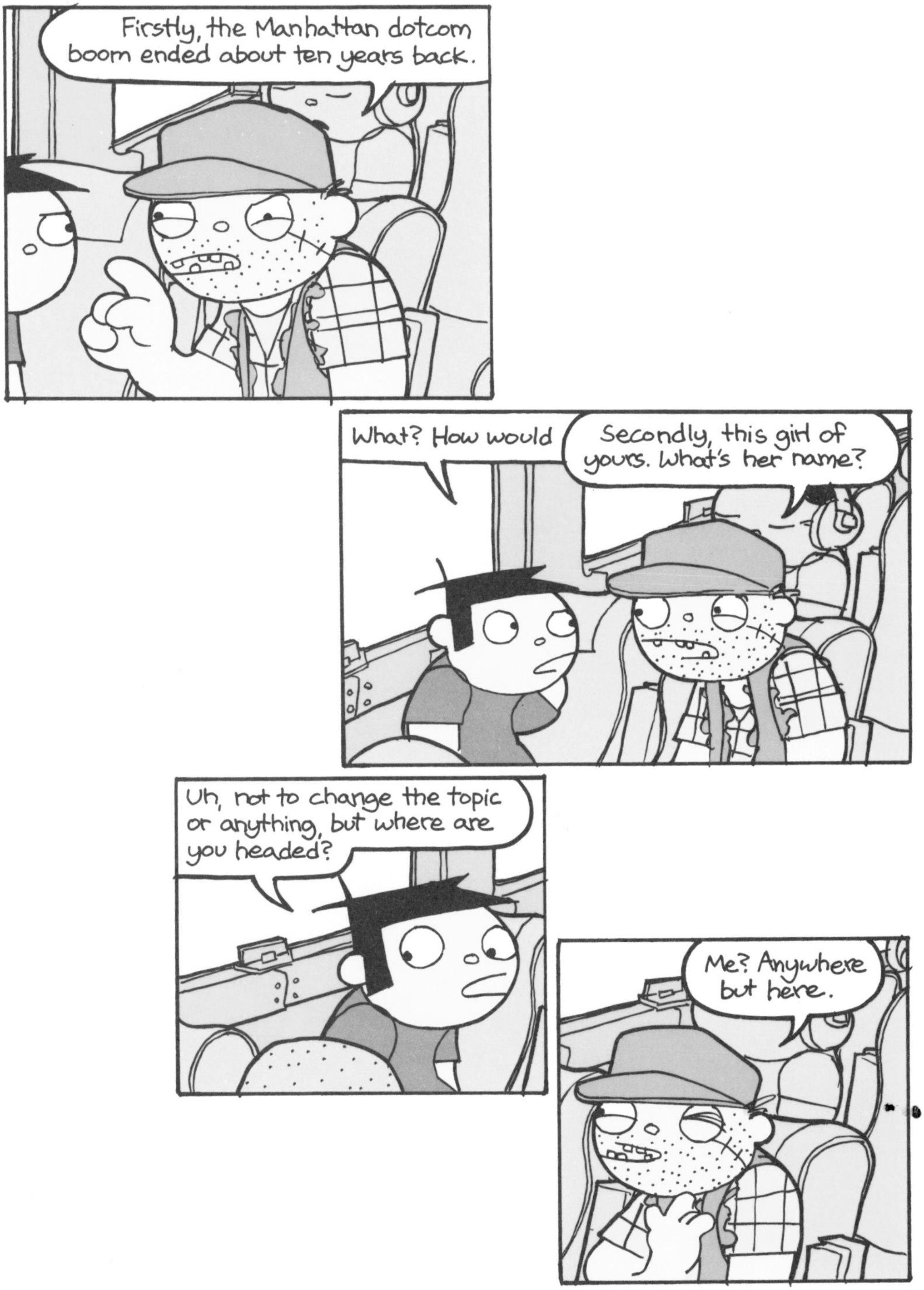
Firstly, the Manhattan dotcom boom ended about ten years back.
What? How would
Secondly, this girl of yours. What's her name?
Uh, not to change the topic or anything, but where are you headed?
Me? Anywhere but here.

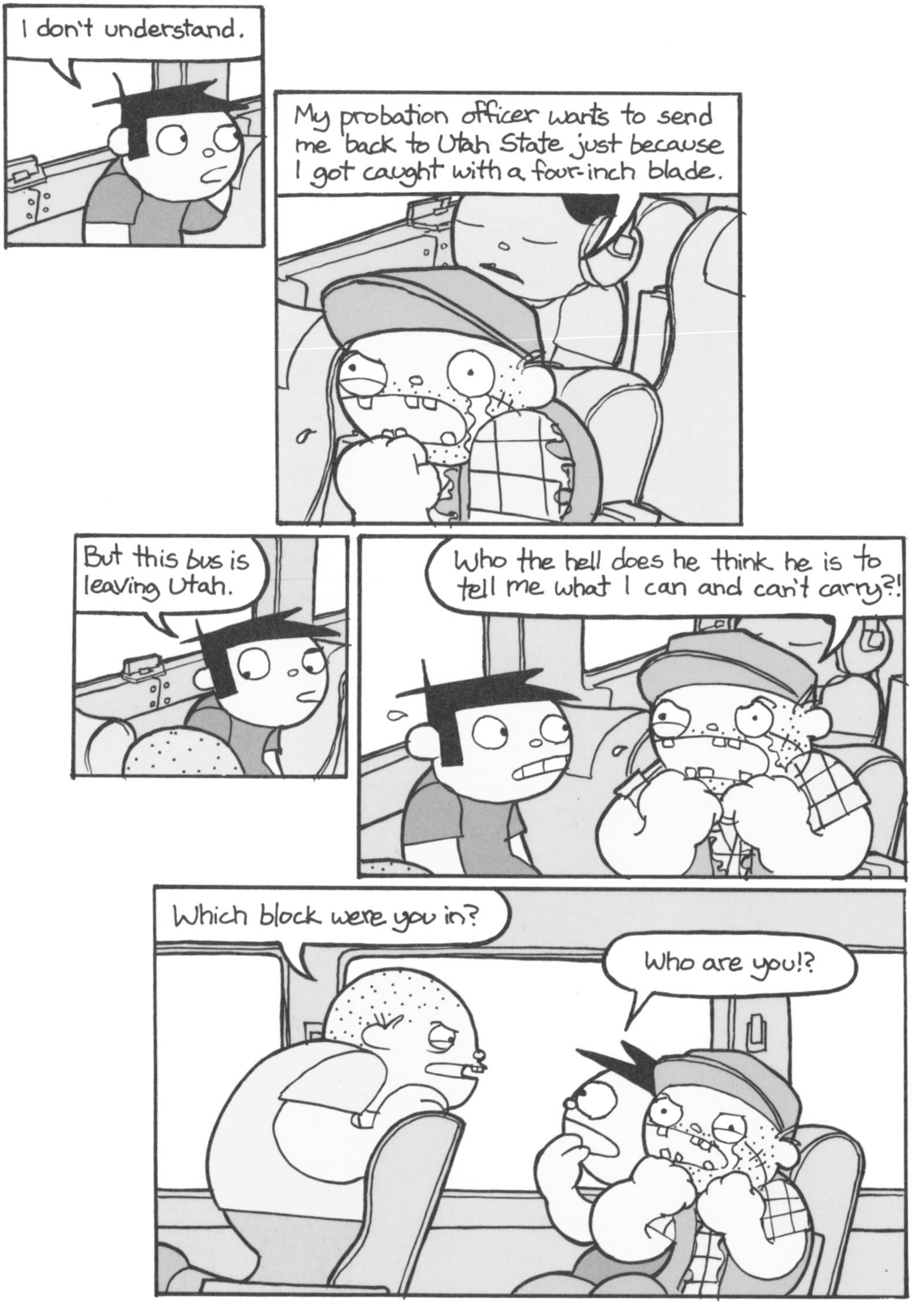
I don't understand.
My probation officer wants to send me back to Utah State just because I got caught with a four-inch blade.
But this bus is leaving Utah.
Who the hell does he think he is to tell me what I can and can't carry?!
Which block were you in?
Who are you!?

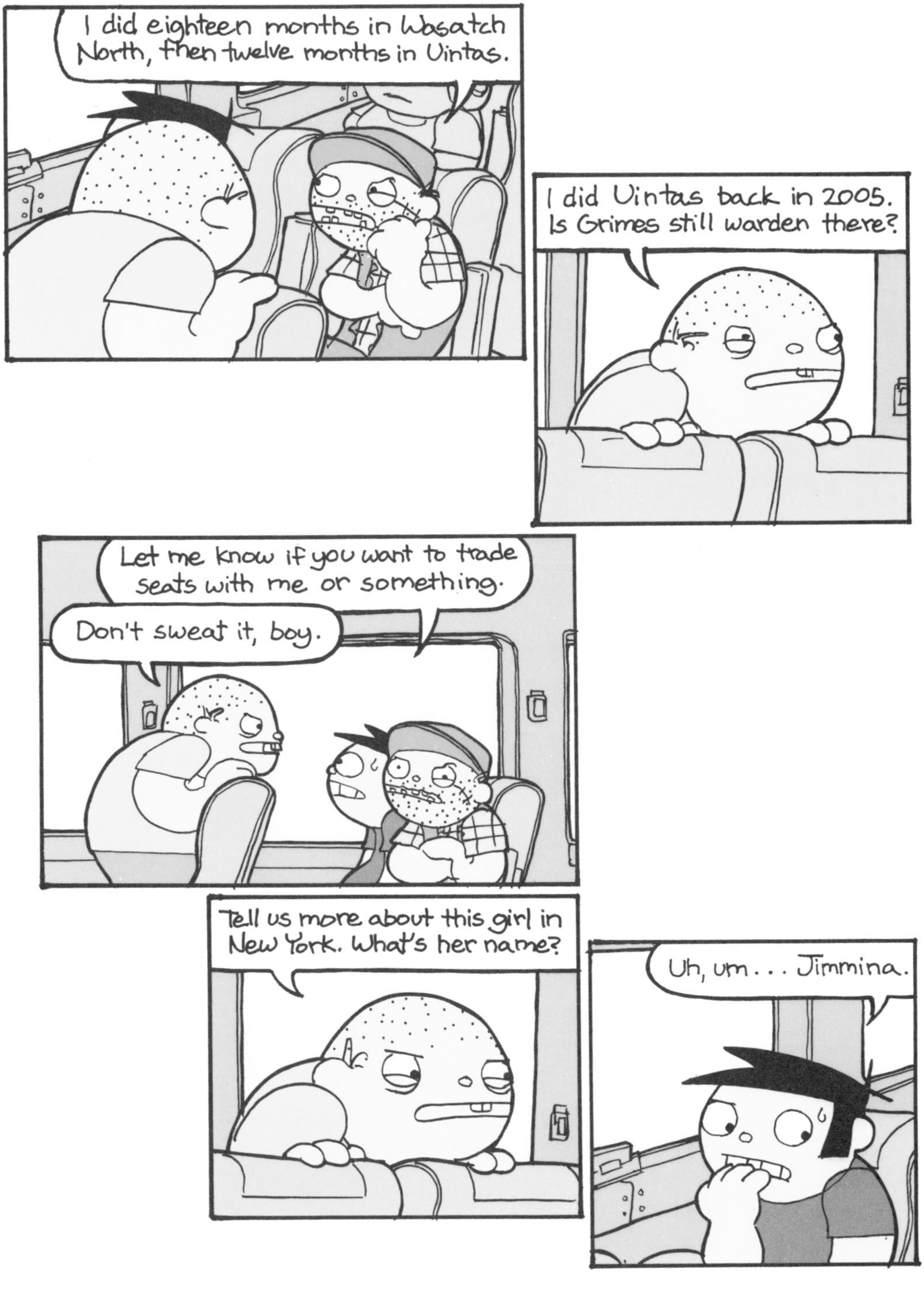

I did eighteen months in Wasatch North, then twelve months in Uintas.
I did Uintas back in 2005. Is Grimes still warden there?
Let me know if you want to trade seats with me or something.
Don't sweat it, boy.
Tell us more about this girl in New York. What's her name?
Uh, um . . . Jimmina.

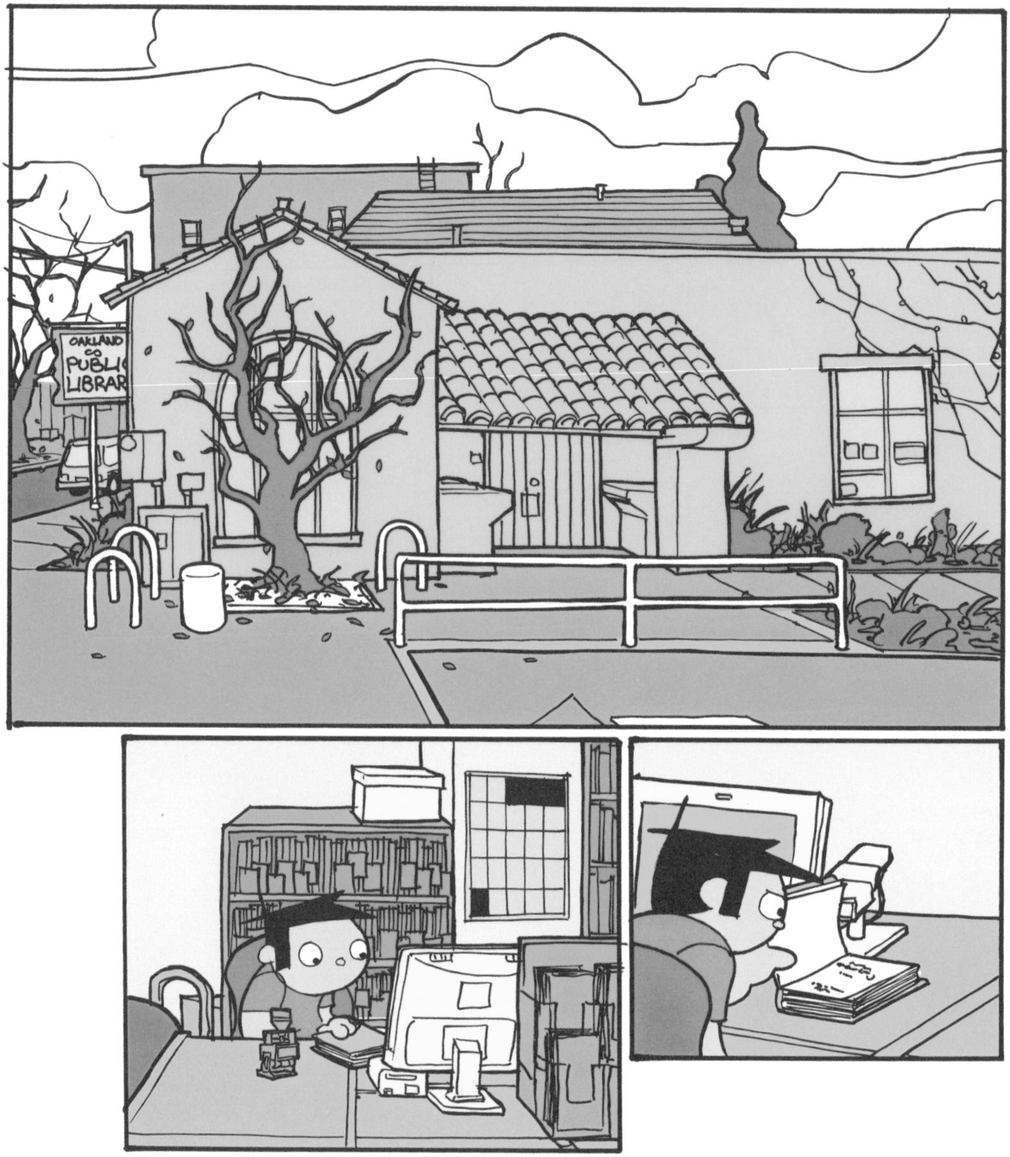
OAKLAND
CO
PUBLIC
LIBRAR

A Brief History of
American Sign Language

Lisa Cross

Red House Educational Series, Inc.

New York

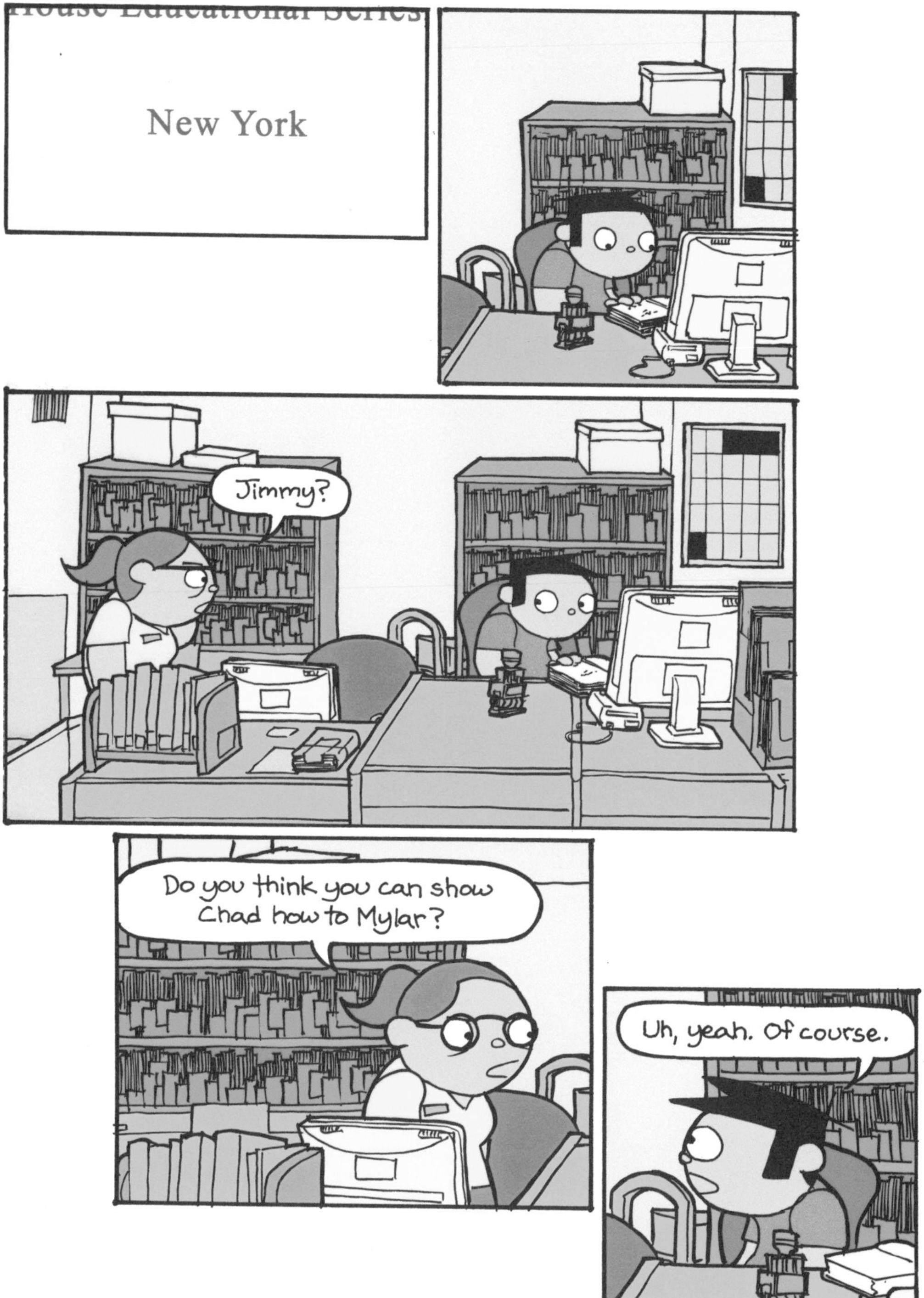
New York
Jimmy?
Do you think you can show Chad how to Mylar?
Uh, yeah. Of course.

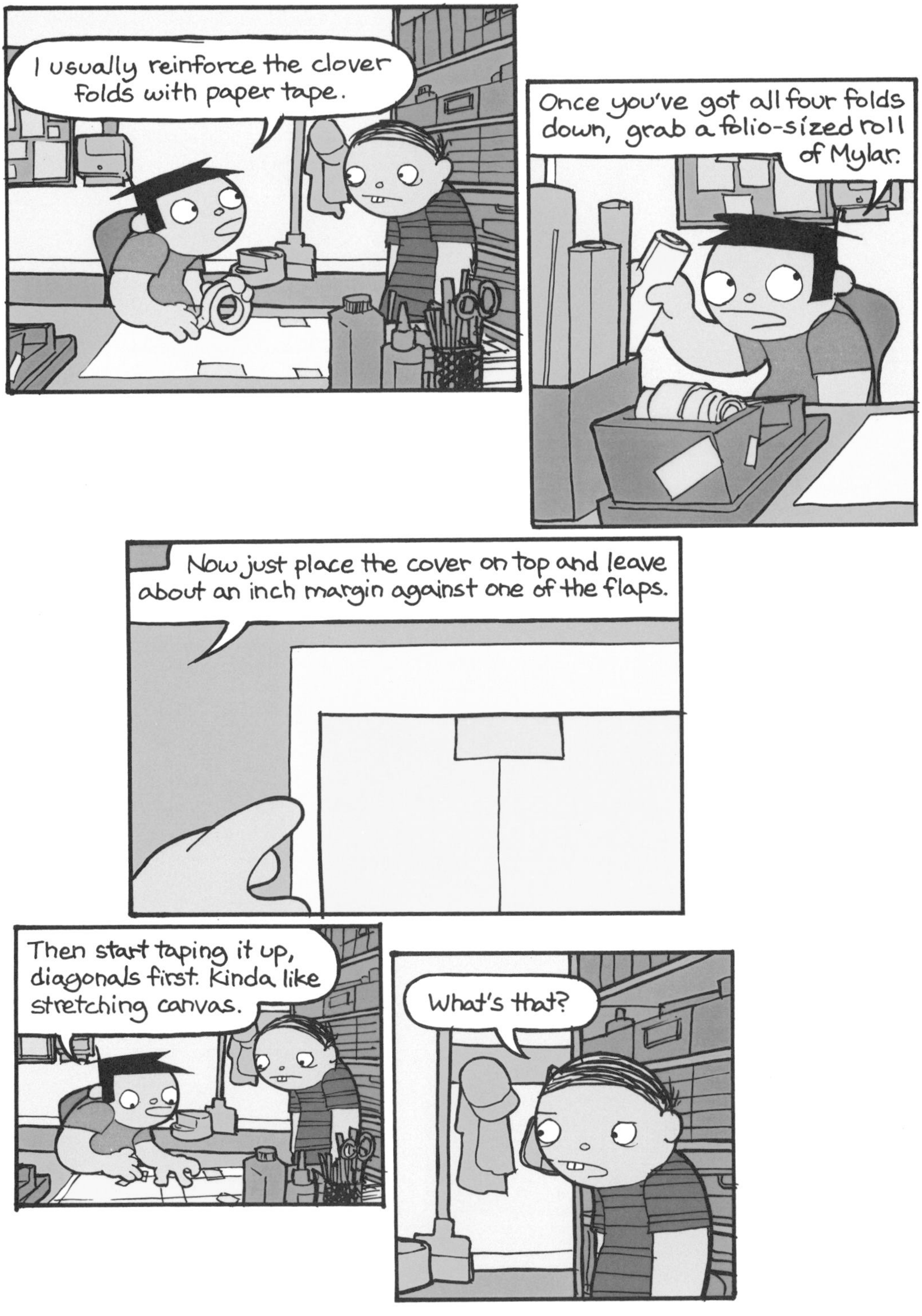
I usually reinforce the clover folds with paper tape.
Once you've got all four folds down, grab a folio-sized roll of Mylar.
Now just place the cover on top and leave about an inch margin against one of the flaps.
Then start taping it up, diagonals first. Kinda like stretching canvas.
What's that?

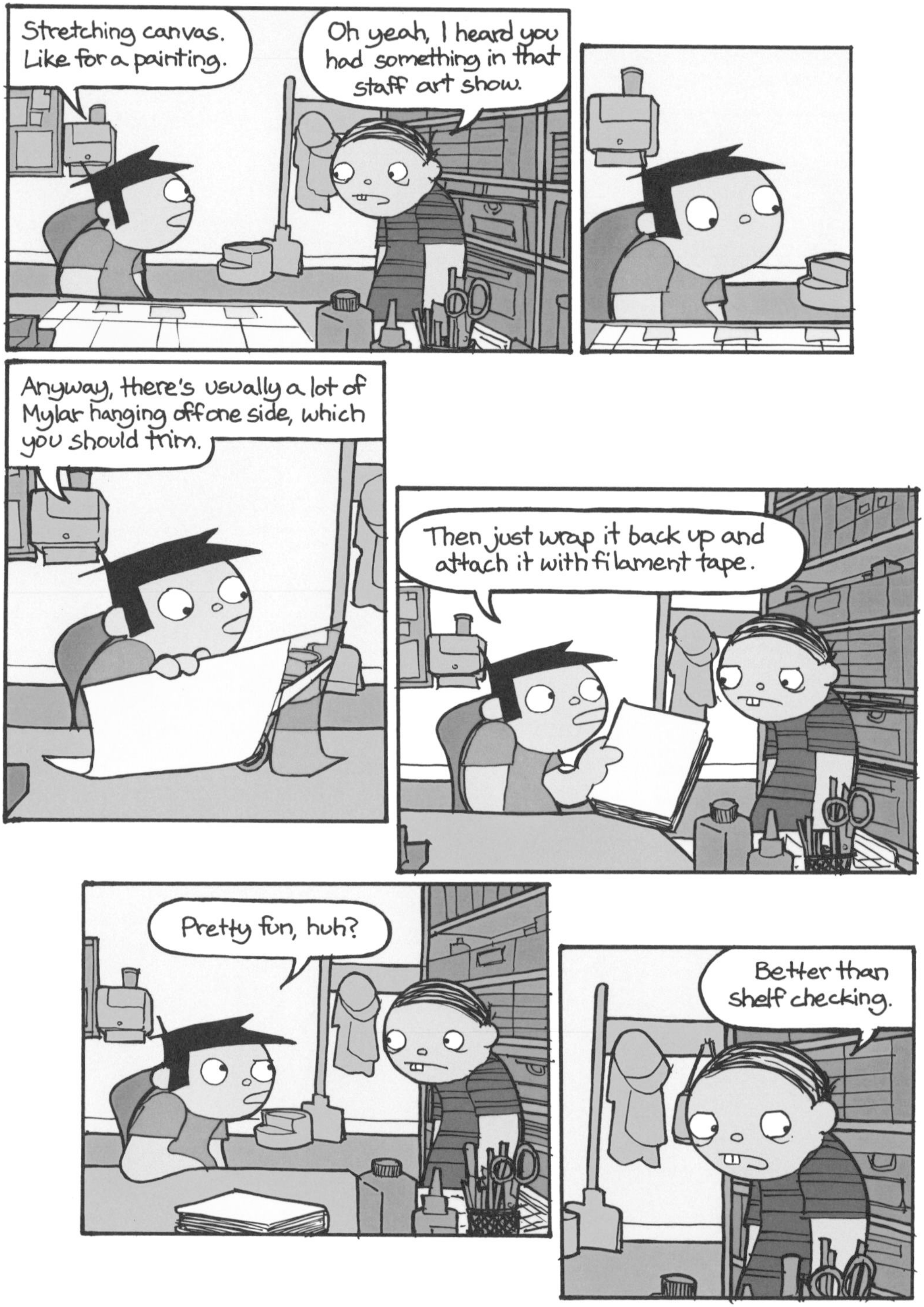
Stretching canvas. Like for a painting.
Oh yeah, I heard you had something in that staff art show.
Anyway, there's usually a lot of Mylar hanging off one side, which you should trim.
Then just wrap it back up and attach it with filament tape.
Pretty fun, huh?
Better than shelf checking.

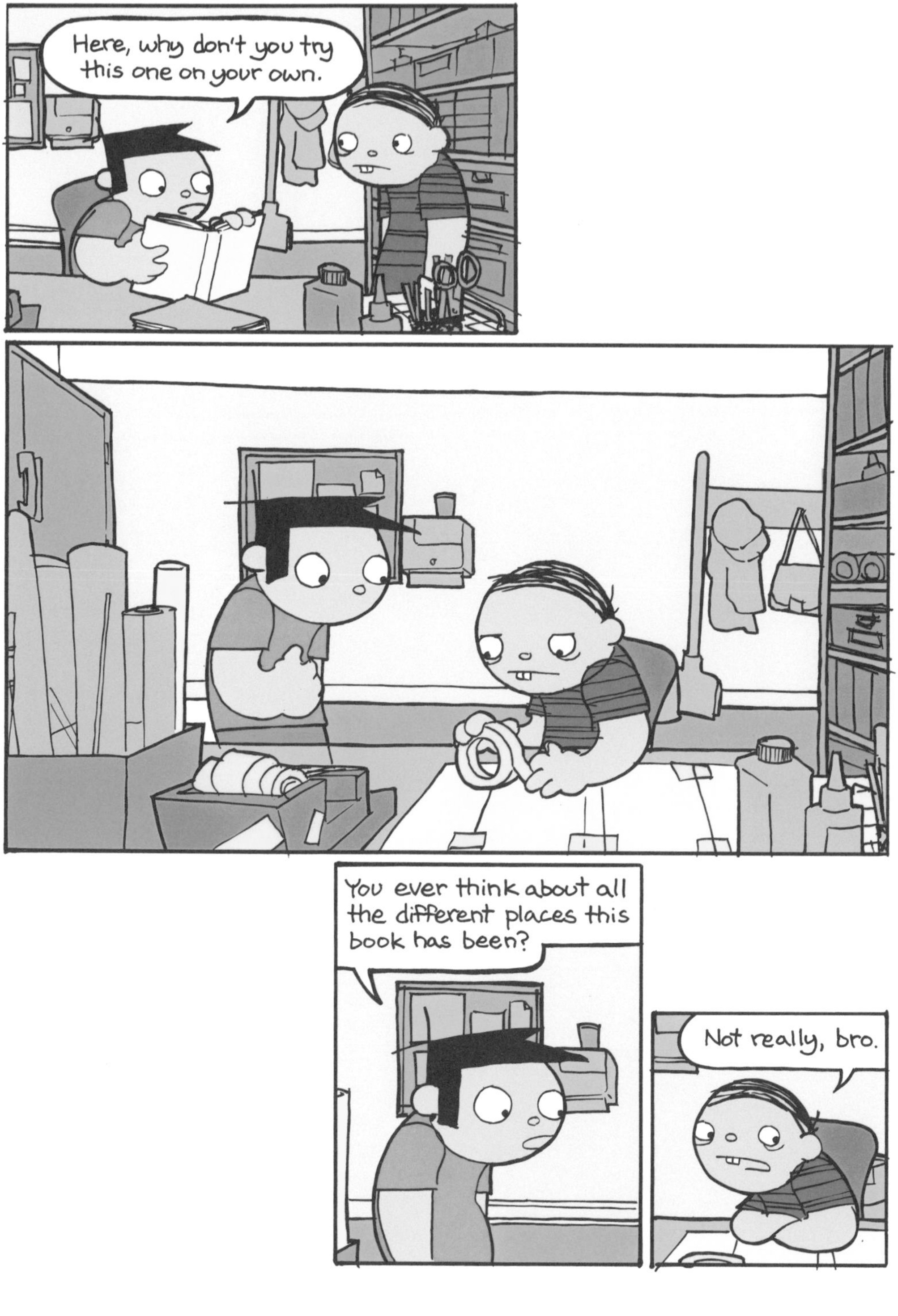
Here, why don't you try this one on your own.
You ever think about all the different places this book has been?
Not really, bro.

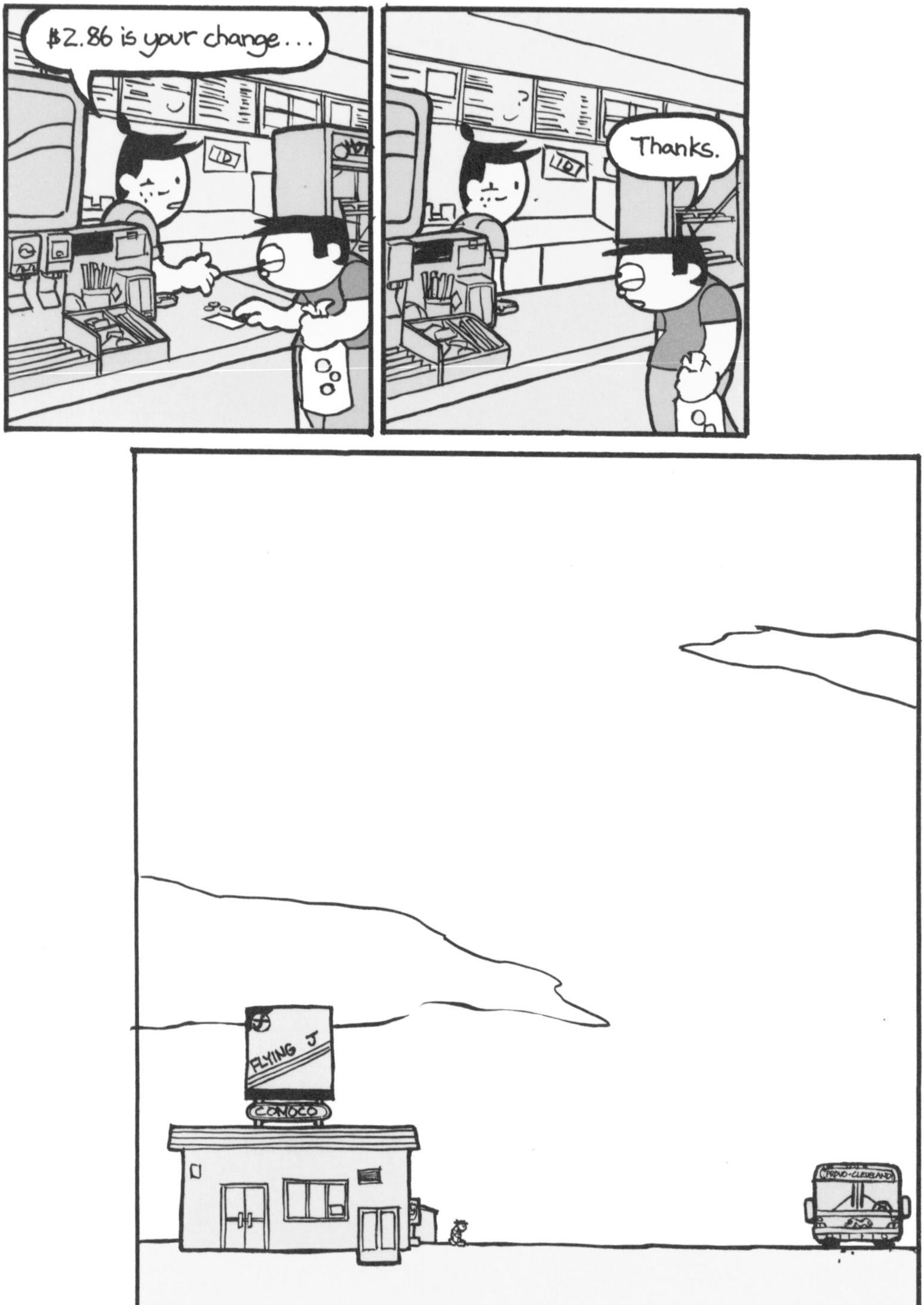
$2.86 is your change...
Thanks.
FLYING J
CONOCO
PROVO-CLEVELAND

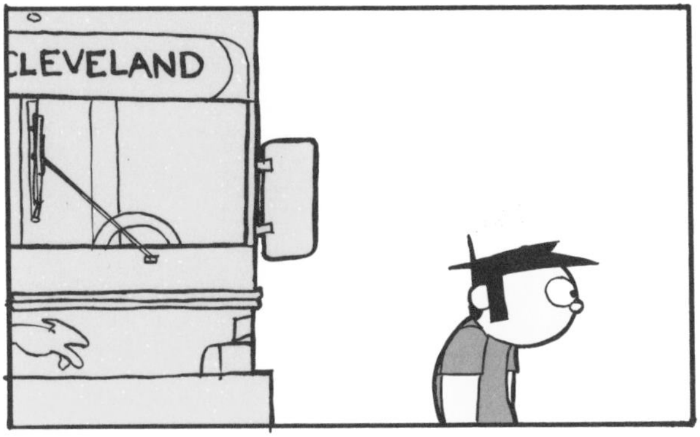
CLEVELAND

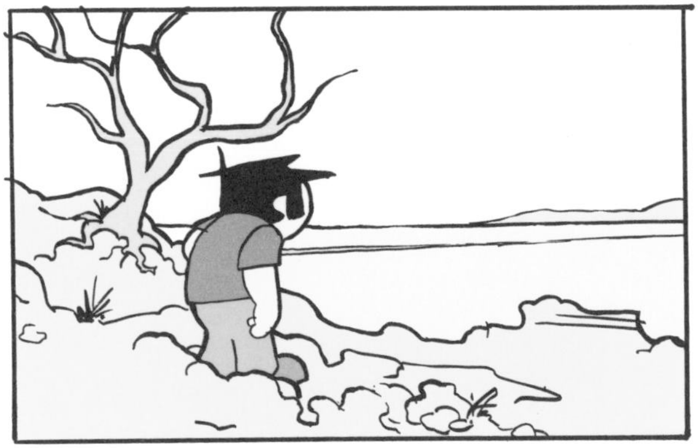

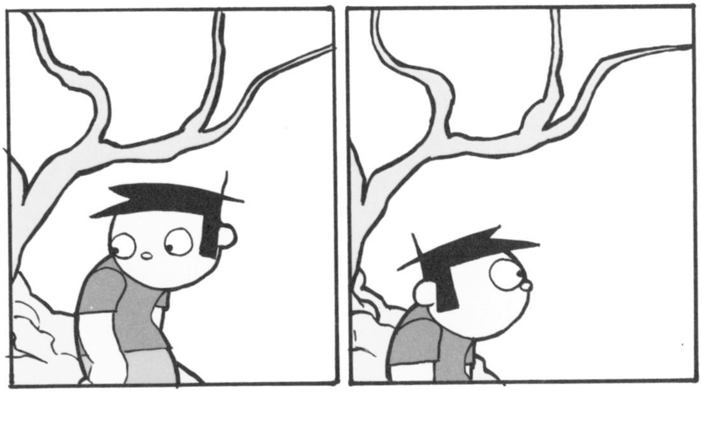

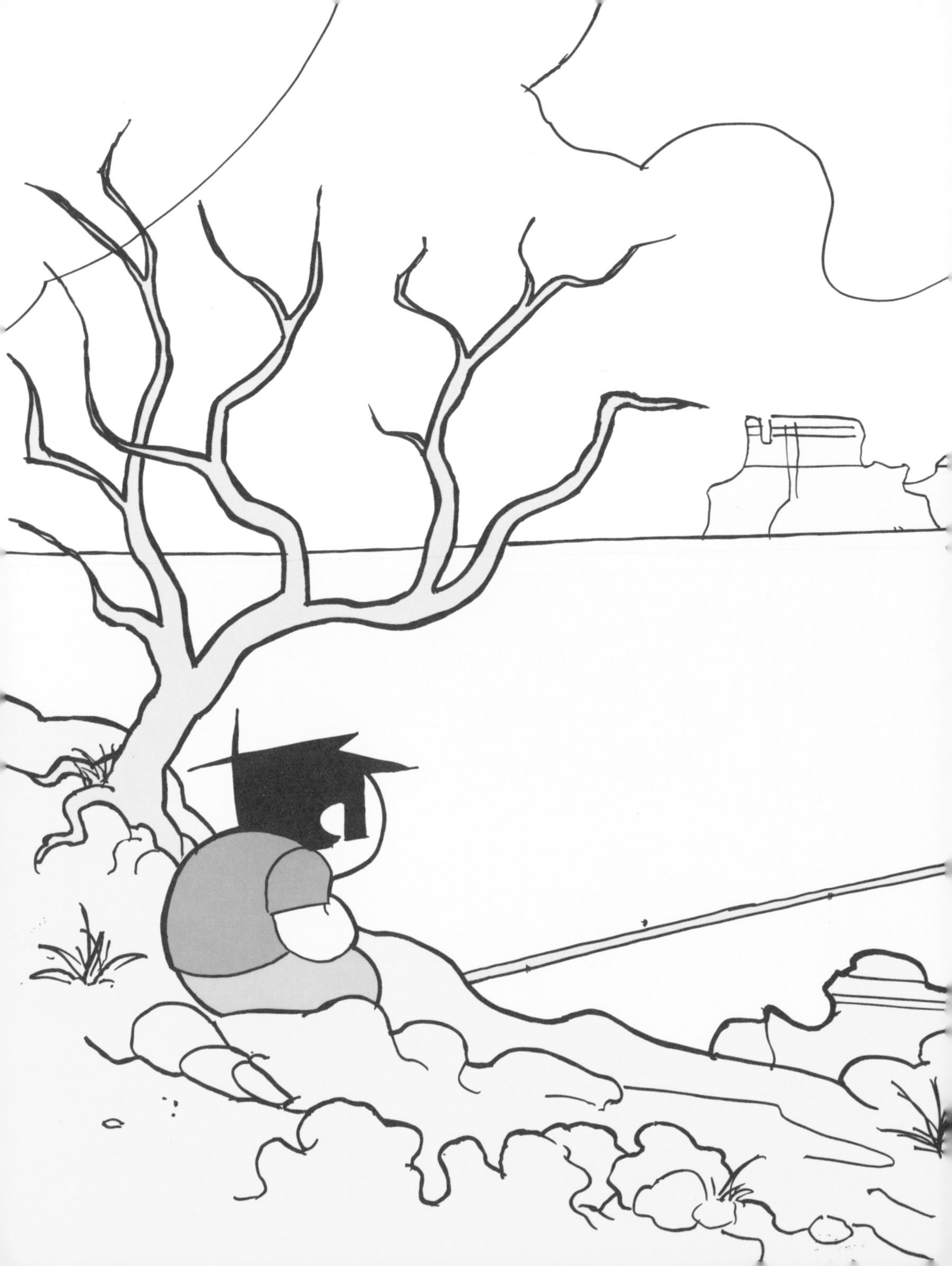

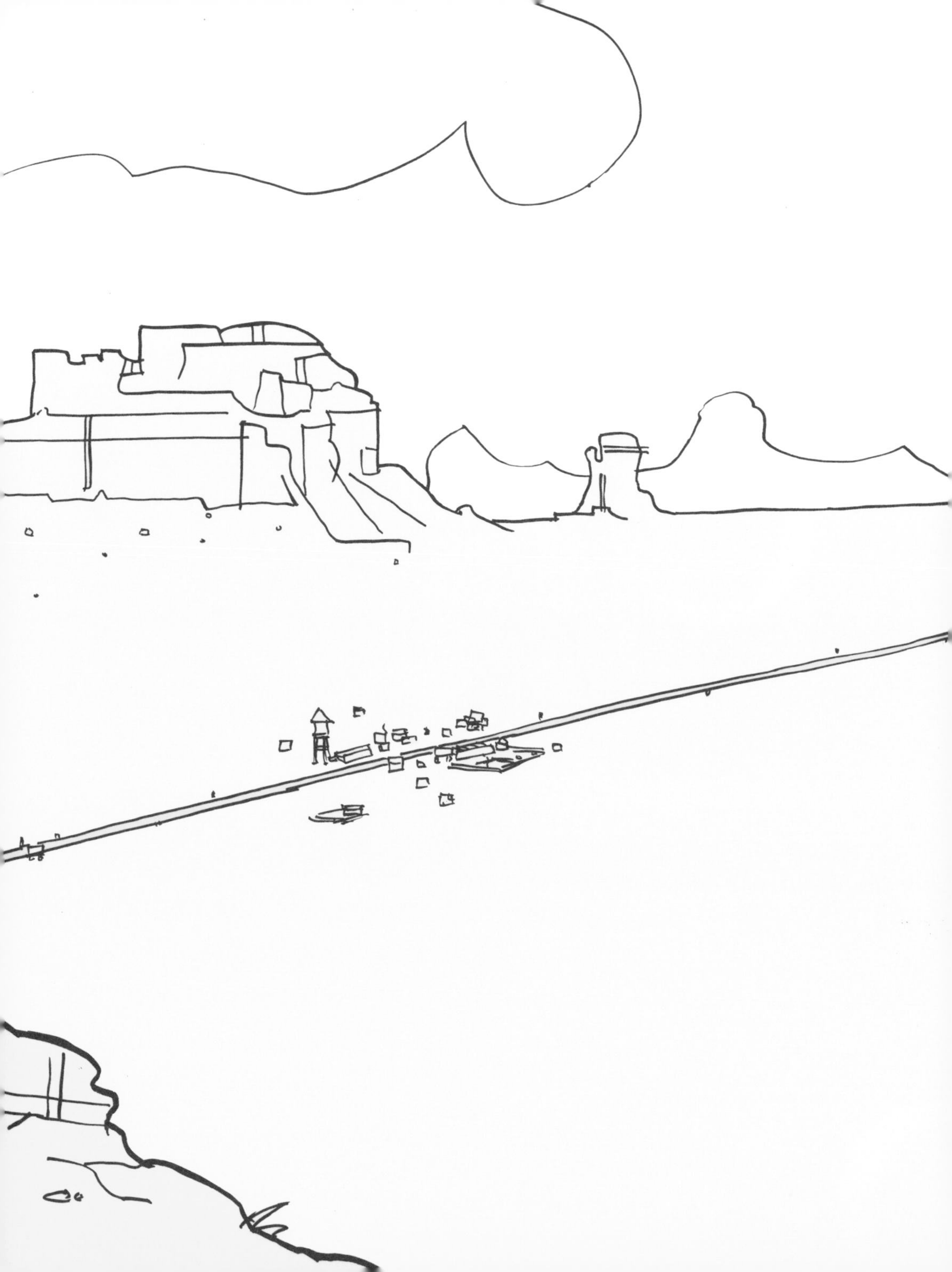

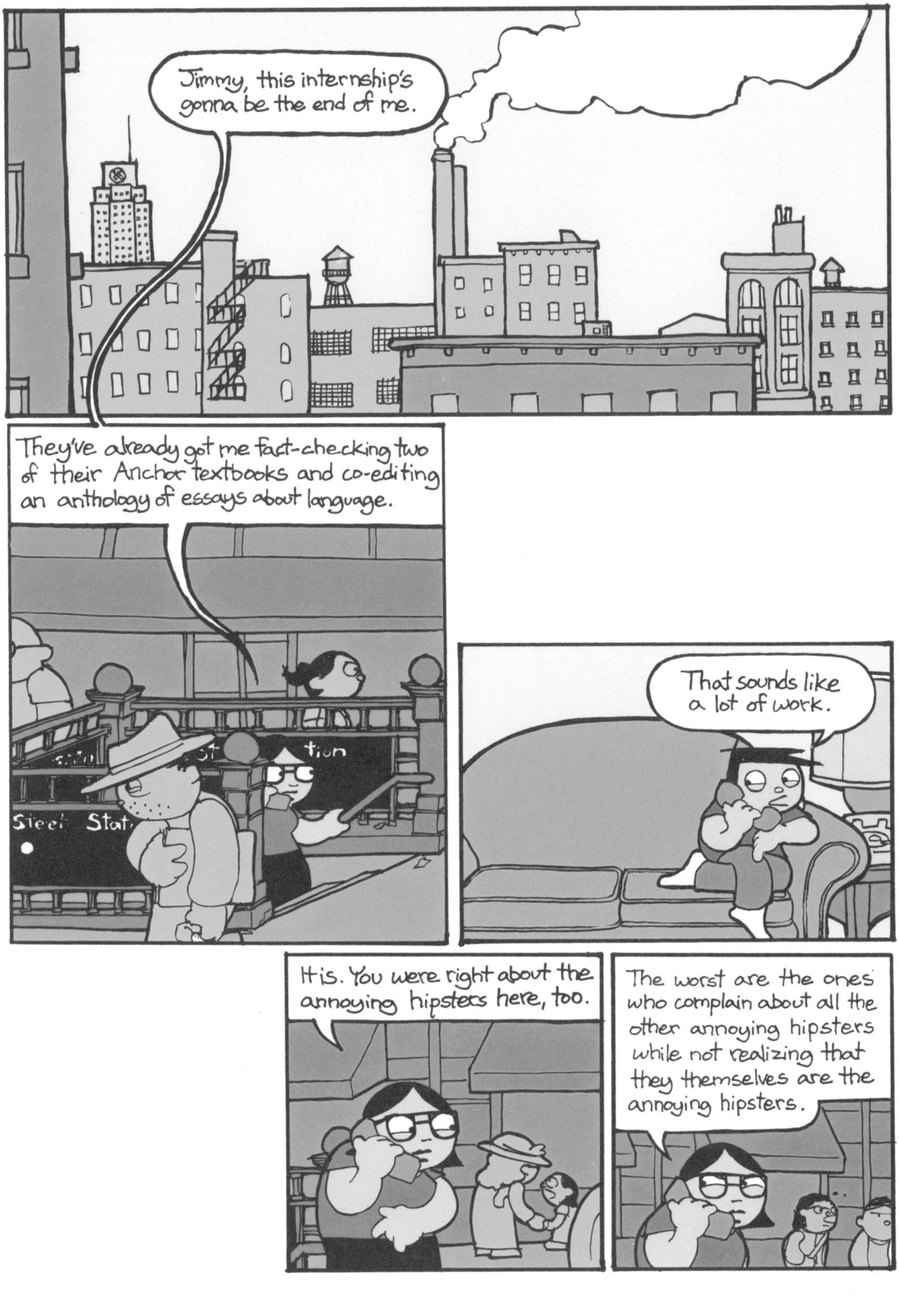
Jimmy, this internship's gonna be the end of me.
They've already got me fact-checking two of their Anchor textbooks and co-editing an anthology of essays about language.
That sounds like a lot of work.
It is. You were right about the annoying hipsters here, too.
The worst are the ones who complain about all the other annoying hipsters while not realizing that they themselves are the annoying hipsters.

Have you met any famous authors?

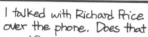

I talked with Richard Price over the phone. Does that count?

Sure.

Who else... John McWhorter, Akeel Bilgrami. Basically all the New York contributors to the language anthology.

Jimmy, this anthology is so much work! There's over 40 contributors whittled down from about 200. I'm reading literally 150-plus pages of submissions a day.

I don't think I read that much in a week.

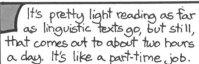

It's pretty light reading as far as linguistic texts go, but still, that comes out to about two hours a day. It's like a part-time job.

What about yourself, what are you up to these days?

You know. Same old stuff. Still working at the library. Still working on my website. Still eating dinner with the folks every Monday.

You should come and visit.

Really?

Yes, really. You could bring your design portfolio and shop it around town while you're here.

That's not gonna happen.

I remember the first time we met you told me that it was your dream to become an artist or a designer.

I'll be frank. Being an artist is tough here, but there's a zillion little design studios in Manhattan alone.

I'm not; I just can't pick up and leave that easily.

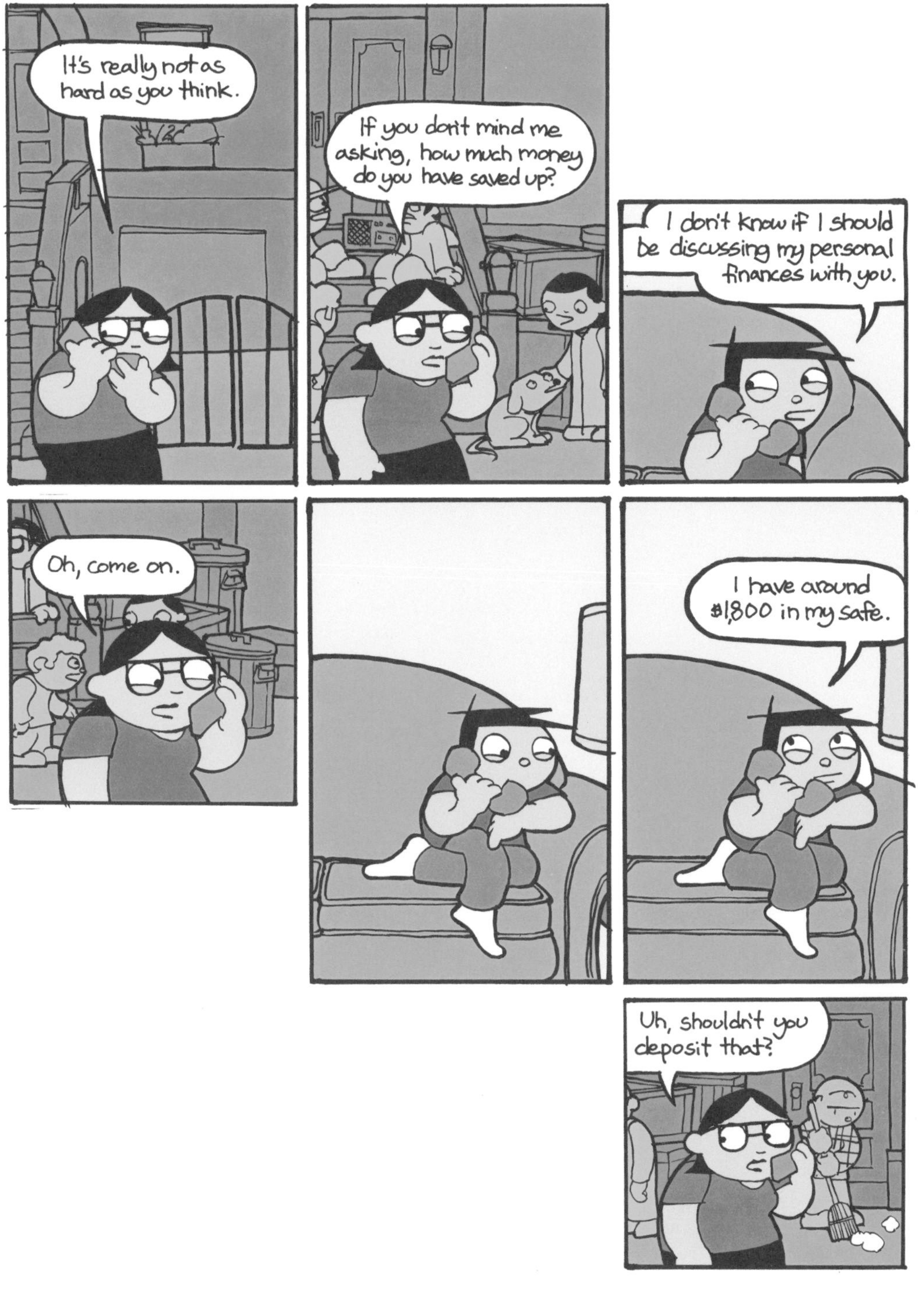
It's really not as hard as you think.
If you don't mind me asking, how much money do you have saved up?
I don't know if I should be discussing my personal finances with you.
Oh, come on.
I have around $1,800 in my safe.
Uh, shouldn't you deposit that?

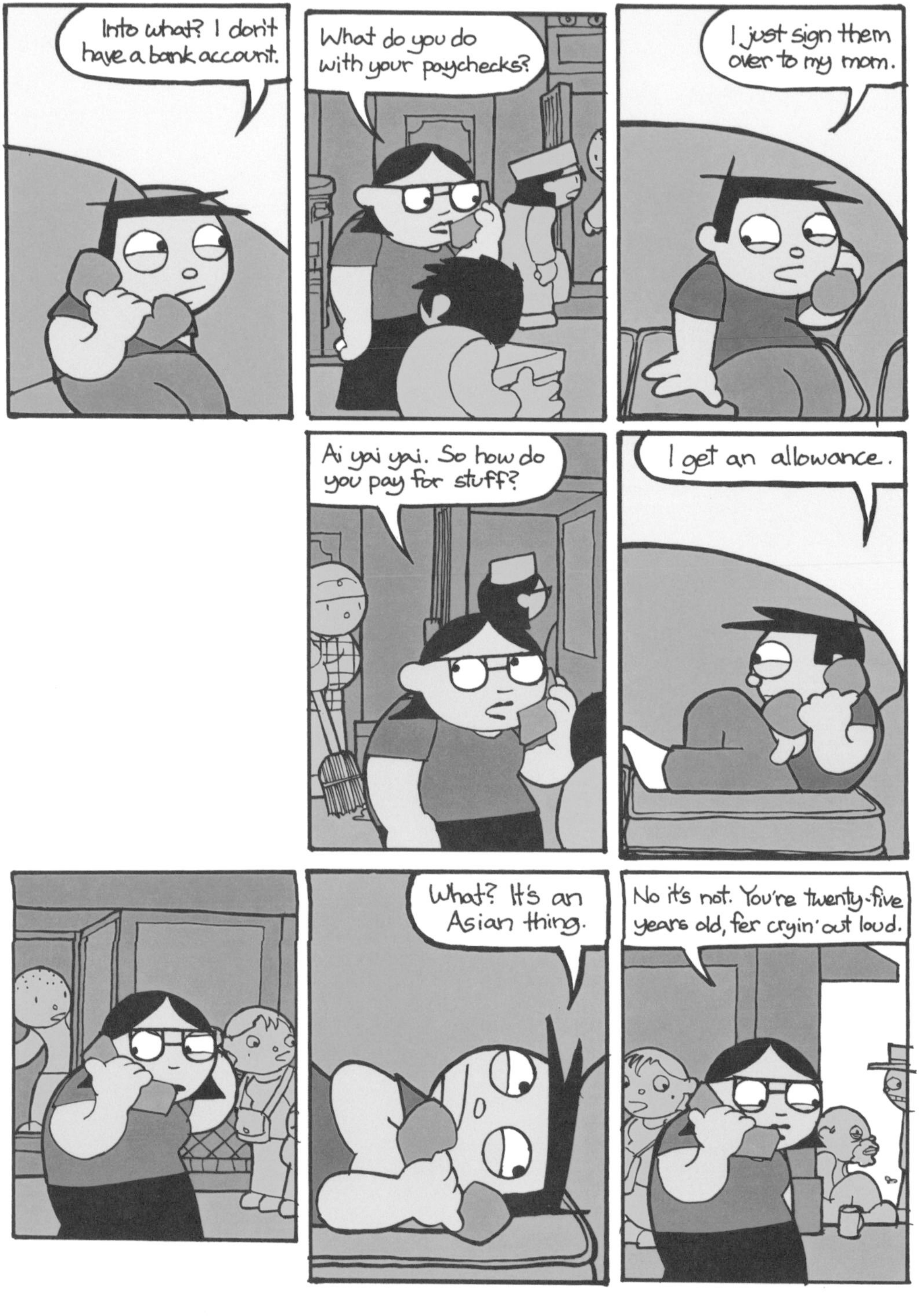
Into what? I don't have a bank account.
What do you do with your paychecks?
I just sign them over to my mom.
Ai yai yai. So how do you pay for stuff?
I get an allowance.
What? It's an Asian thing.
No it's not. You're twenty-five years old, fer cryin' out loud.

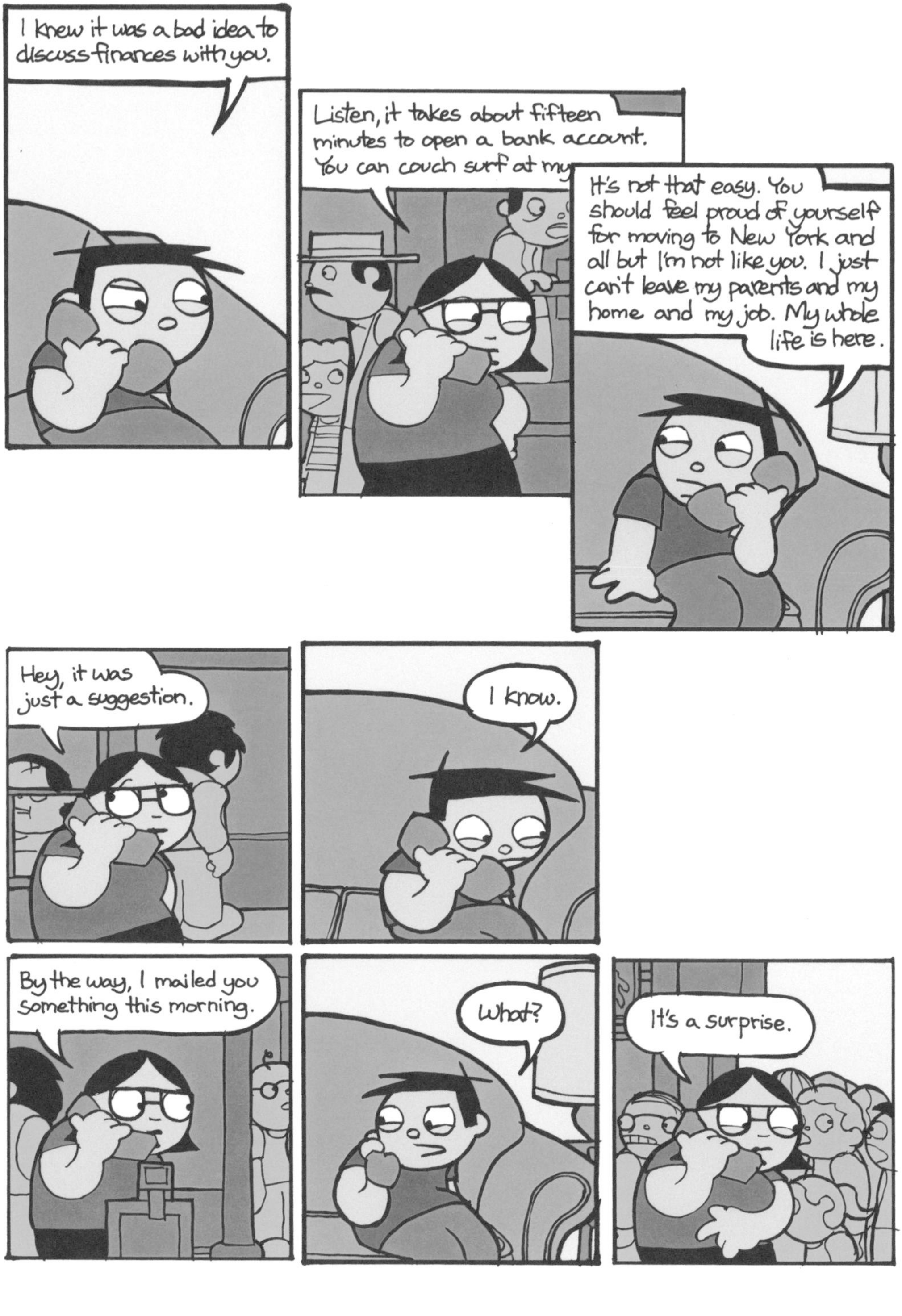
I knew it was a bad idea to discuss finances with you.
Listen, it takes about fifteen minutes to open a bank account. You can couch surf at my
It's not that easy. You should feel proud of yourself for moving to New York and all but I'm not like you. I just can't leave my parents and my home and my job. My whole life is here.
Hey, it was just a suggestion.
I know.
By the way, I mailed you something this morning.
What?
It's a surprise.

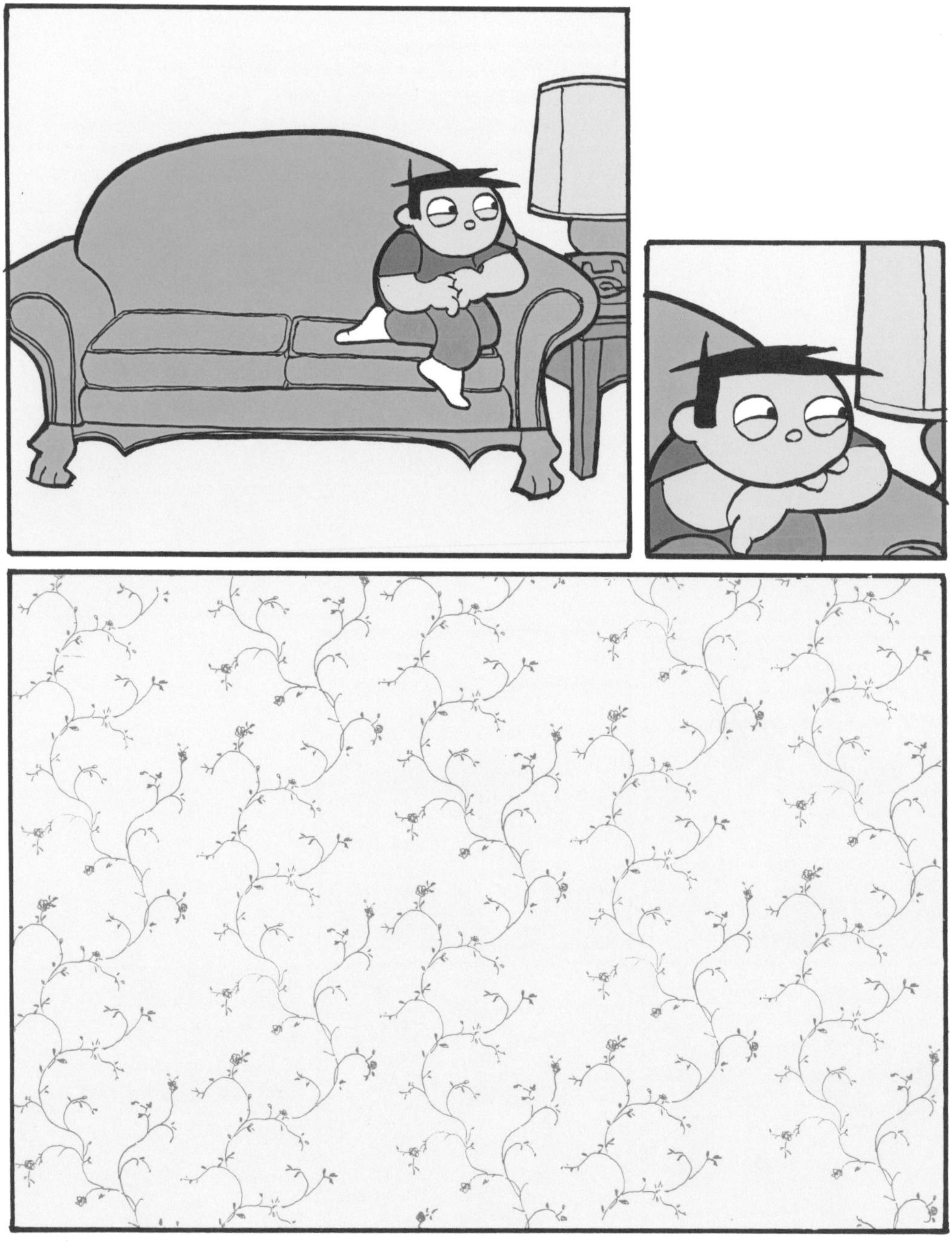

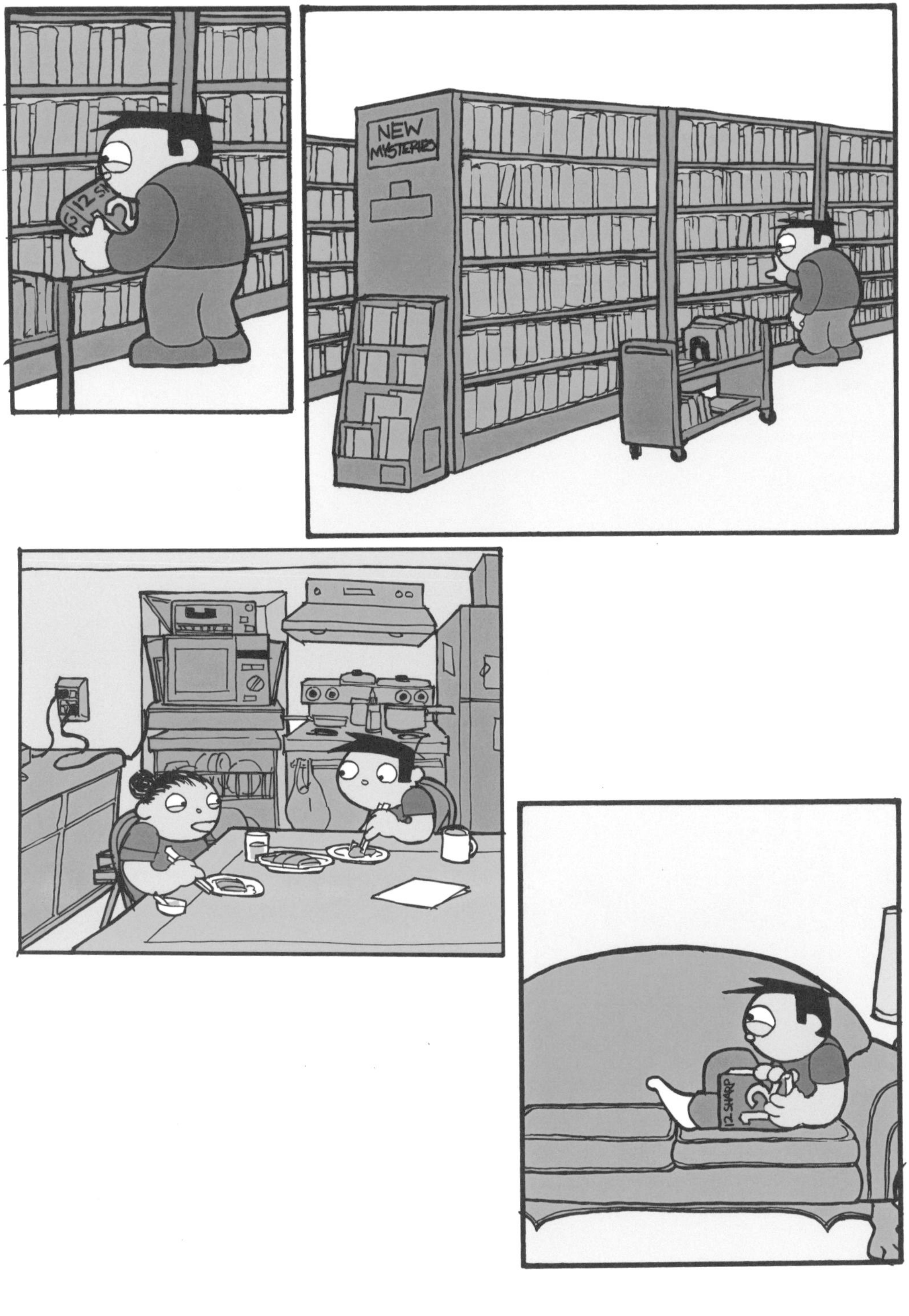
NEW MYSTERIES
12 SHARP

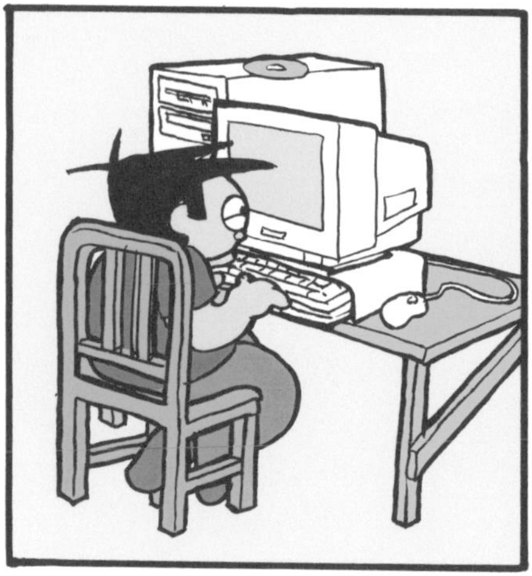

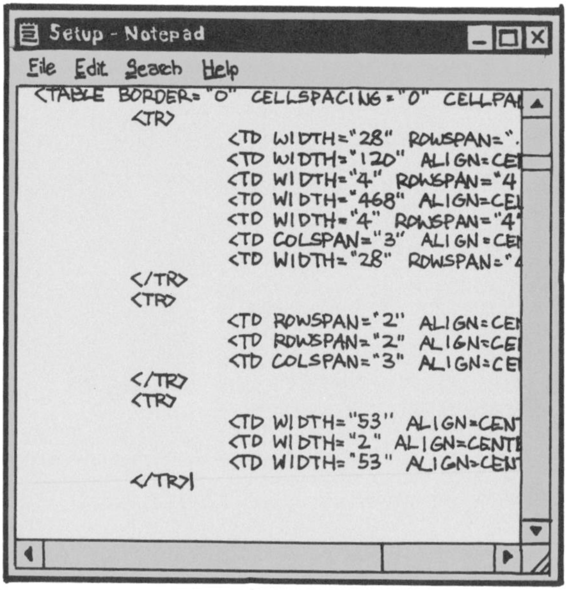

Setup - Notepad
File Edit Search Help
<TABLE BORDER="0" CELLSPACING="0" CELLPA
<TR>
<TD WIDTH="28" ROWSPAN=".
<TD WIDTH="120" ALIGN=CE
<TD WIDTH="4" ROWSPAN="4
<TD WIDTH="468" ALIGN=CEL
<TD WIDTH="4" ROWSPAN="4"
<TD COLSPAN="3" ALIGN=CE
<TD WIDTH="28" ROWSPAN="4
</TR>
<TR>
<TD ROWSPAN="2" ALIGN=CE
<TD ROWSPAN="2" ALIGN=CE
<TD COLSPAN="3" ALIGN=CE
</TR>
<TR>
<TD WIDTH="53" ALIGN=CENT
<TD WIDTH="2" ALIGN=CENTE
<TD WIDTH="53" ALIGN=CENT
</TR>|

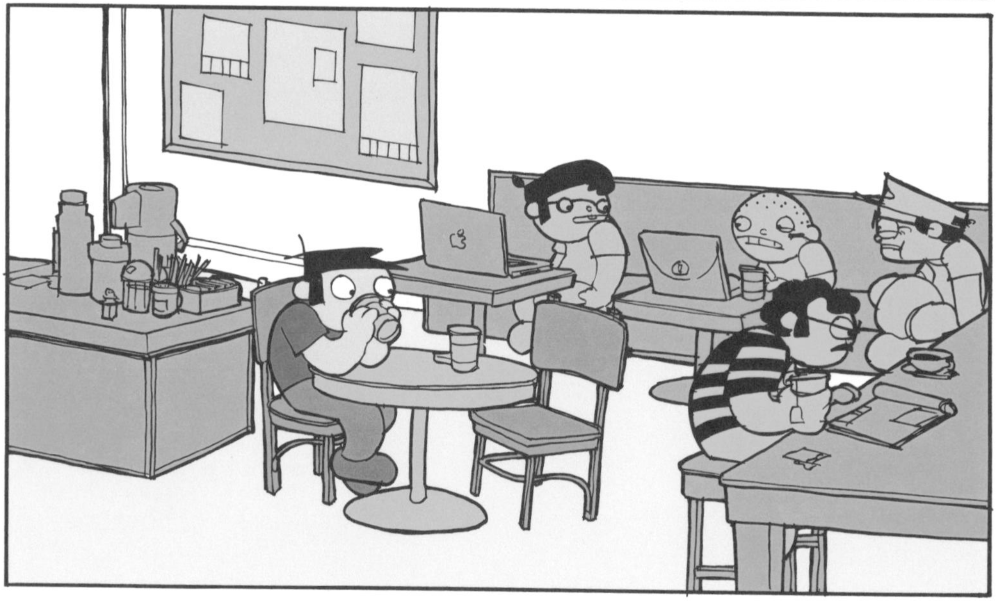

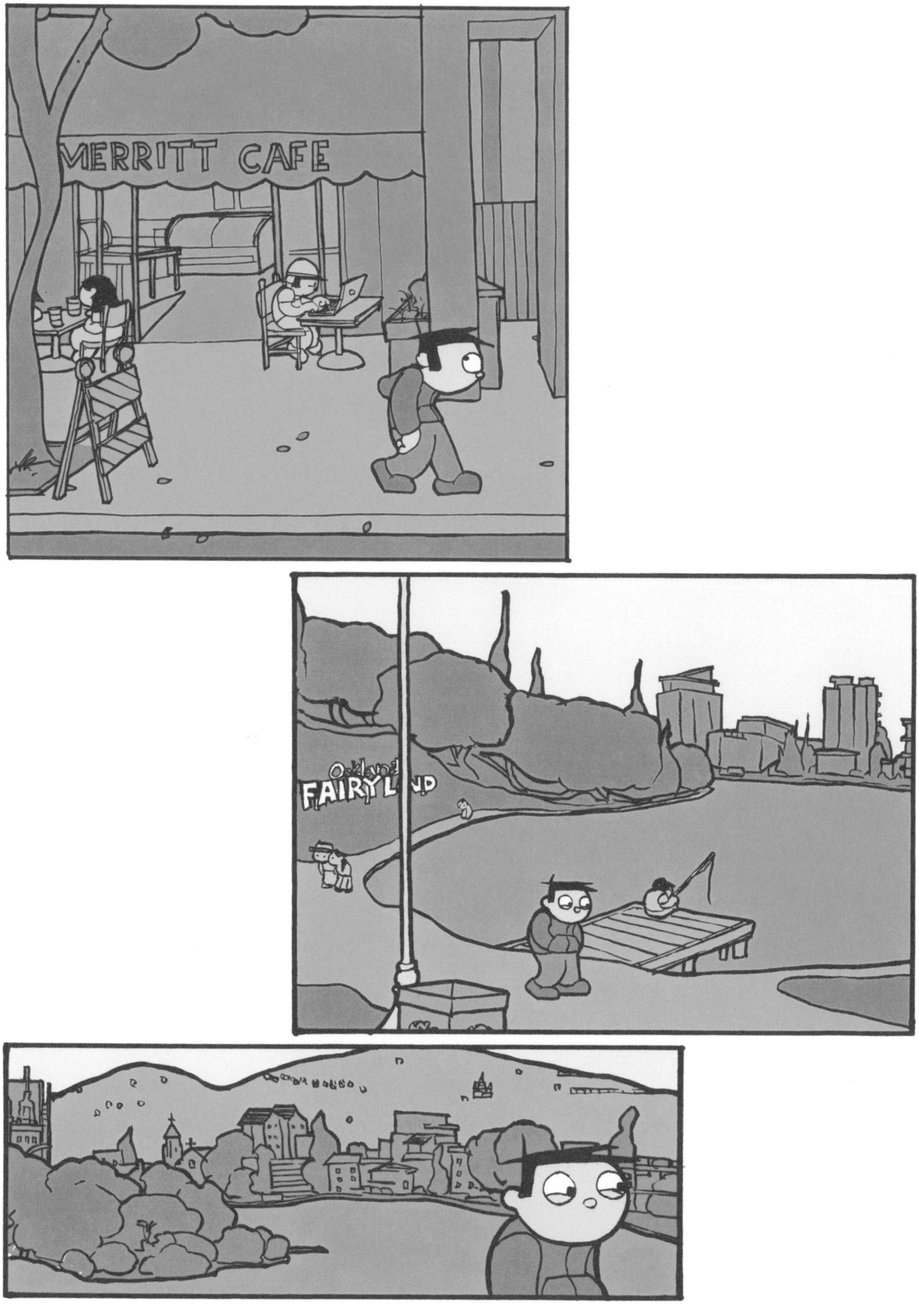
MERRITT CAFE
Oakland

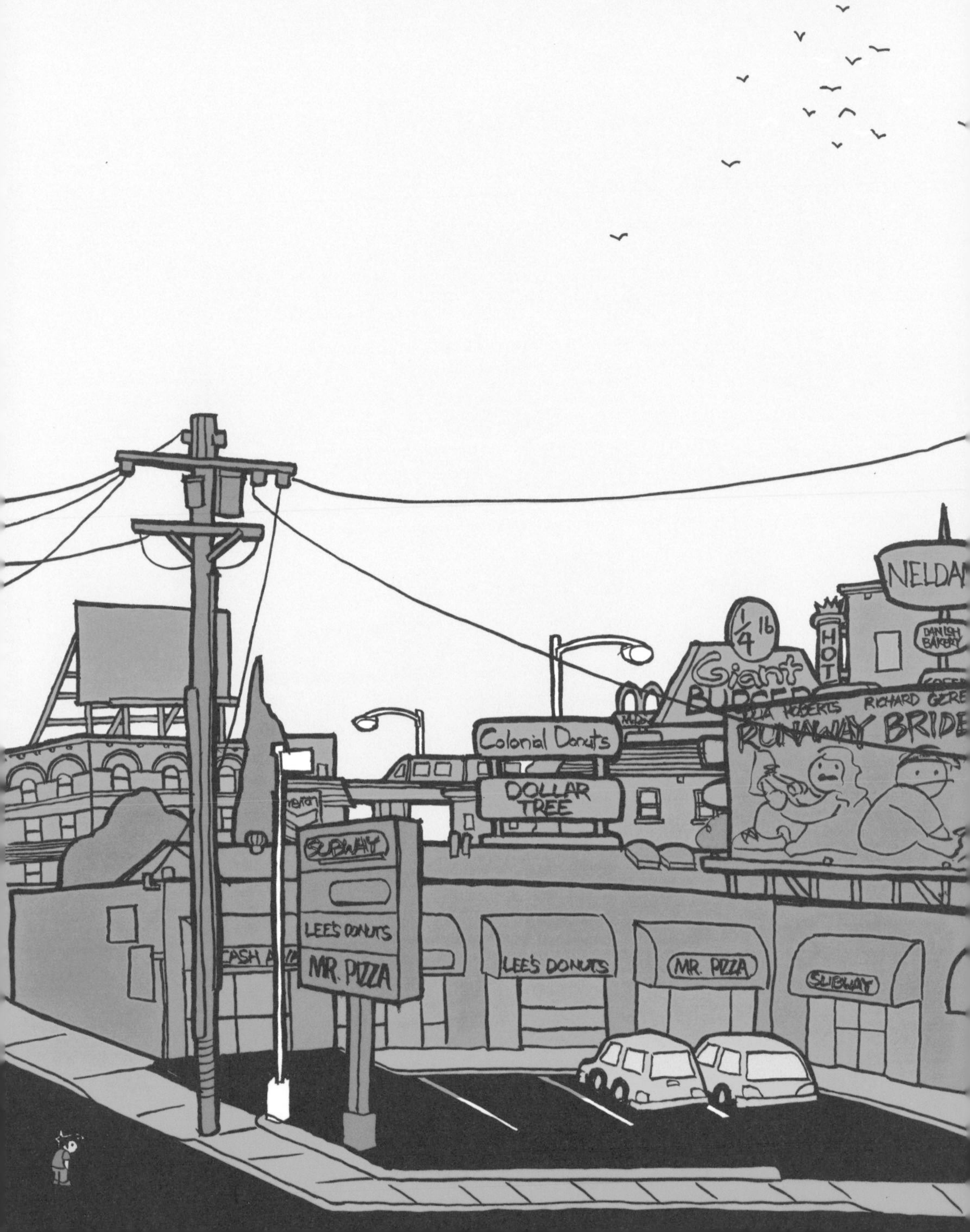

HOT
Giant
RICHARD GERE
RUNAWAY BRIDE
Colonial Donuts
DOLLAR TREE
SUBWAY
LEE'S DONUTS
MR. PIZZA
LEE'S DONUTS
MR. PIZZA
SUBWAY

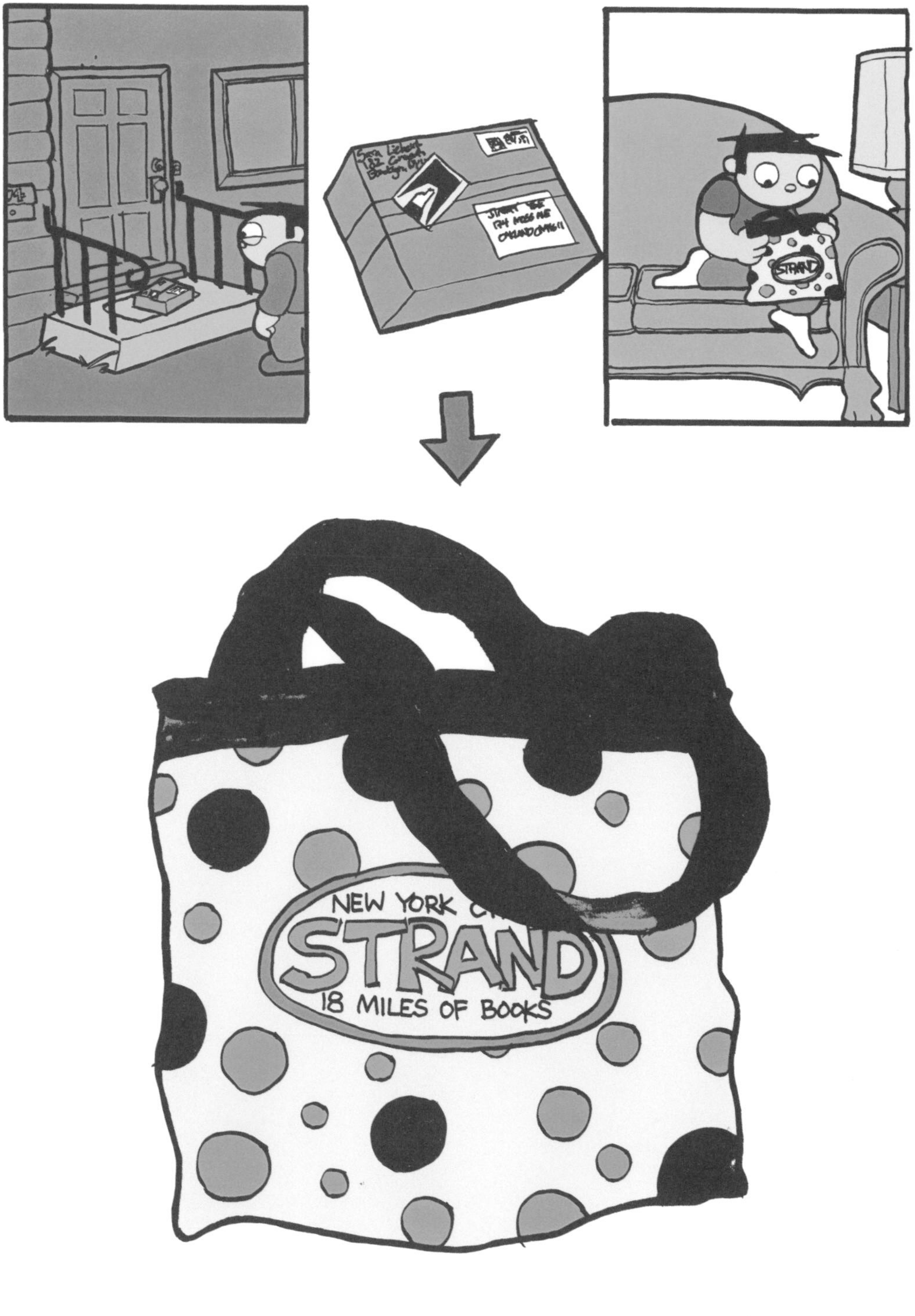
NEW YORK
STRAND
18 MILES OF BOOKS

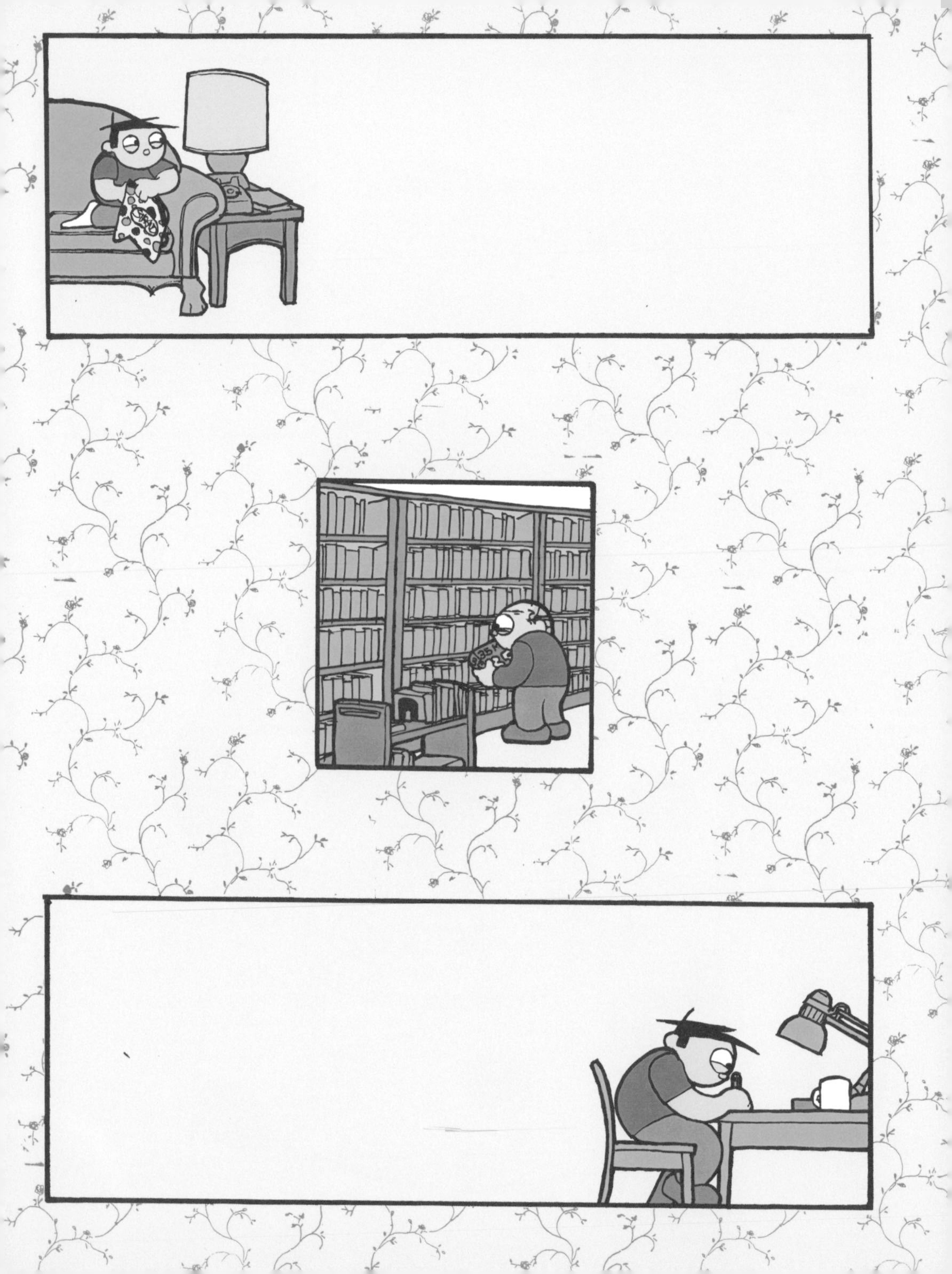

Dear Sara,

By the time you read this I will be in a bus traveling through the ~~salt flats~~ Salt Flats of Utah. You're probably wondering why.

I really don't know how else to put it other than to say that you're my best friend and I miss you. I had a weird dream the other morning that we were holding hands and running ~~through~~ a field of daisies. It felt nice, but then I woke up holding my own hand. Even if I called in sick and went back to sleep, I'd probably have a completely different dream about my teeth falling out or a giant snake in a vest. ~~or the 21~~

I thought a lot about what you said last week about moving to NY. And if you'd asked me a few years ago I would have imagined I'd have an equal chance of moving to Mars. But just by thinking about you, I feel like I can climb the highest mountain and swim to the deepest depths of the ocean. I'm an Oakland boy and I'll always be an Oakland boy, but if being close to you means traveling into the festering hellhole that is New York, then to the festering hellhole I shall go.

Remember when you were at my place and we watched "Sleepless in Seattle" and I started to cry at the end and you started laughing at me and saying that "Kate and Leopold" was more realistic. ~~even though they failed to resolve the grandfather paradox or the bootstrap~~ Well, I still maintain the ending was quite plausible and I'd like to meet you at the top of the Empire State Building February 21st — President's Day — at sunset as a proof of concept (I know it was Valentine's Day in the movie but the 14th just passed). I realize I'm being simultaneously unoriginal and psychotic. I also realize this could be the creepiest letter you've ever read and you'll forever feel uncomfortable around me. I'll wait for you at the Empire State Building, you'll never show; I'll head back to Oakland, grow old, die alone, and call it a life. But at least fifty years from now as I lie on my deathbed, decrepit and alone with a morphine drip sticking out of my arm, I won't regret not having tried.

P.S.: Thanks for the canvas bag!

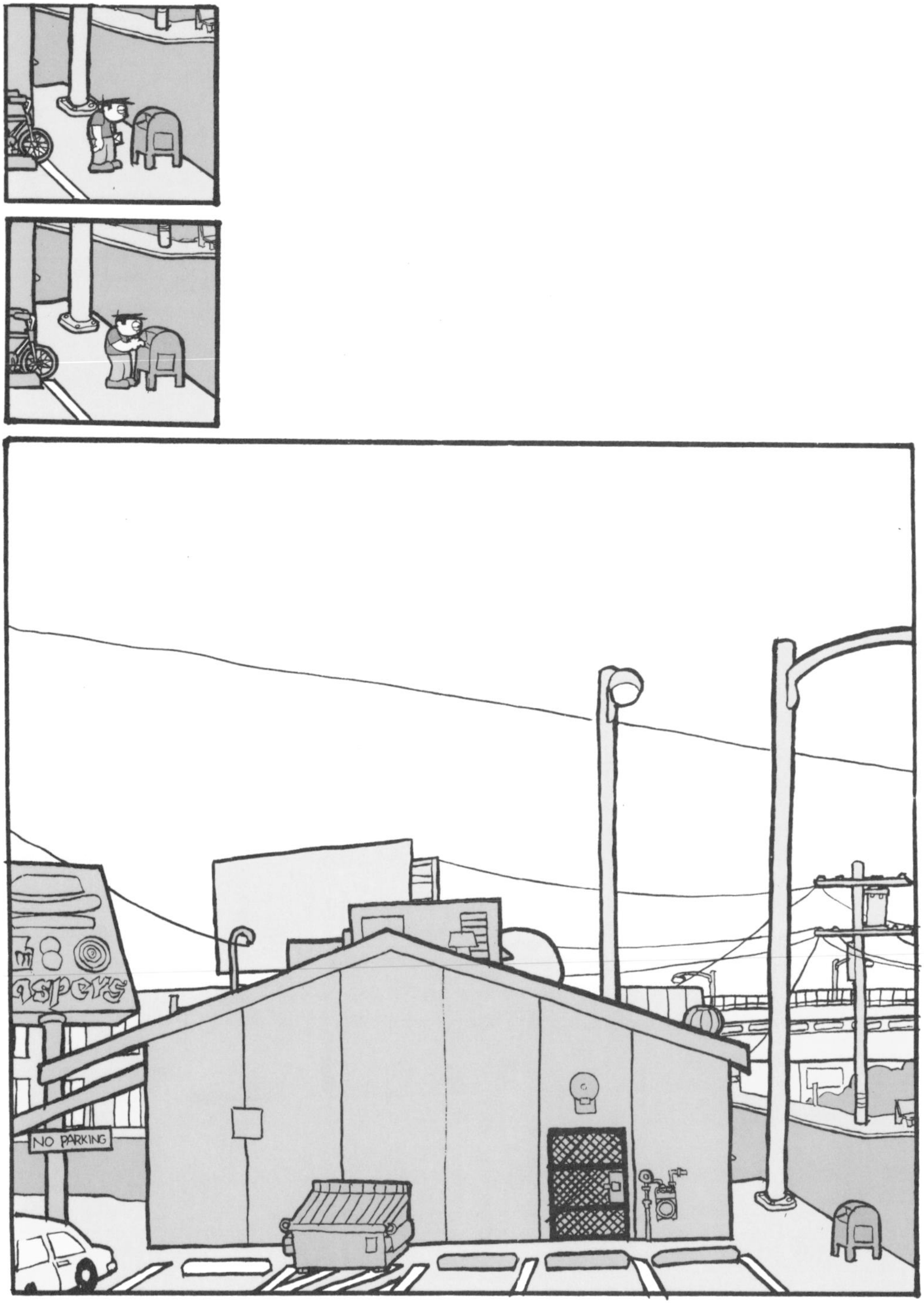
NO PARKING

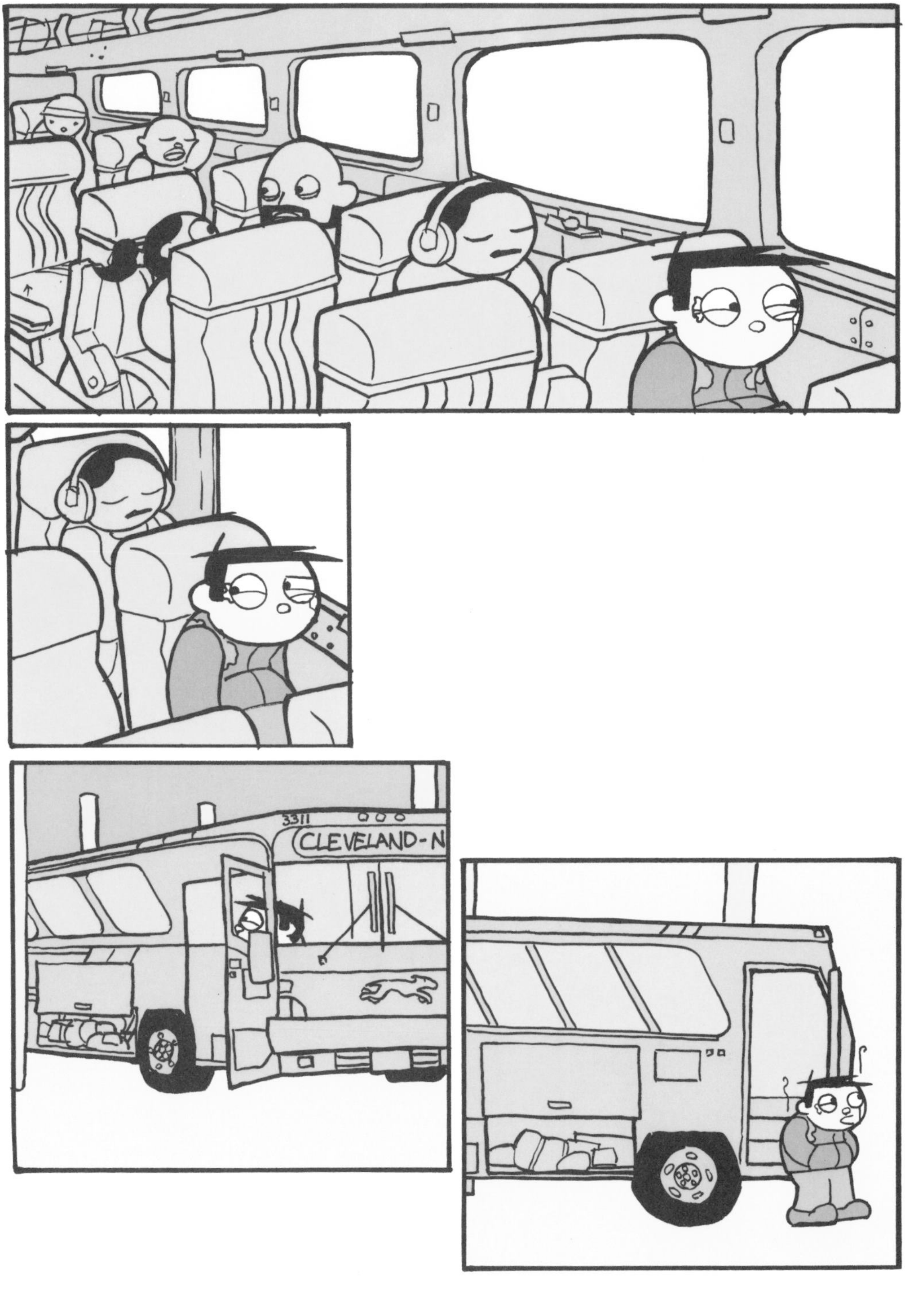
3311
CLEVELAND-N

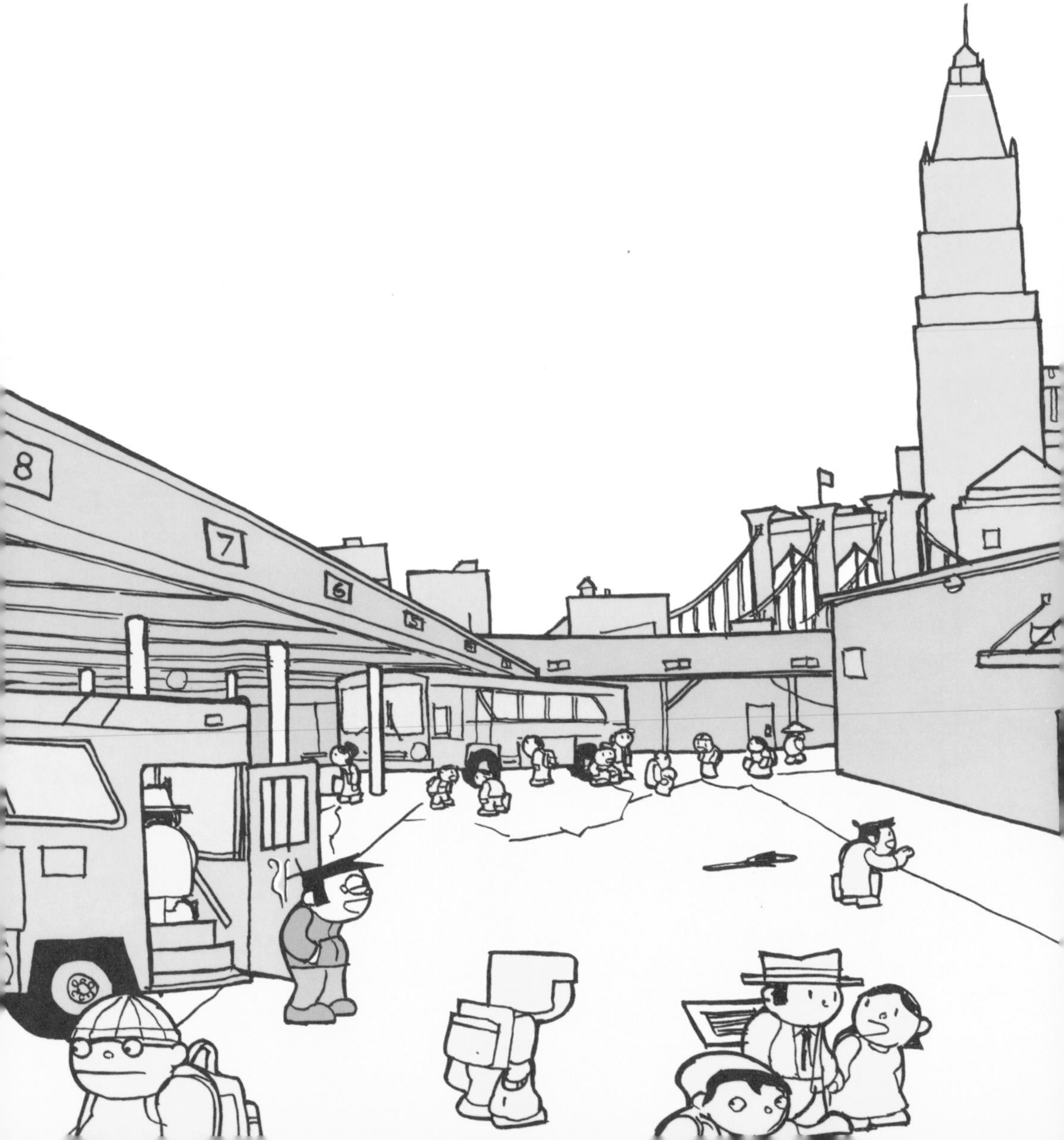
8
7
6

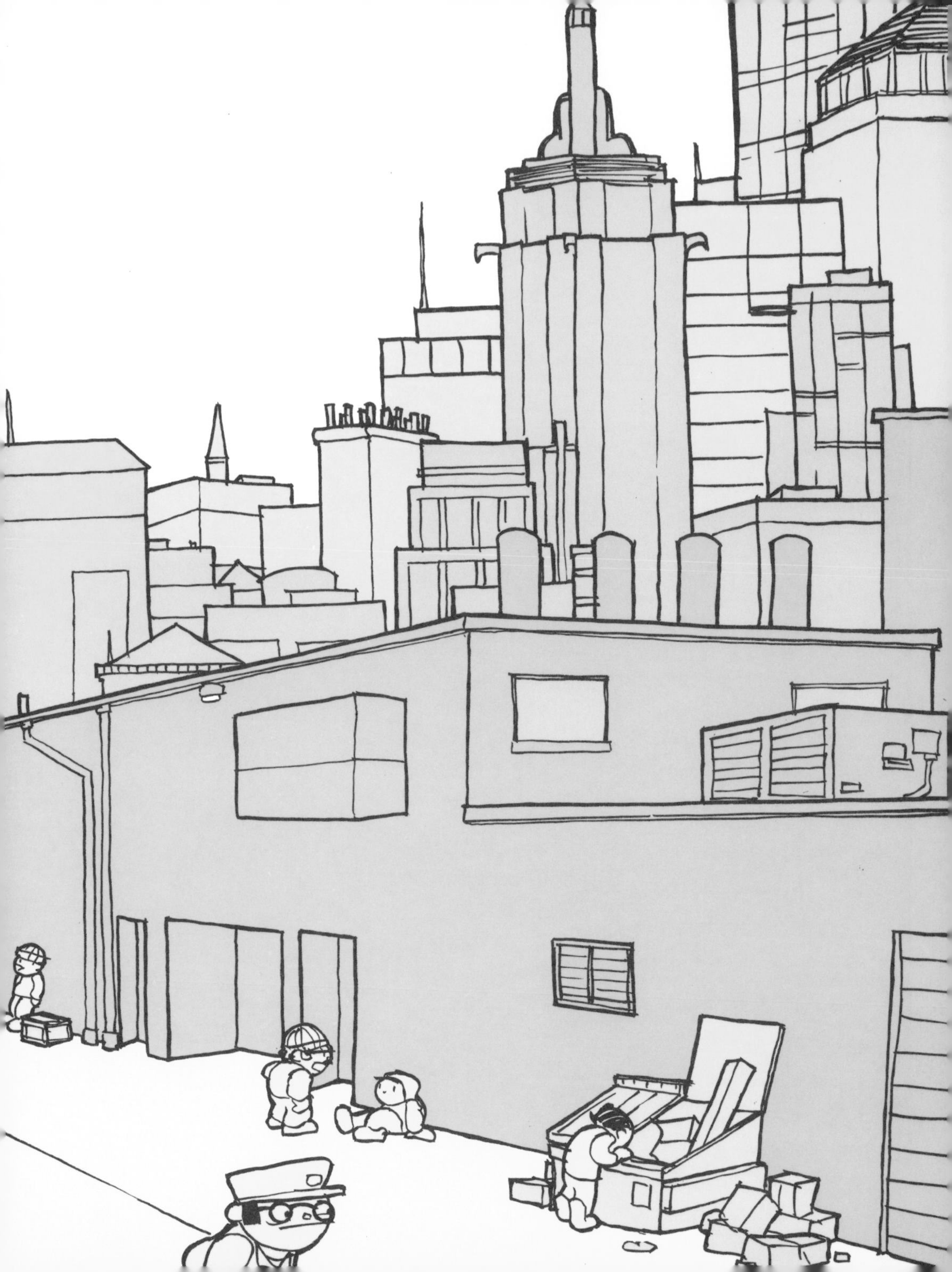

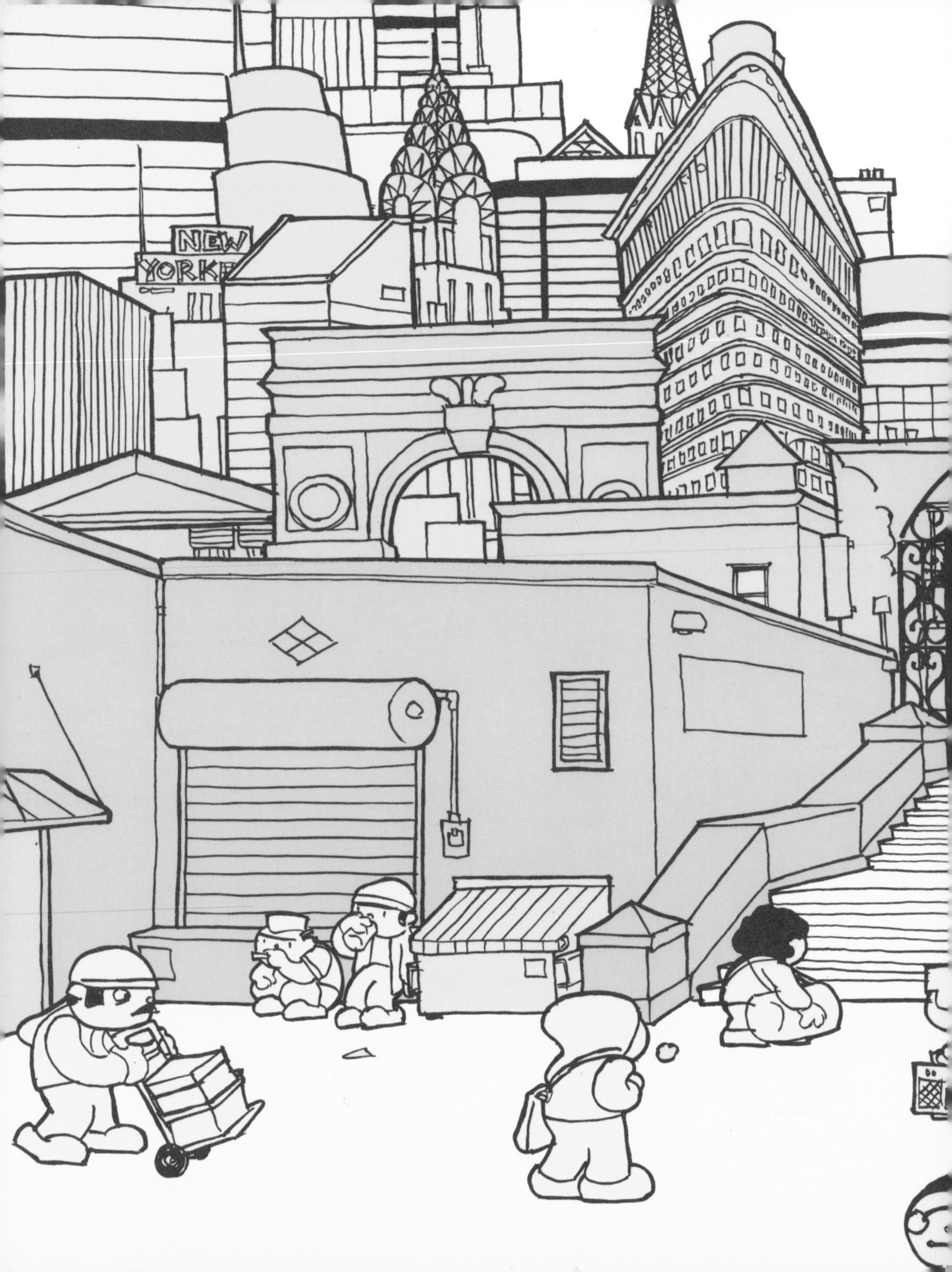
NEW

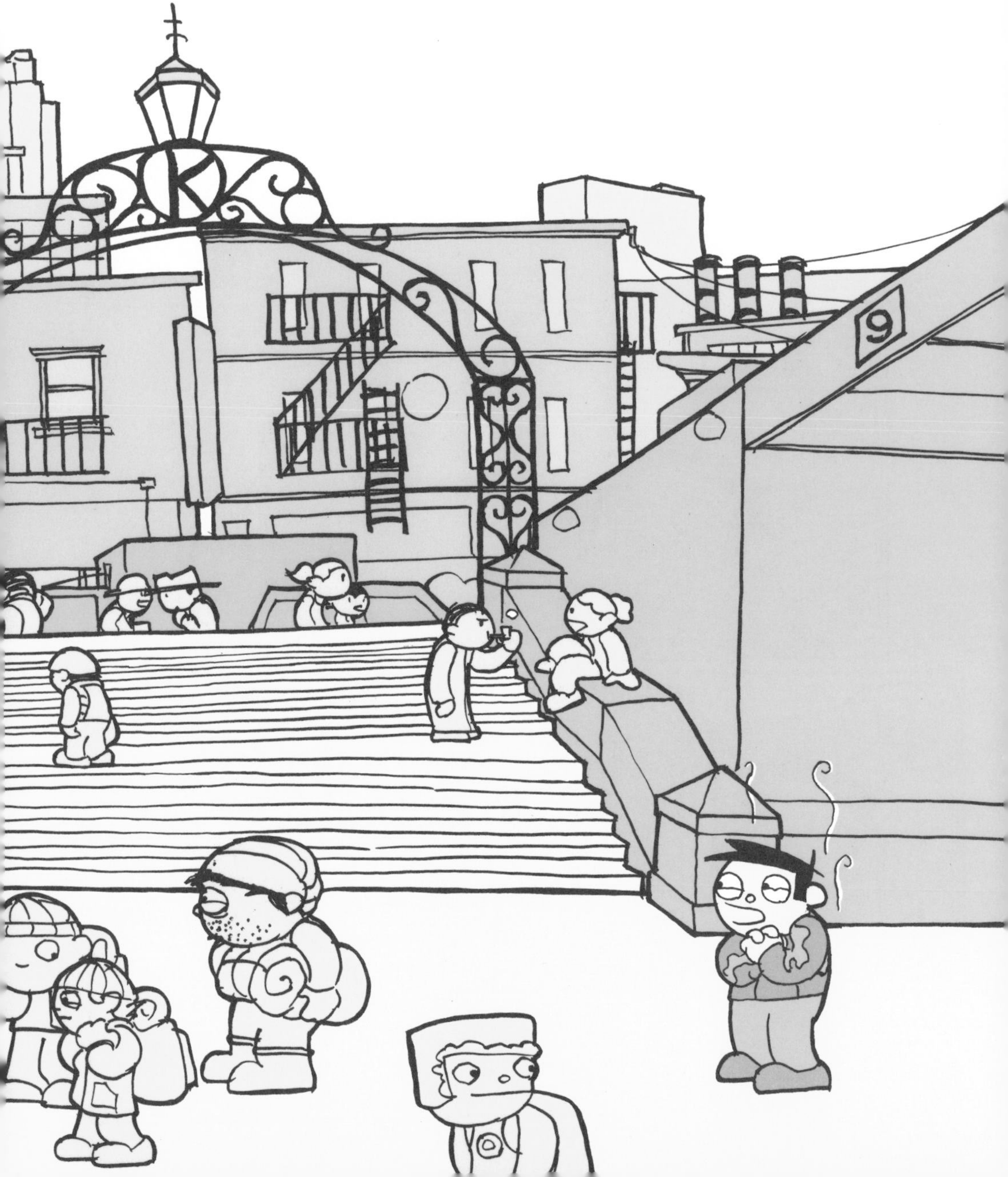
9

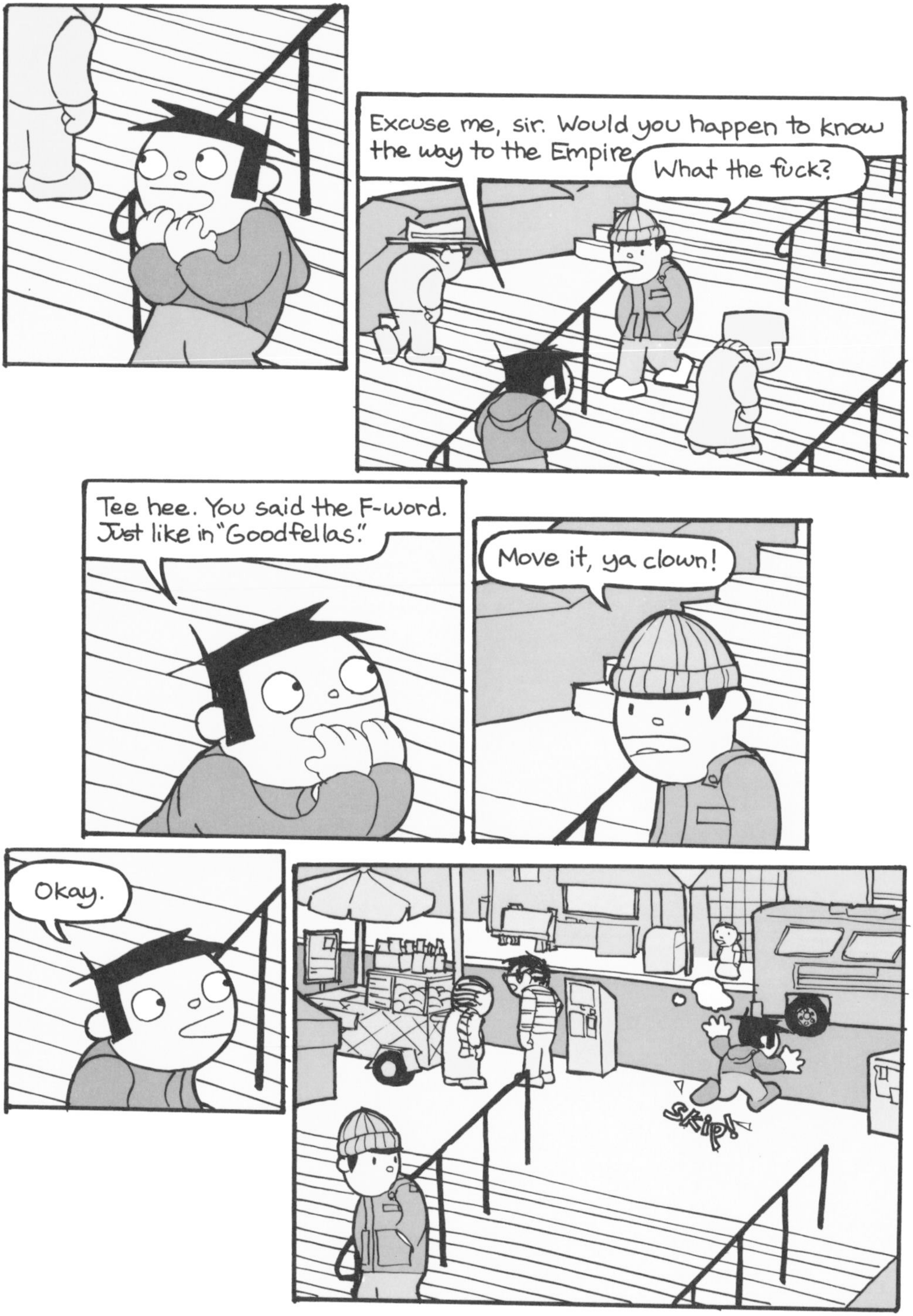
Excuse me, sir. Would you happen to know the way to the Empire
What the fuck?
Tee hee. You said the F-word. Just like in "Goodfellas."
Move it, ya clown!
Okay.
SKIP!

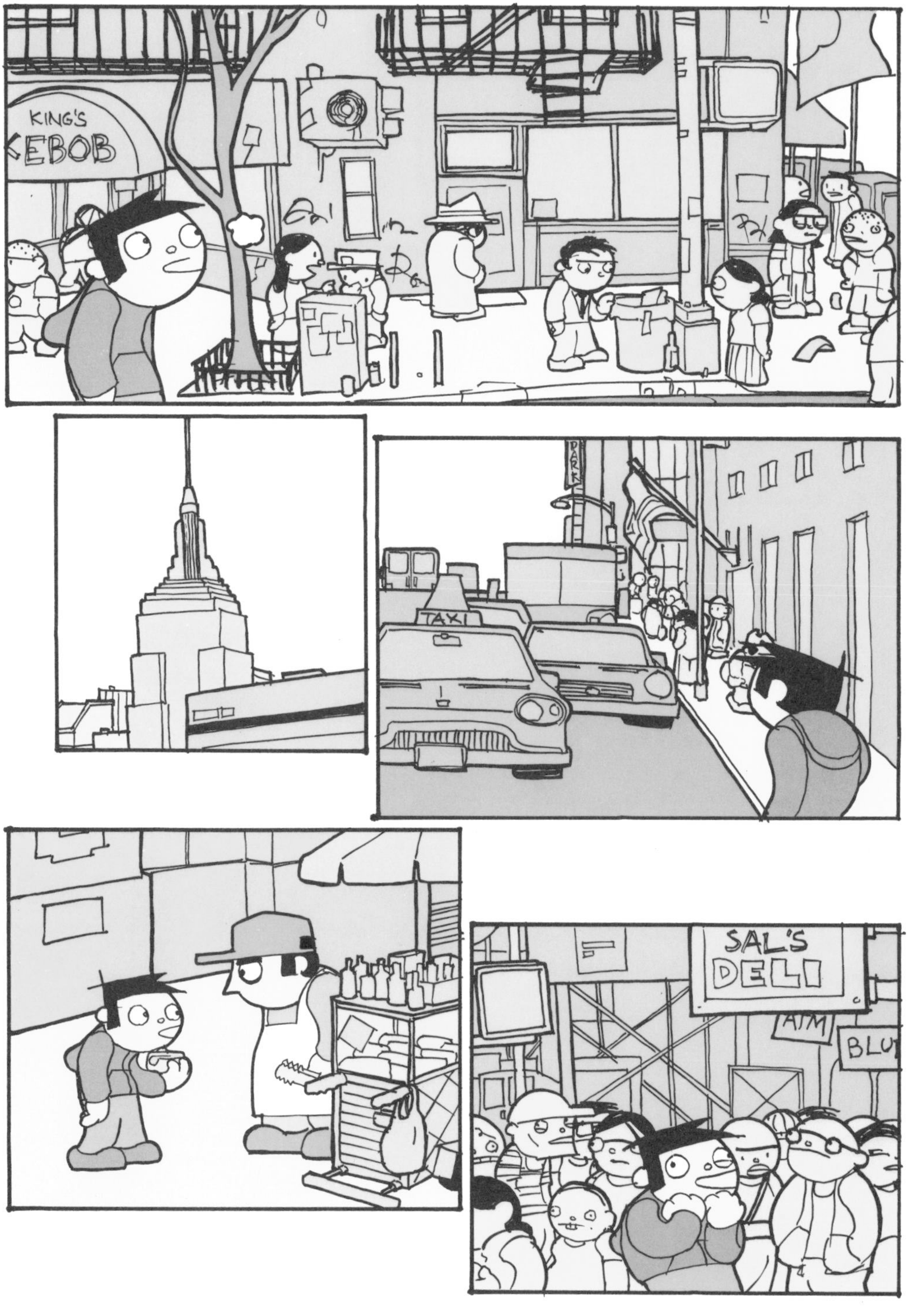

KING'S
EBOB
PARK
TAXI
SAL'S
DELI
ATM
BLU

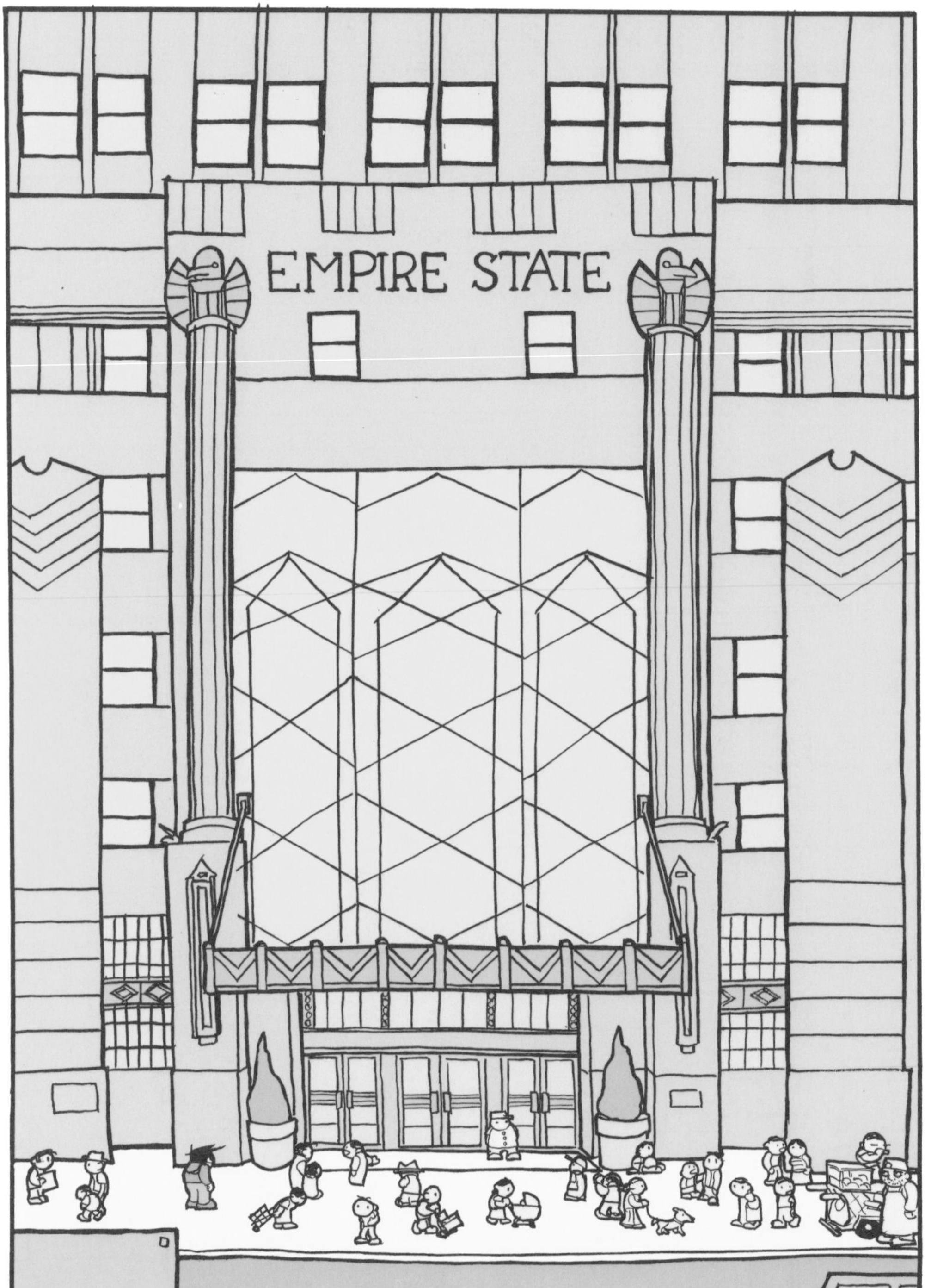
EMPIRE STATE

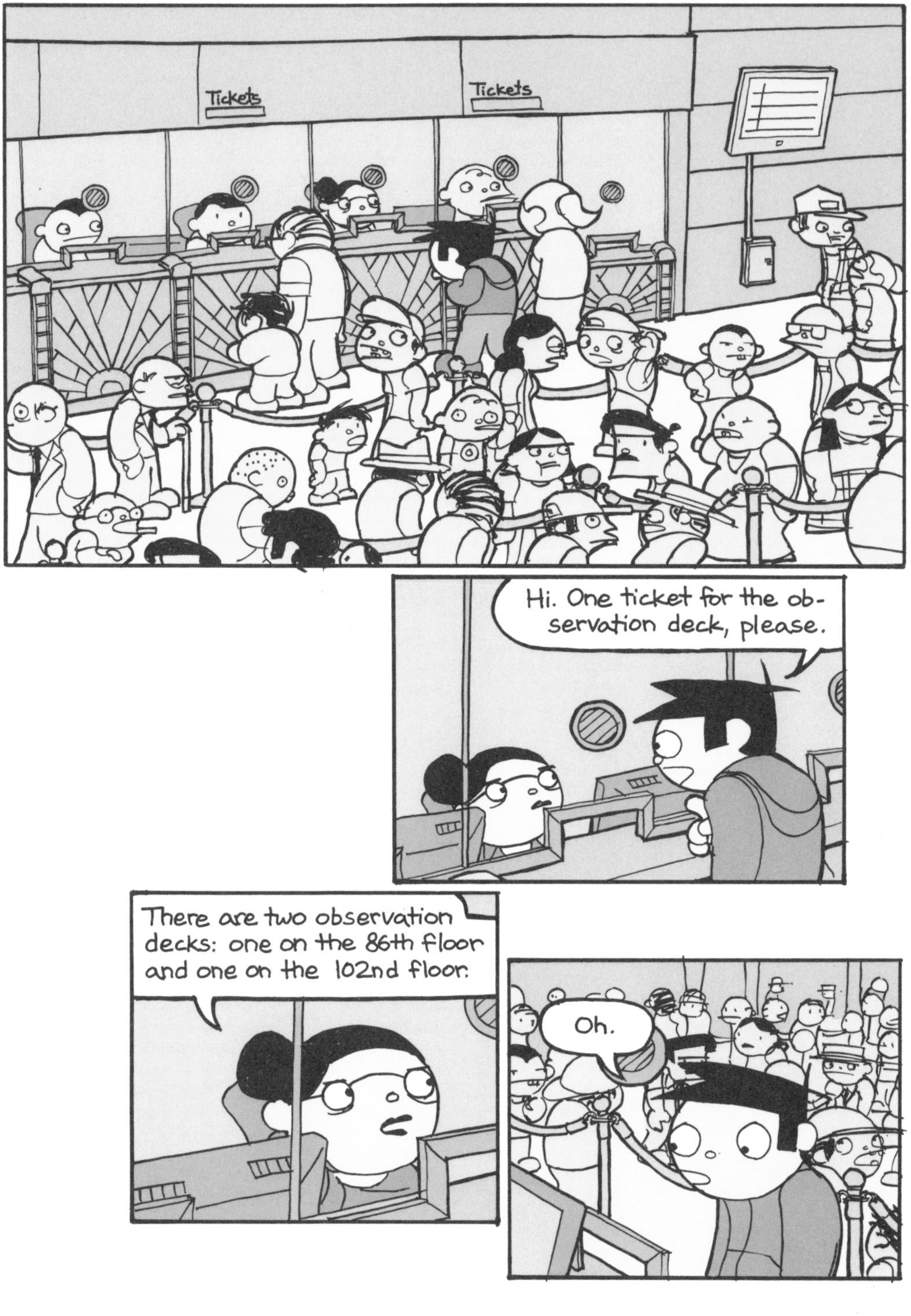
Tickets
Tickets
Hi. One ticket for the observation deck, please.
There are two observation decks: one on the 86th floor and one on the 102nd floor.
Oh.

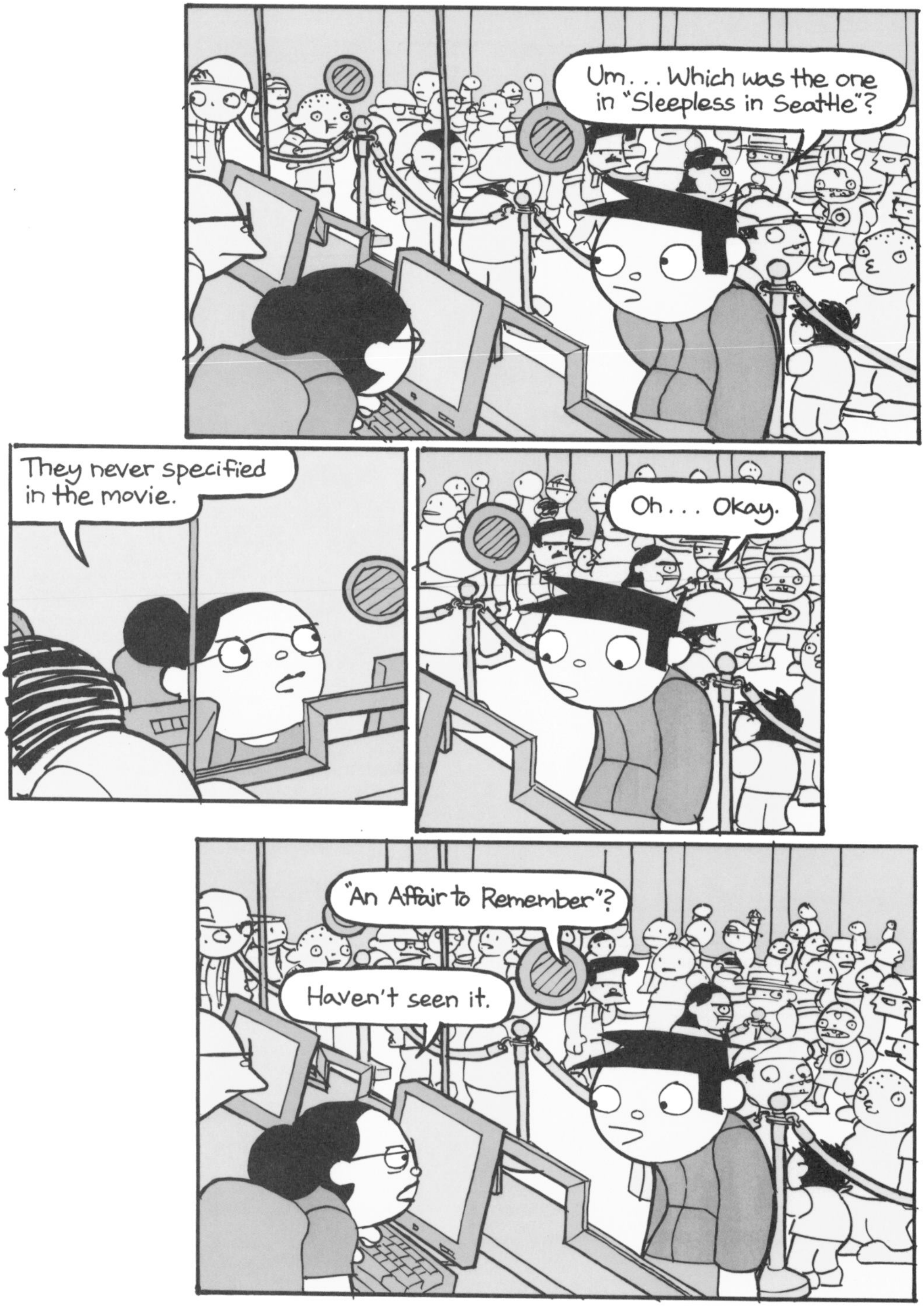
Um. . . Which was the one in "Sleepless in Seattle"?
They never specified in the movie.
Oh . . . Okay.
"An Affair to Remember"?
Haven't seen it.

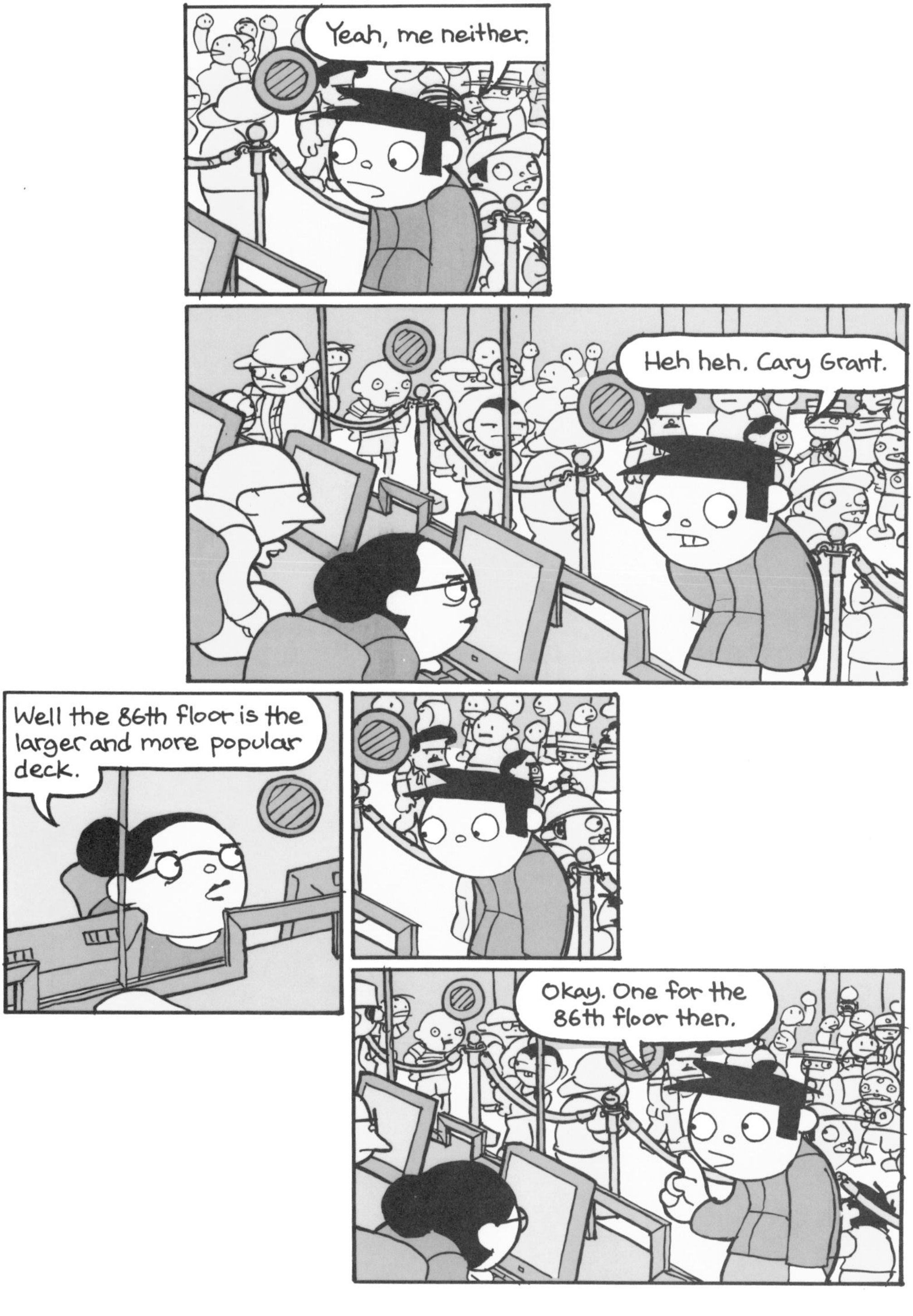

Yeah, me neither.
Heh heh. Cary Grant.
Well the 86th floor is the larger and more popular deck.
Okay. One for the 86th floor then.

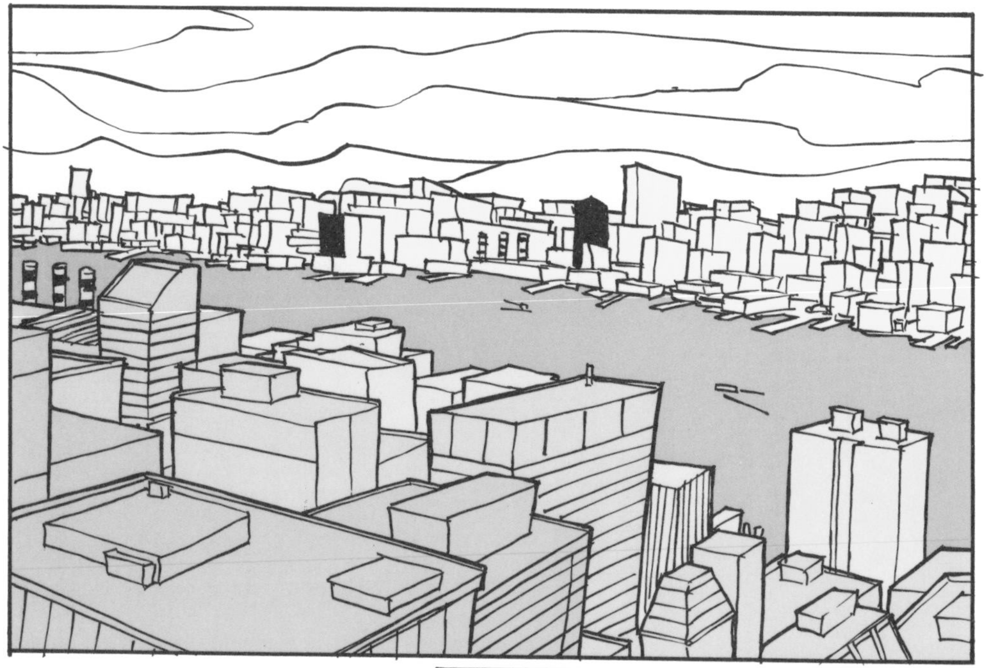

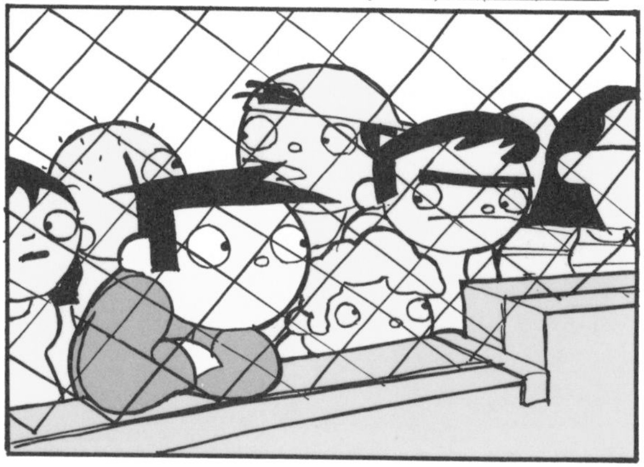

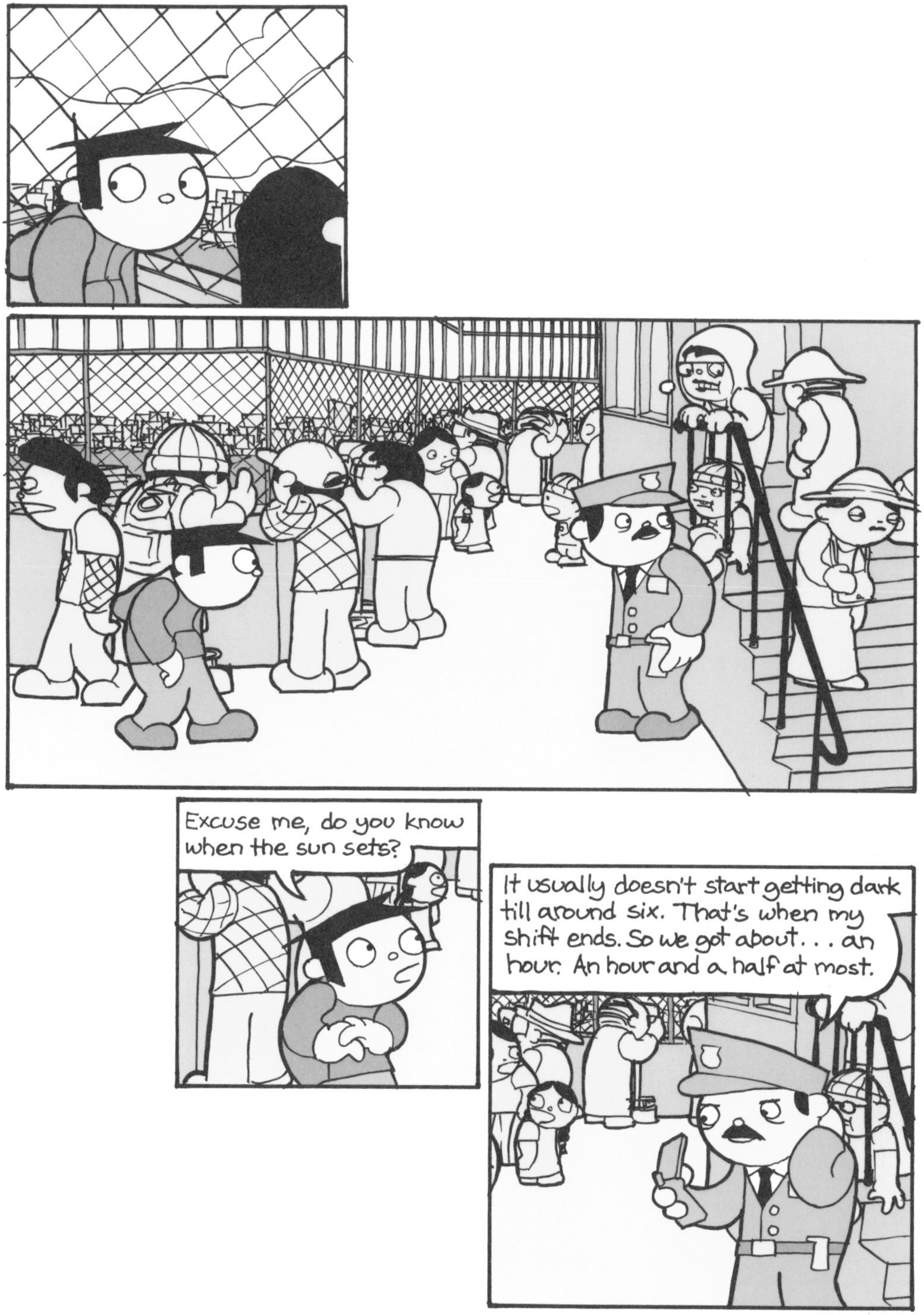
Excuse me, do you know when the sun sets?
It usually doesn't start getting dark till around six. That's when my shift ends. So we got about. . . an hour. An hour and a half at most.

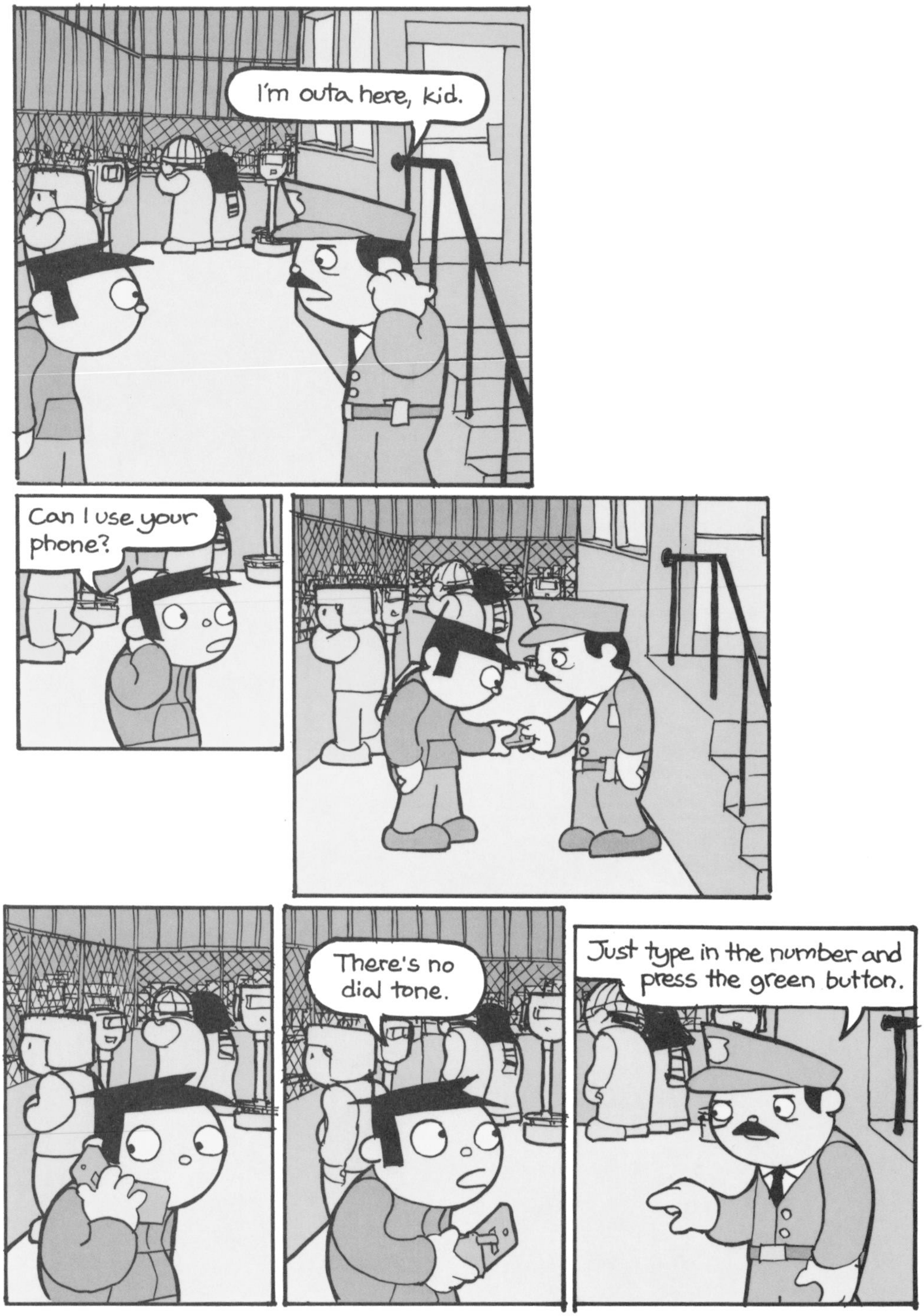
I'm outa here, kid.
Can I use your phone?
There's no dial tone.
Just type in the number and press the green button.

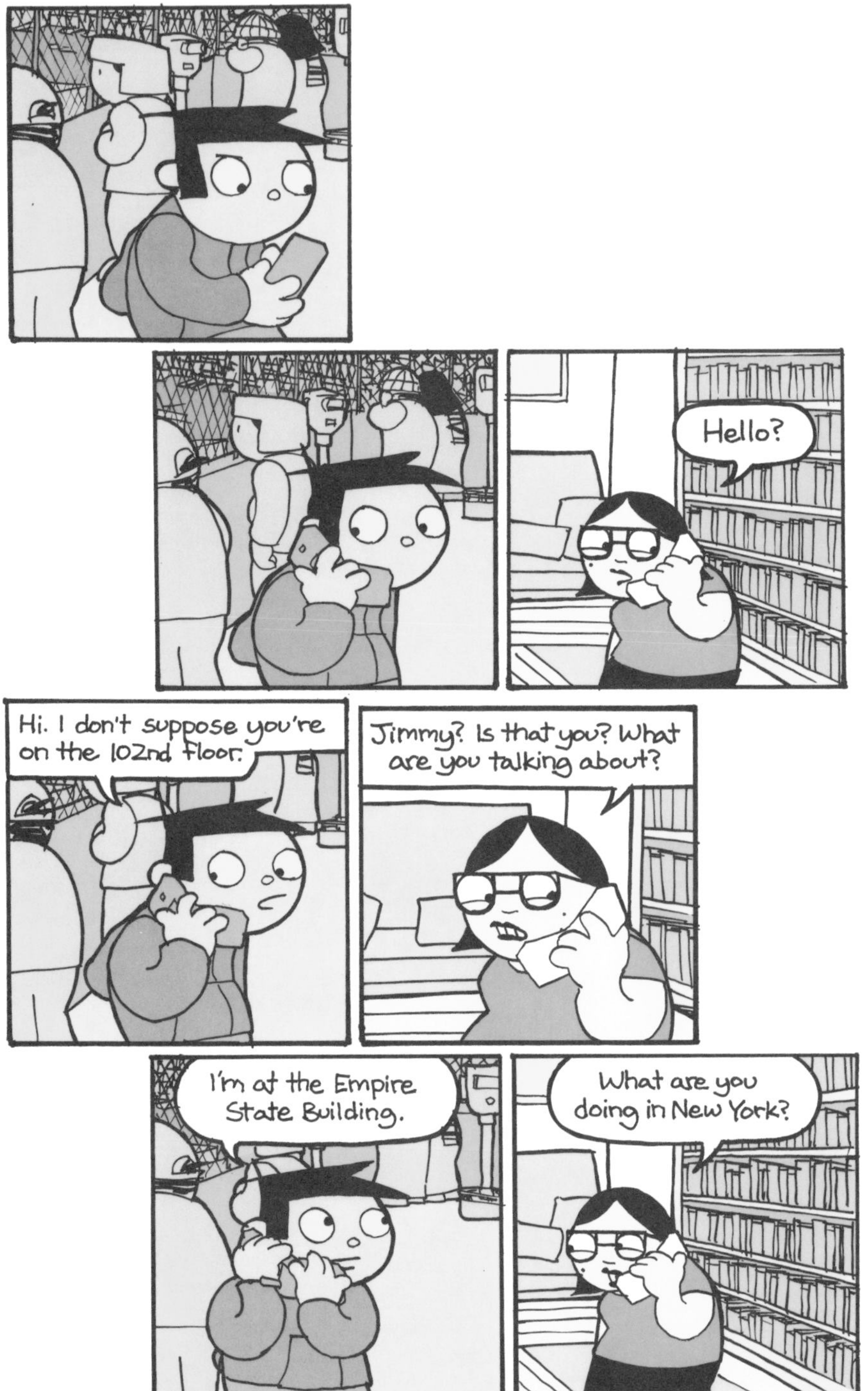
Hello?
Hi. I don't suppose you're on the 102nd floor.
Jimmy? Is that you? What are you talking about?
I'm at the Empire State Building.
What are you doing in New York?

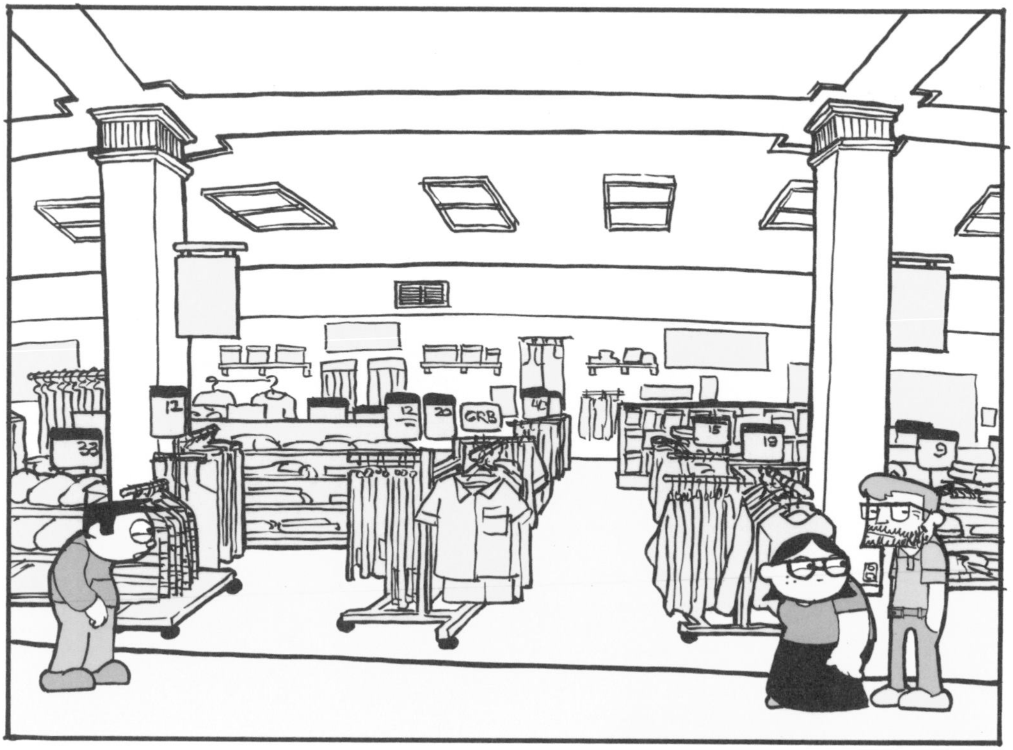

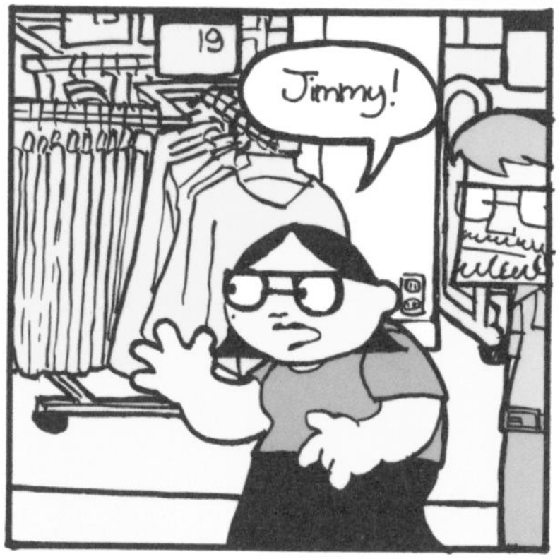
Jimmy!

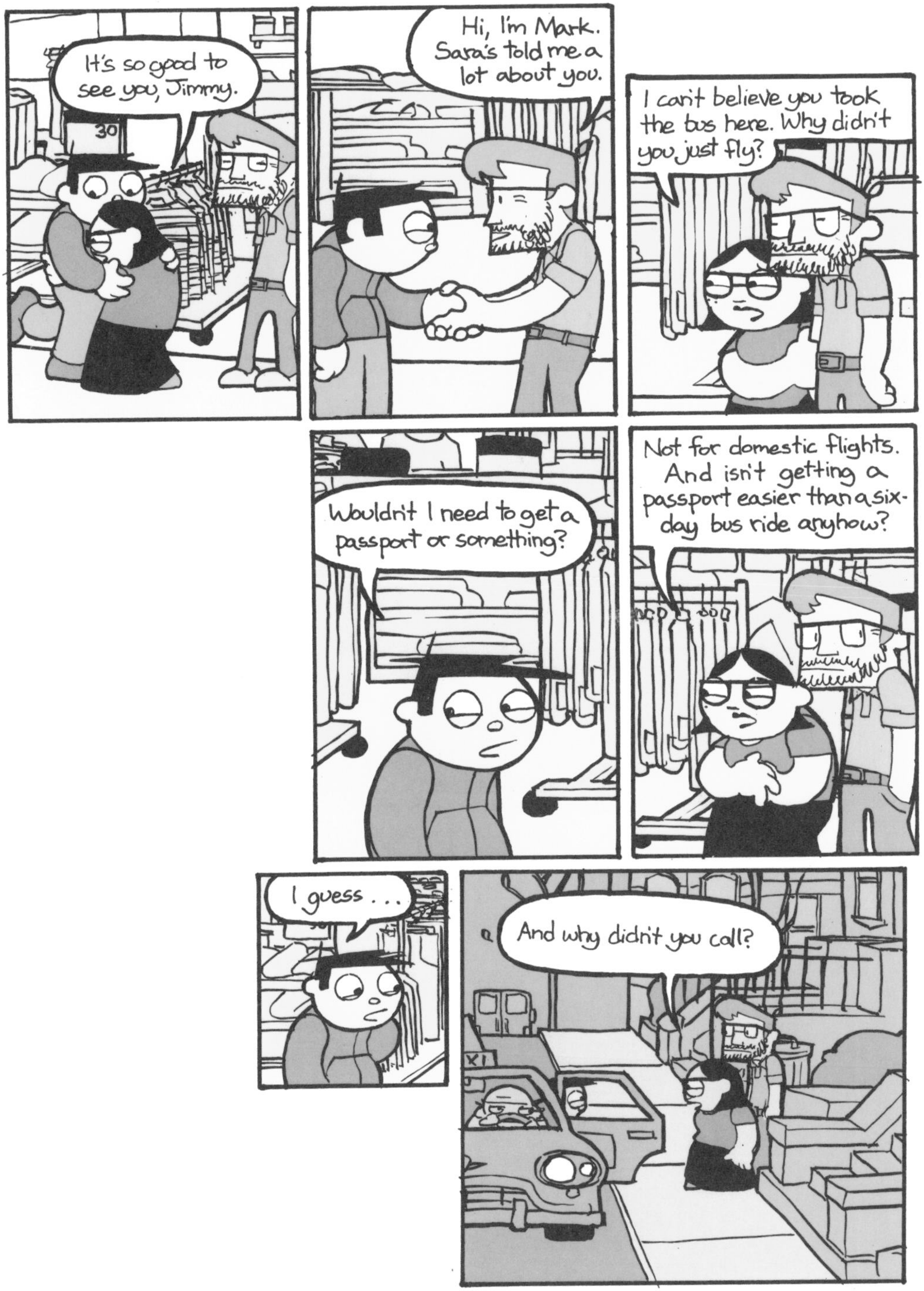
It's so good to see you, Jimmy.
Hi, I'm Mark. Sara's told me a lot about you.
I can't believe you took the bus here. Why didn't you just fly?
Wouldn't I need to get a passport or something?
Not for domestic flights. And isn't getting a passport easier than a six-day bus ride anyhow?
I guess . . .
And why didn't you call?

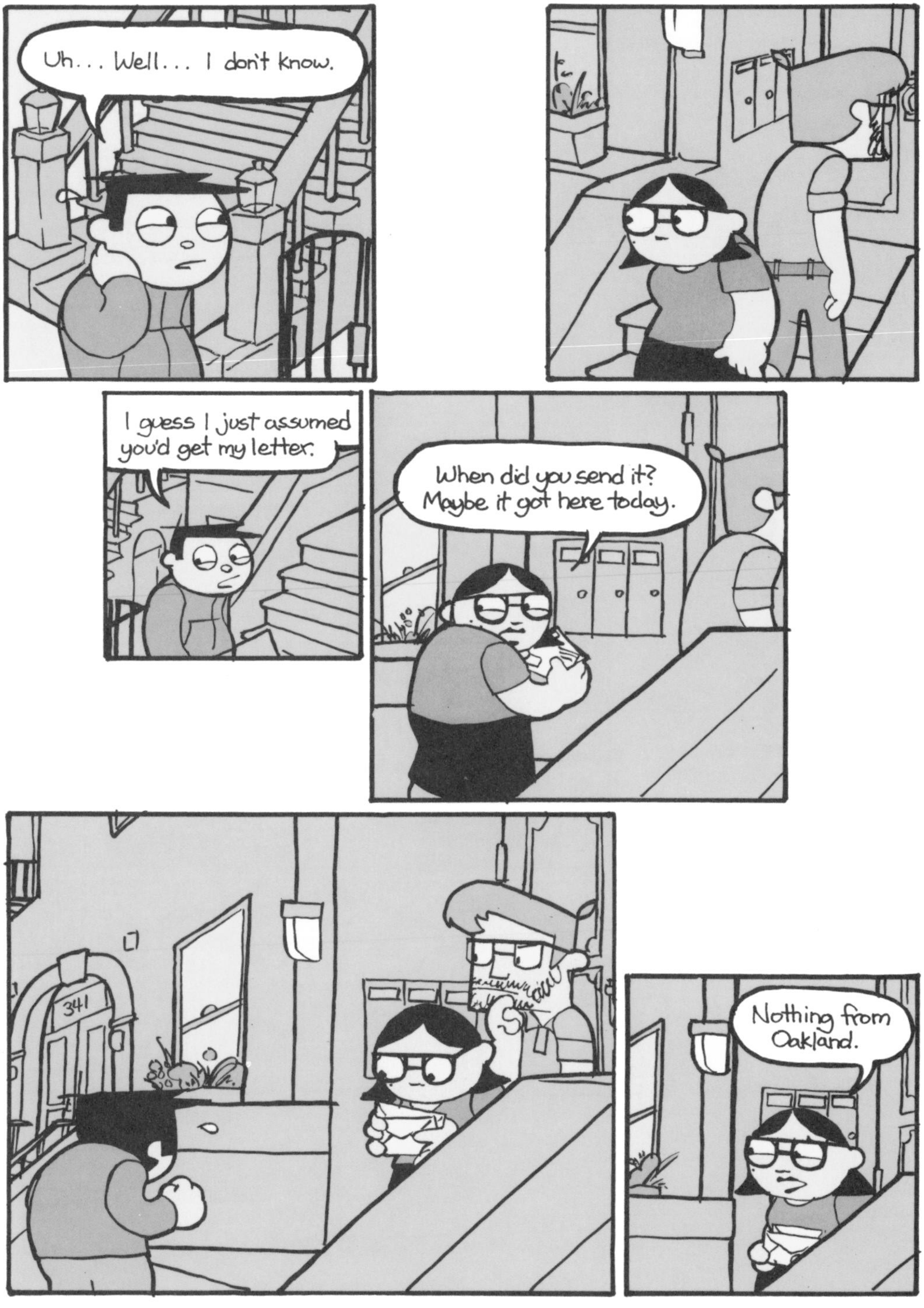
Uh... Well... I don't know.
I guess I just assumed you'd get my letter.
When did you send it? Maybe it got here today.
341
Nothing from Oakland.

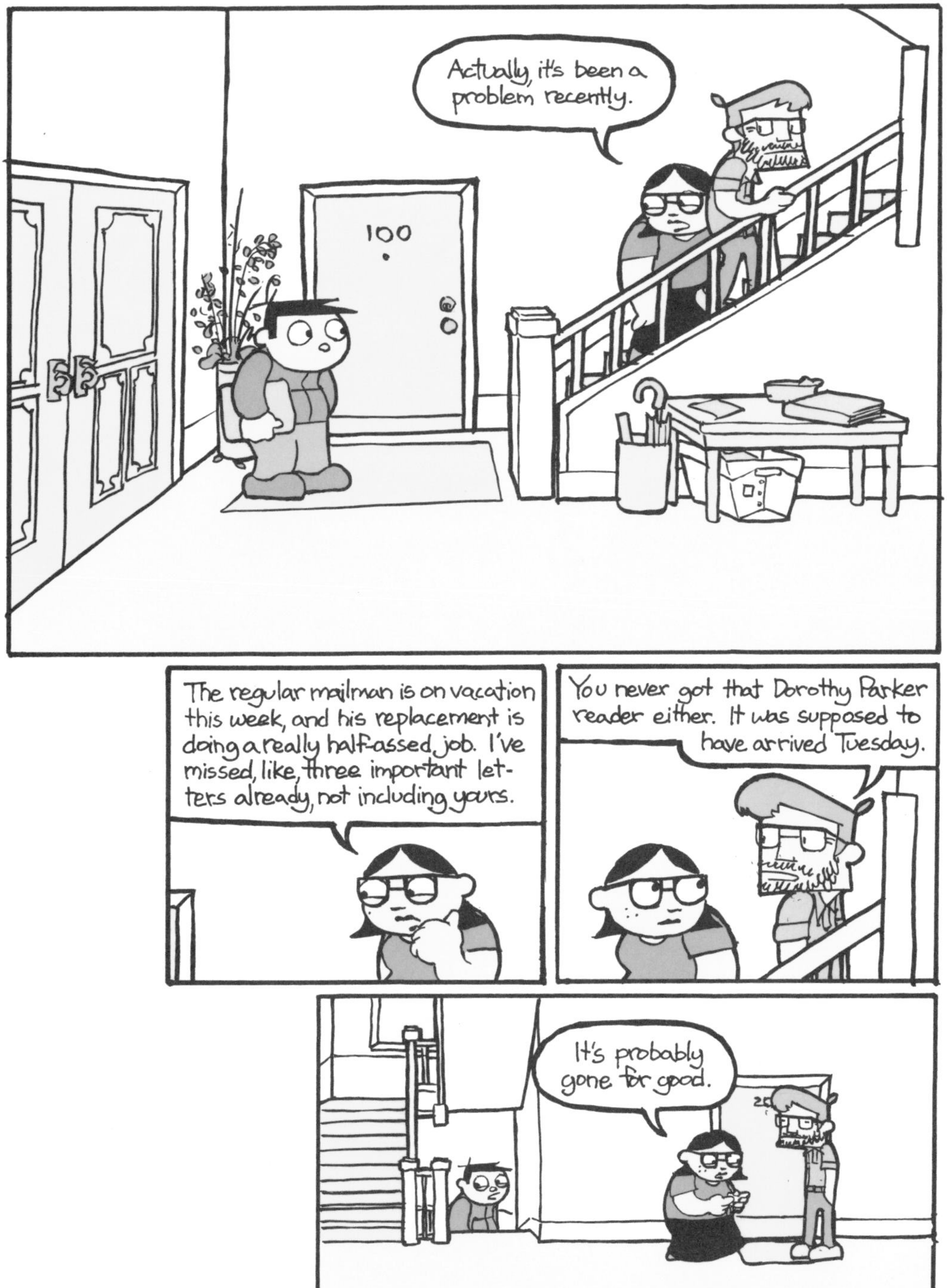
Actually, it's been a problem recently.
The regular mailman is on vacation this week, and his replacement is doing a really half-assed job. I've missed, like, three important letters already, not including yours.
You never got that Dorothy Parker reader either. It was supposed to have arrived Tuesday.
It's probably gone for good.

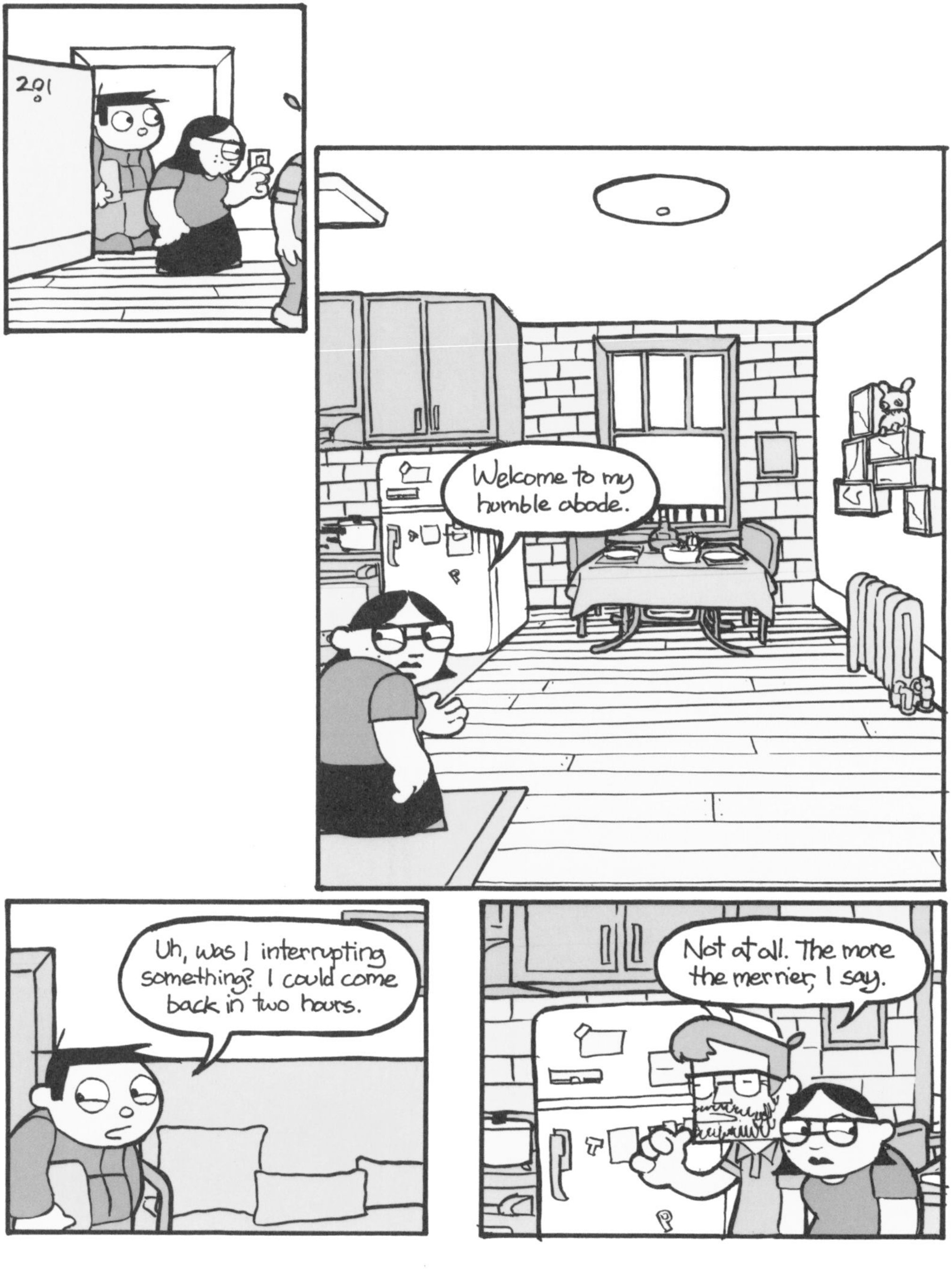
201
Welcome to my humble abode.
Uh, was I interrupting something? I could come back in two hours.
Not at all. The more the merrier, I say.

Thanks. It smells good in here.

I made couscous and chicken pastille.

Uh, do you have any towels? I think I'm gonna take a shower real quick.

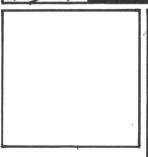

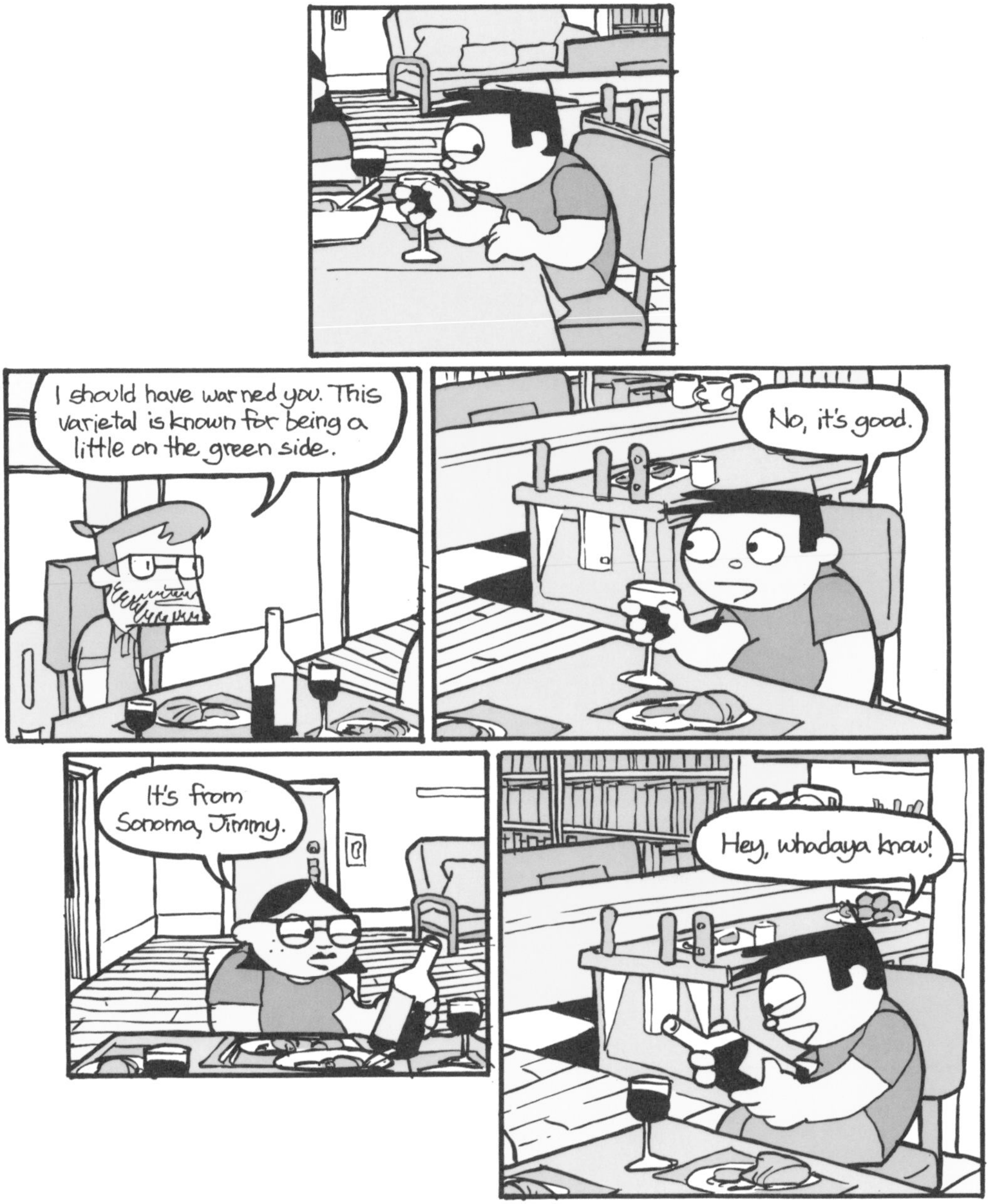
I should have warned you. This varietal is known for being a little on the green side.
No, it's good.
It's from Sonoma, Jimmy.
Hey, whadaya know!

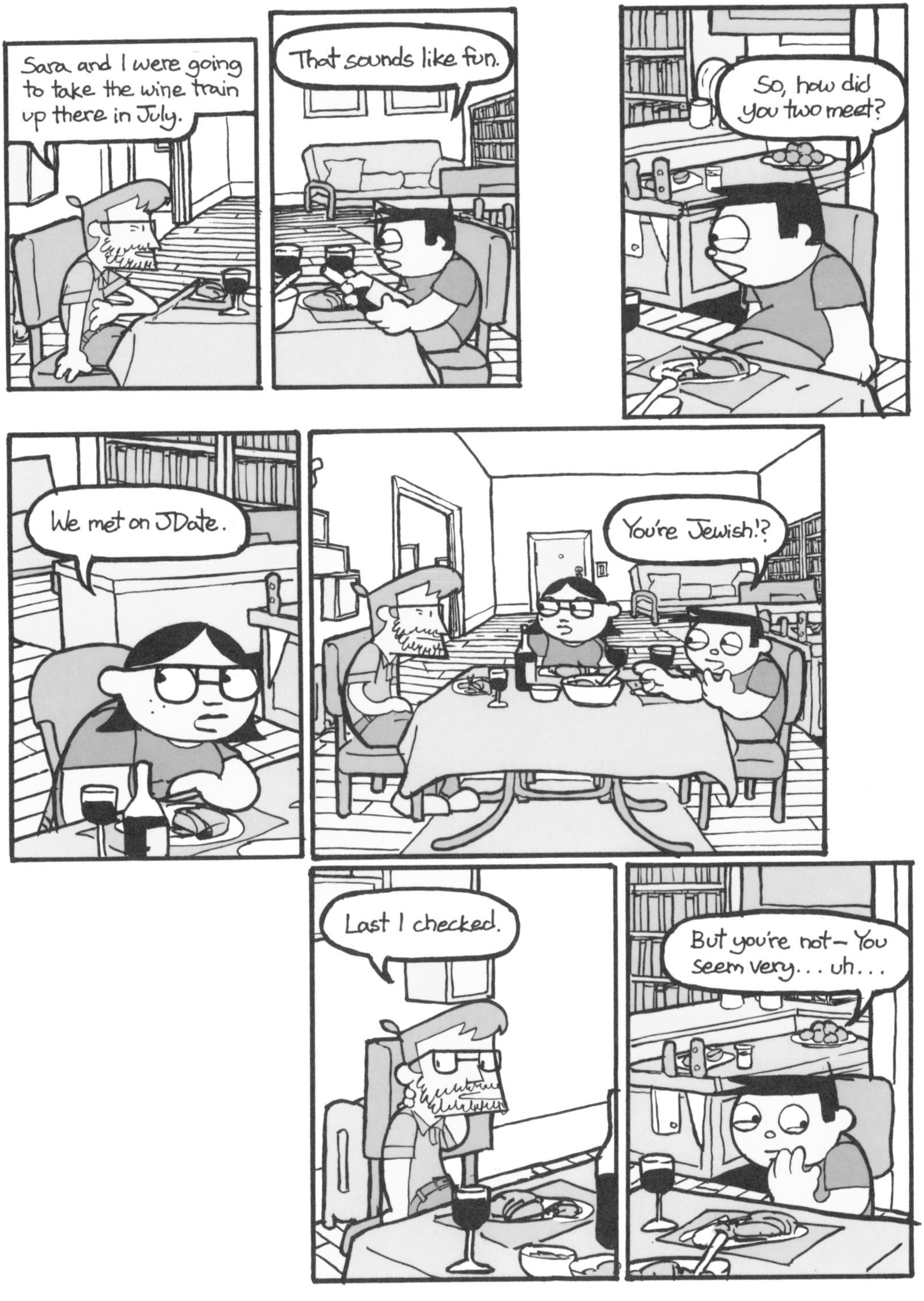
Sara and I were going to take the wine train up there in July.
That sounds like fun.
So, how did you two meet?
We met on JDate.
You're Jewish!?
Last I checked.
But you're not– You seem very... uh...

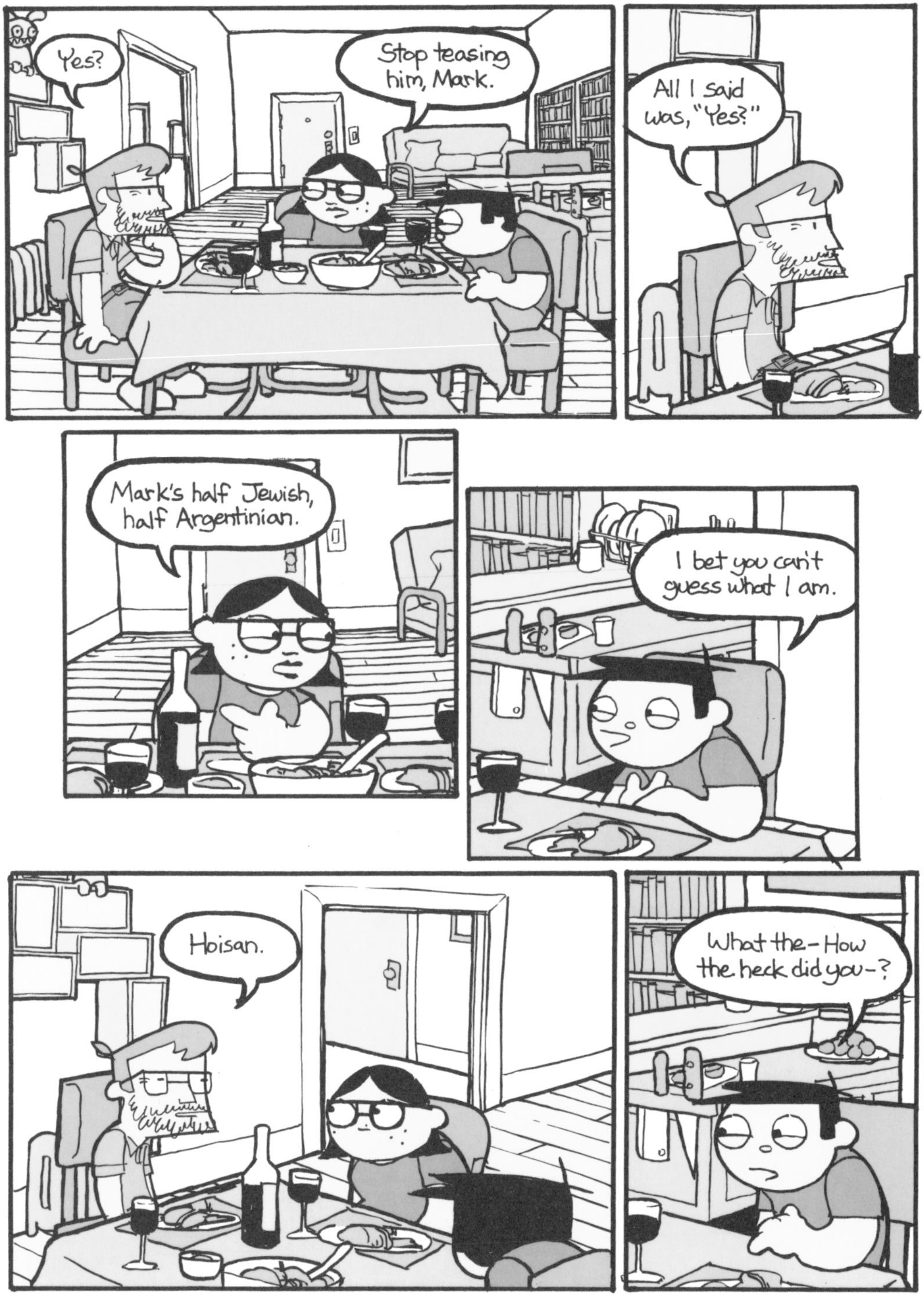
Yes?
Stop teasing him, Mark.
All I said was, "Yes?"
Mark's half Jewish, half Argentinian.
I bet you can't guess what I am.
Hoisan.
What the- How the heck did you-?

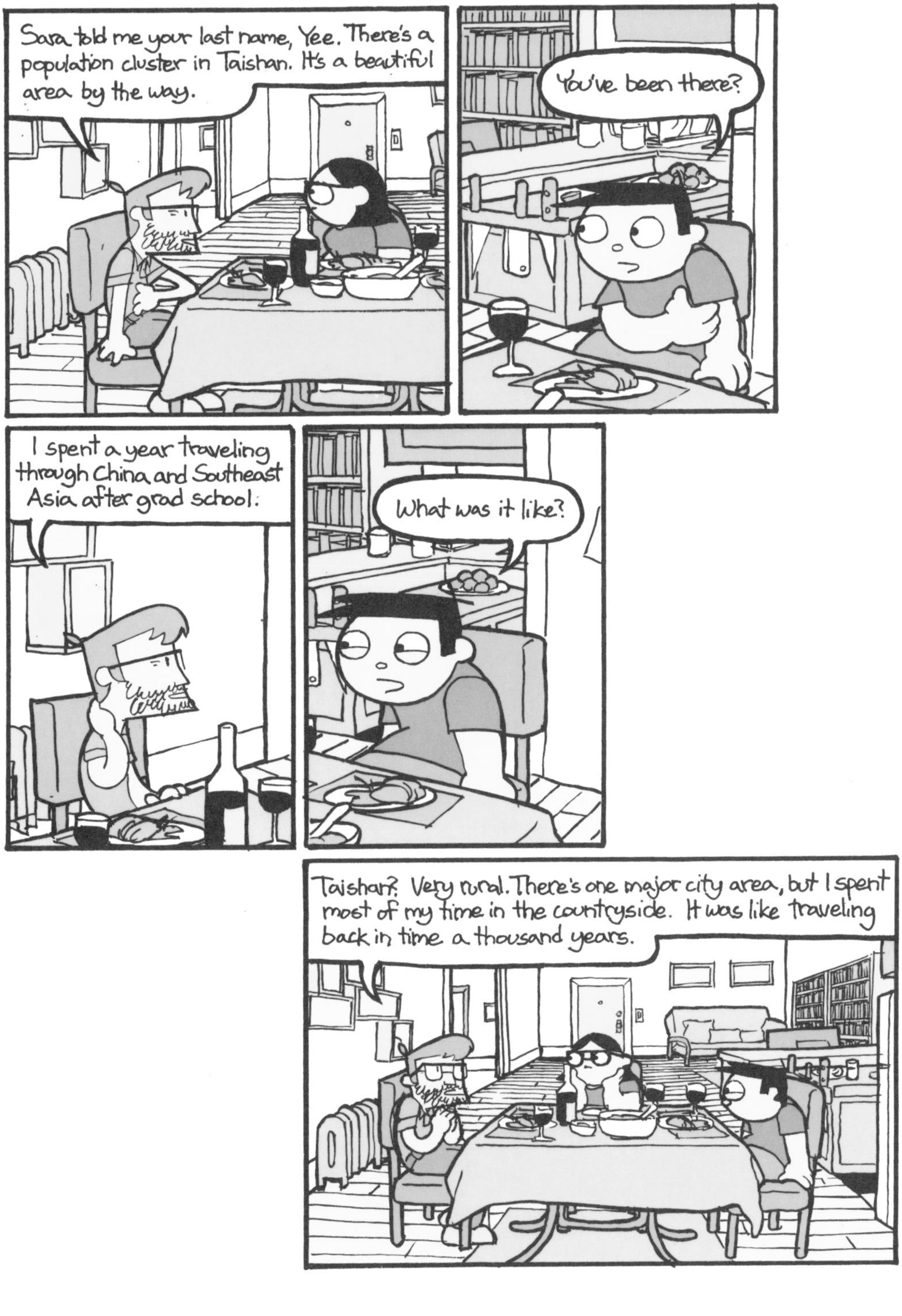
Sara told me your last name, Yee. There's a population cluster in Taishan. It's a beautiful area by the way.
You've been there?
I spent a year traveling through China and Southeast Asia after grad school.
What was it like?
Taishan? Very rural. There's one major city area, but I spent most of my time in the countryside. It was like traveling back in time a thousand years.

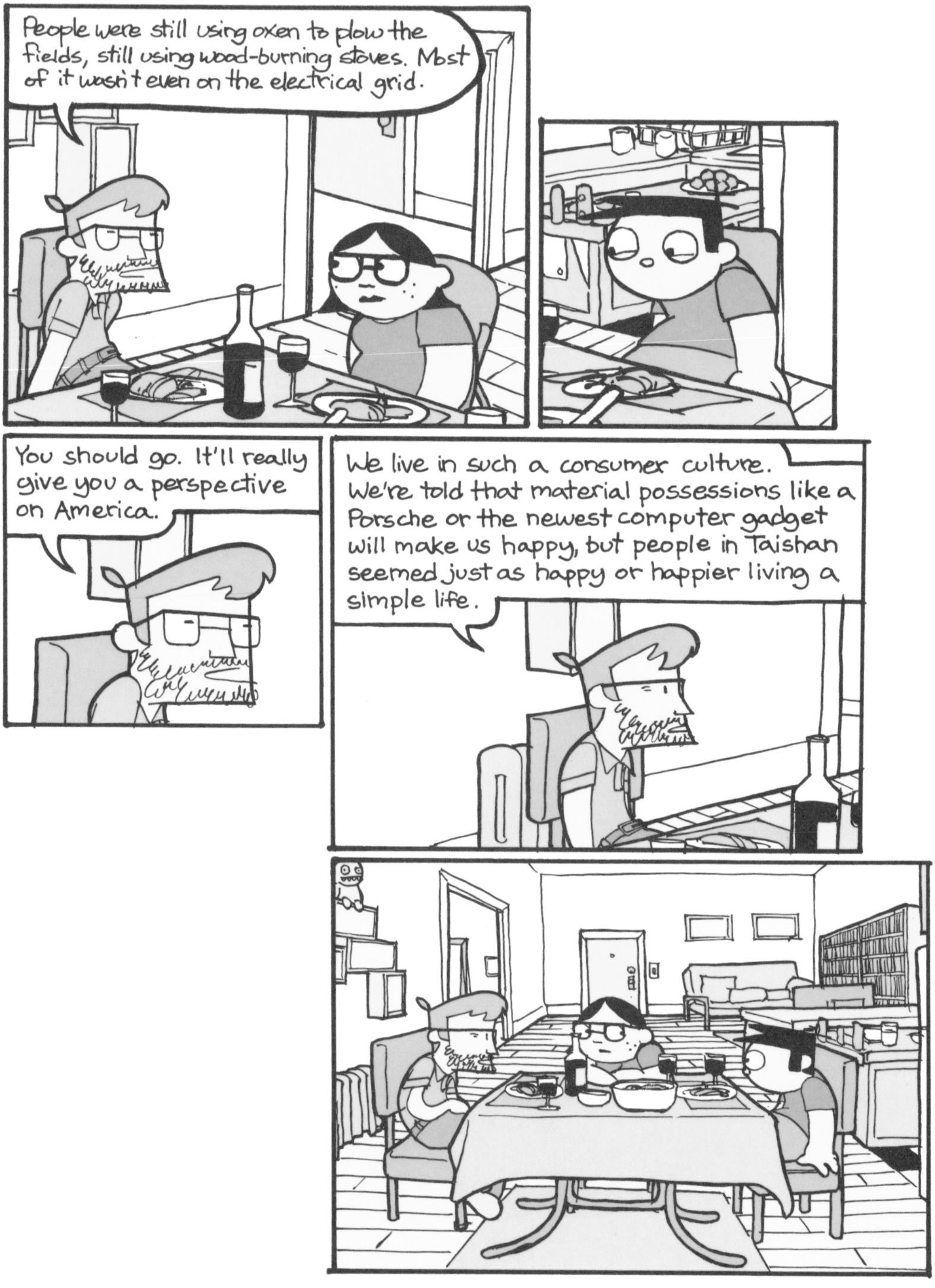
People were still using oxen to plow the fields, still using wood-burning stoves. Most of it wasn't even on the electrical grid.
You should go. It'll really give you a perspective on America.
We live in such a consumer culture. We're told that material possessions like a Porsche or the newest computer gadget will make us happy, but people in Taishan seemed just as happy or happier living a simple life.

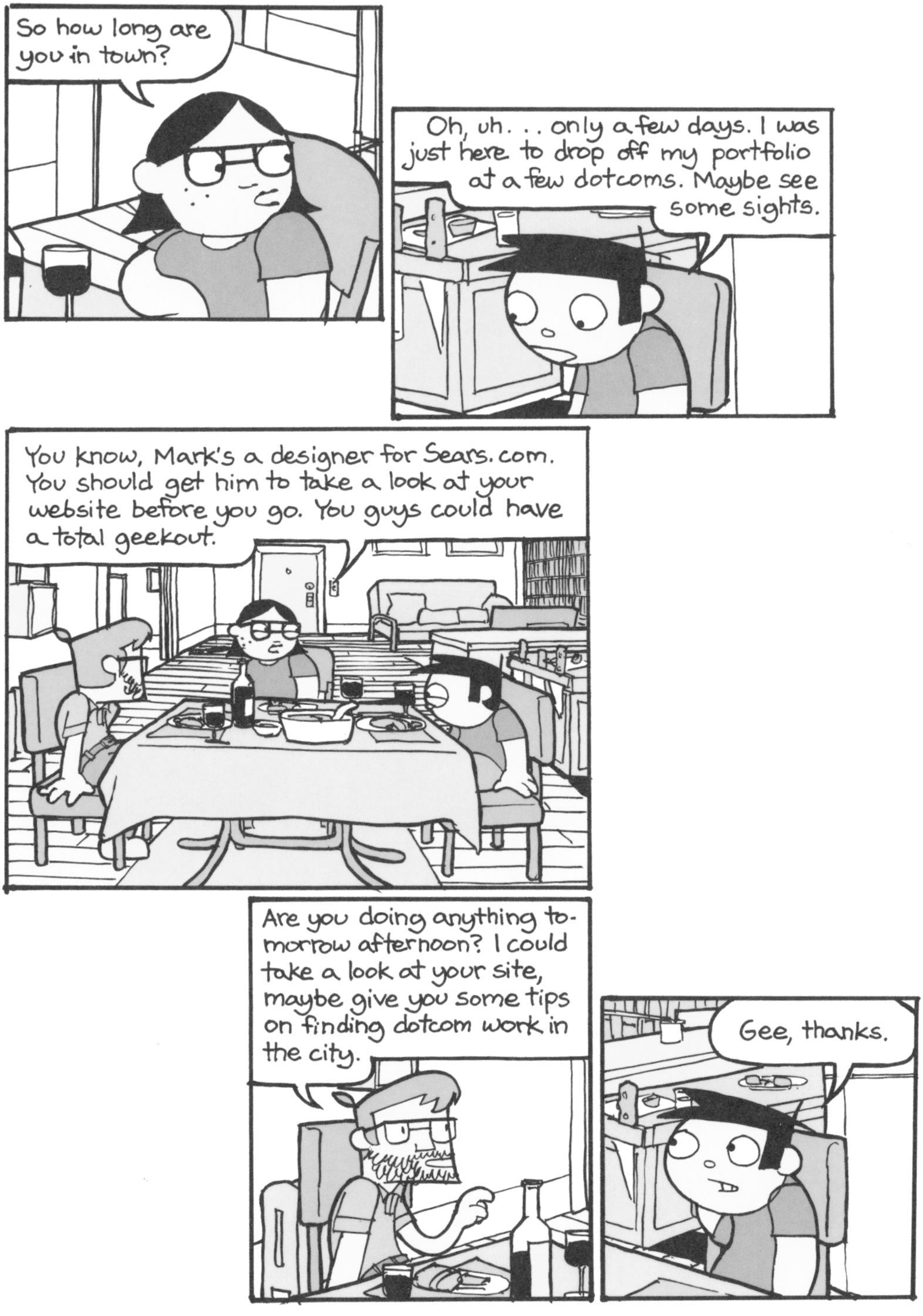
So how long are you in town?
Oh, uh. . . only a few days. I was just here to drop off my portfolio at a few dotcoms. Maybe see some sights.
You know, Mark's a designer for Sears.com. You should get him to take a look at your website before you go. You guys could have a total geekout.
Are you doing anything to-morrow afternoon? I could take a look at your site, maybe give you some tips on finding dotcom work in the city.
Gee, thanks.

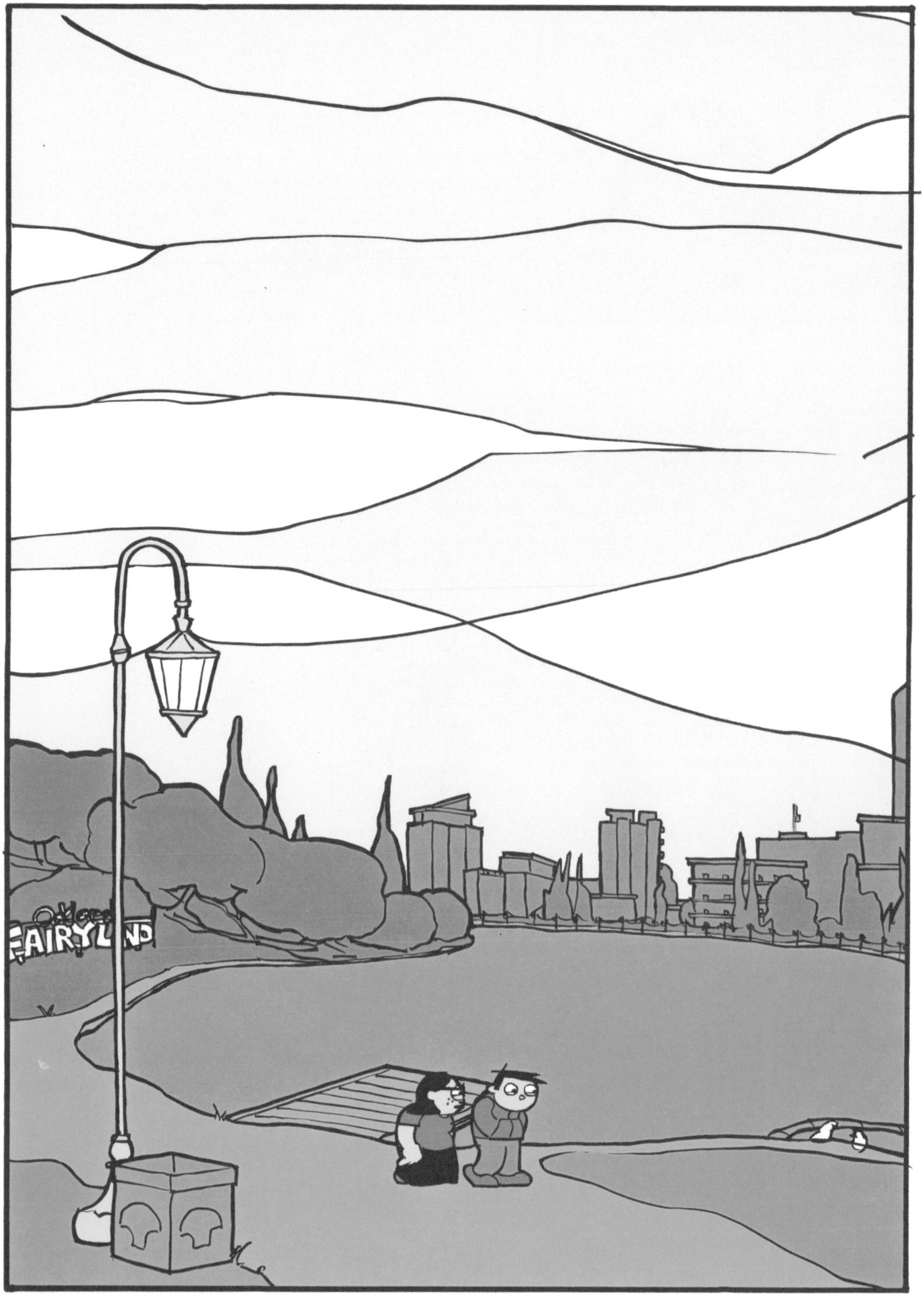

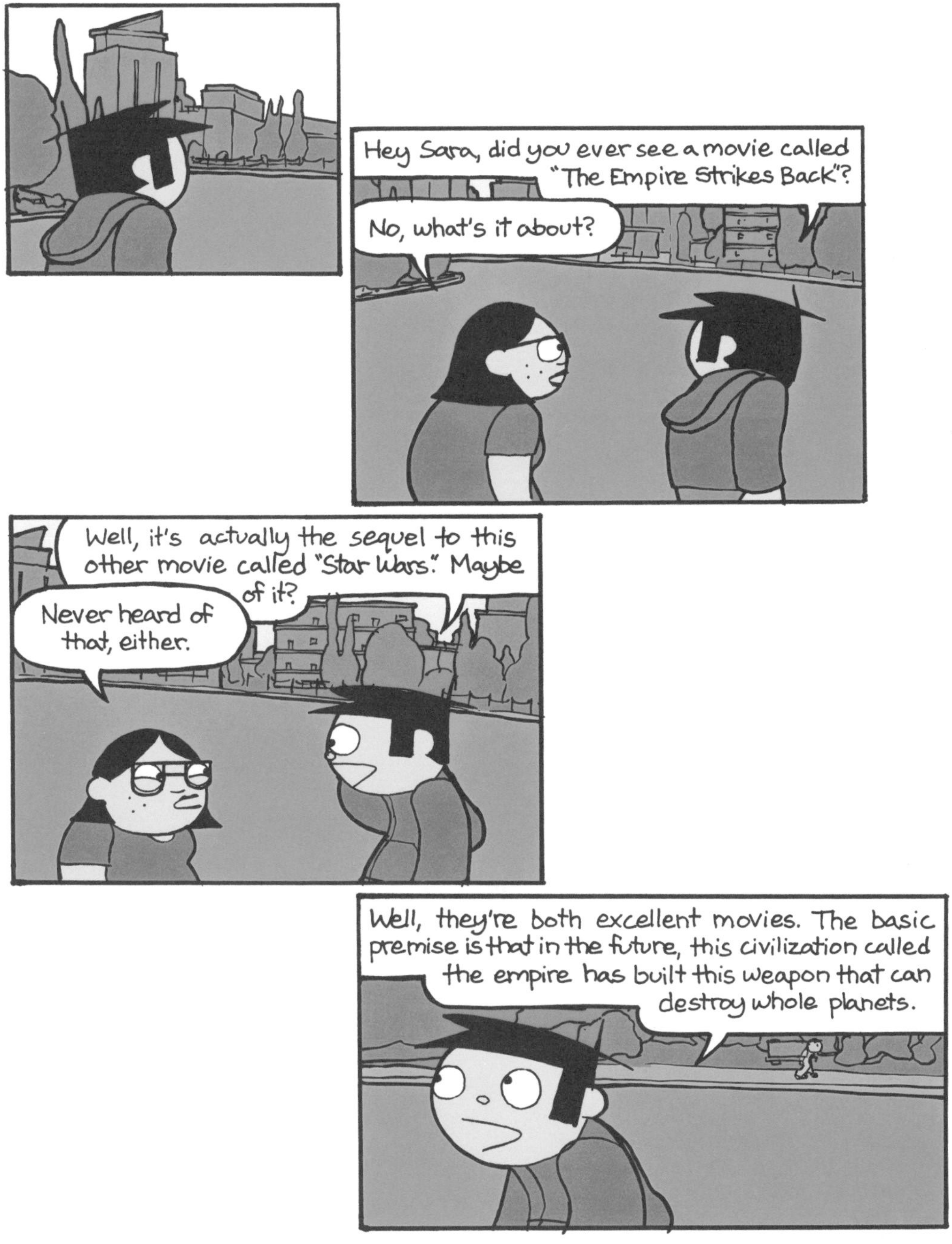
Hey Sara, did you ever see a movie called "The Empire Strikes Back"?
No, what's it about?
Well, it's actually the sequel to this other movie called "Star Wars." Maybe of it?
Never heard of that, either.
Well, they're both excellent movies. The basic premise is that in the future, this civilization called the empire has built this weapon that can destroy whole planets.

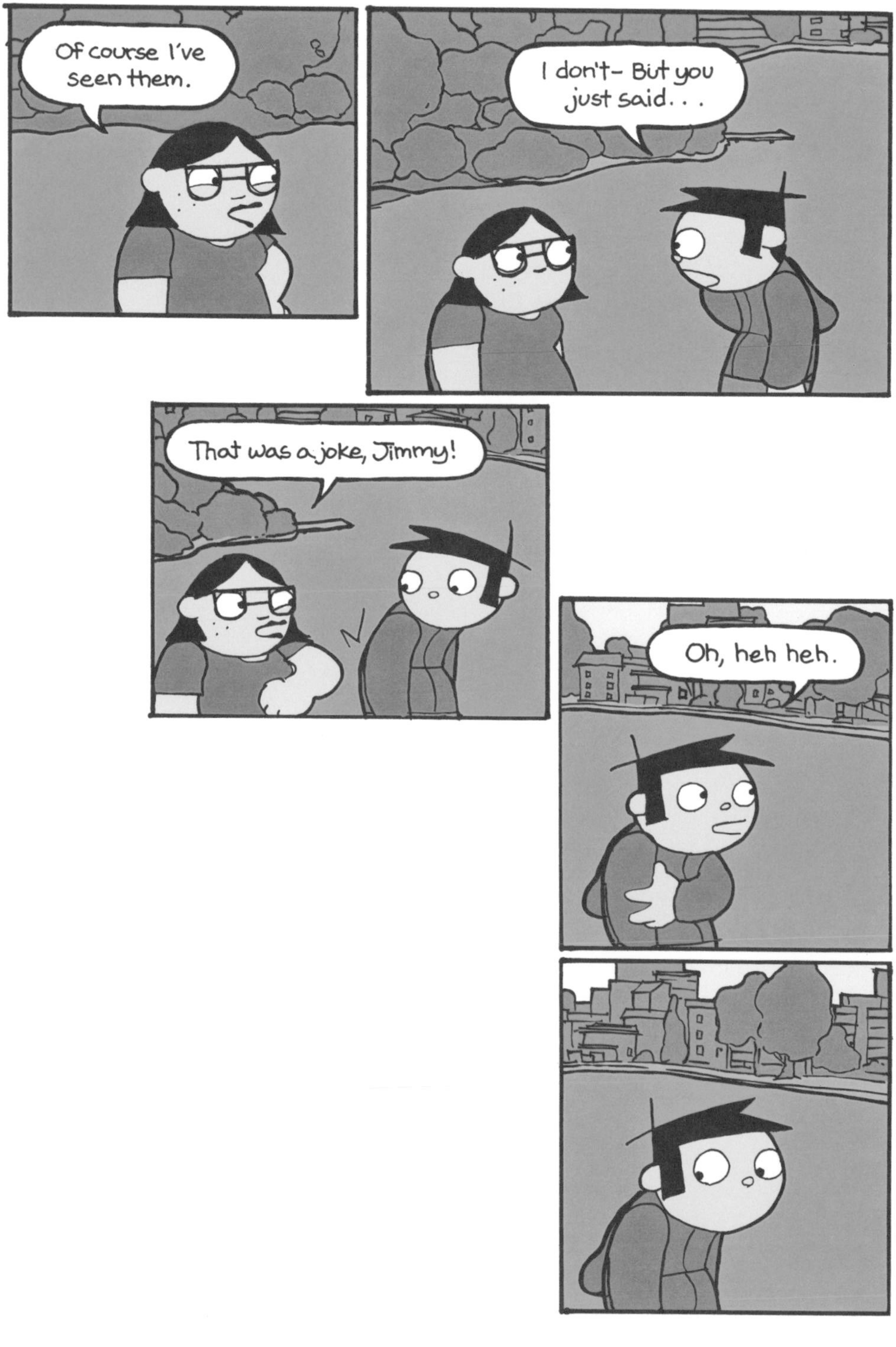
Of course I've seen them.
I don't- But you just said. . .
That was a joke, Jimmy!
Oh, heh heh.

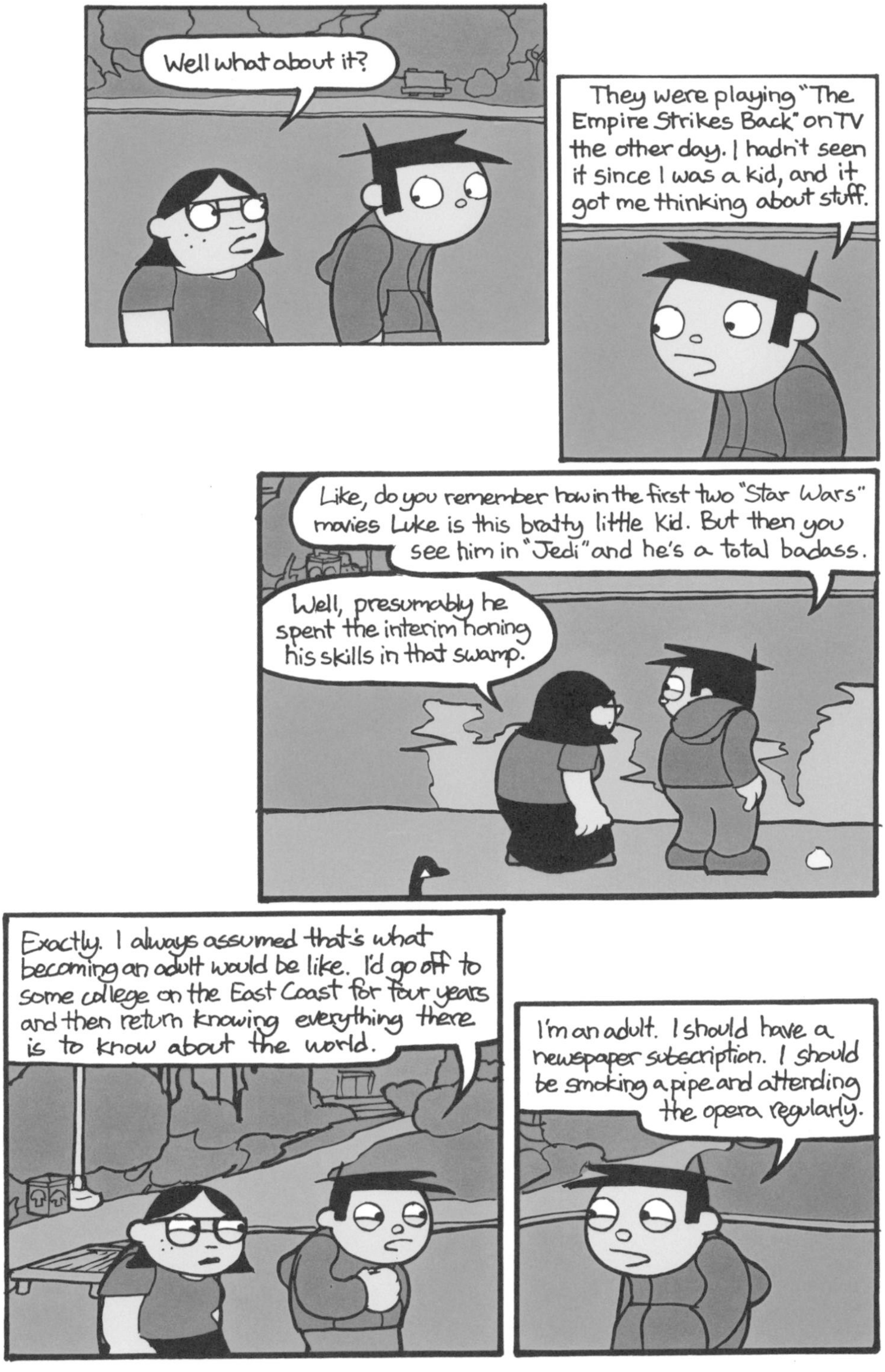
Well what about it?
They were playing "The Empire Strikes Back" on TV the other day. I hadn't seen it since I was a kid, and it got me thinking about stuff.
Like, do you remember how in the first two "Star Wars" movies Luke is this bratty little kid. But then you see him in "Jedi" and he's a total badass.
Well, presumably he spent the interim honing his skills in that swamp.
Exactly. I always assumed that's what becoming an adult would be like. I'd go off to some college on the East Coast for four years and then return knowing everything there is to know about the world.
I'm an adult. I should have a newspaper subscription. I should be smoking a pipe and attending the opera regularly.

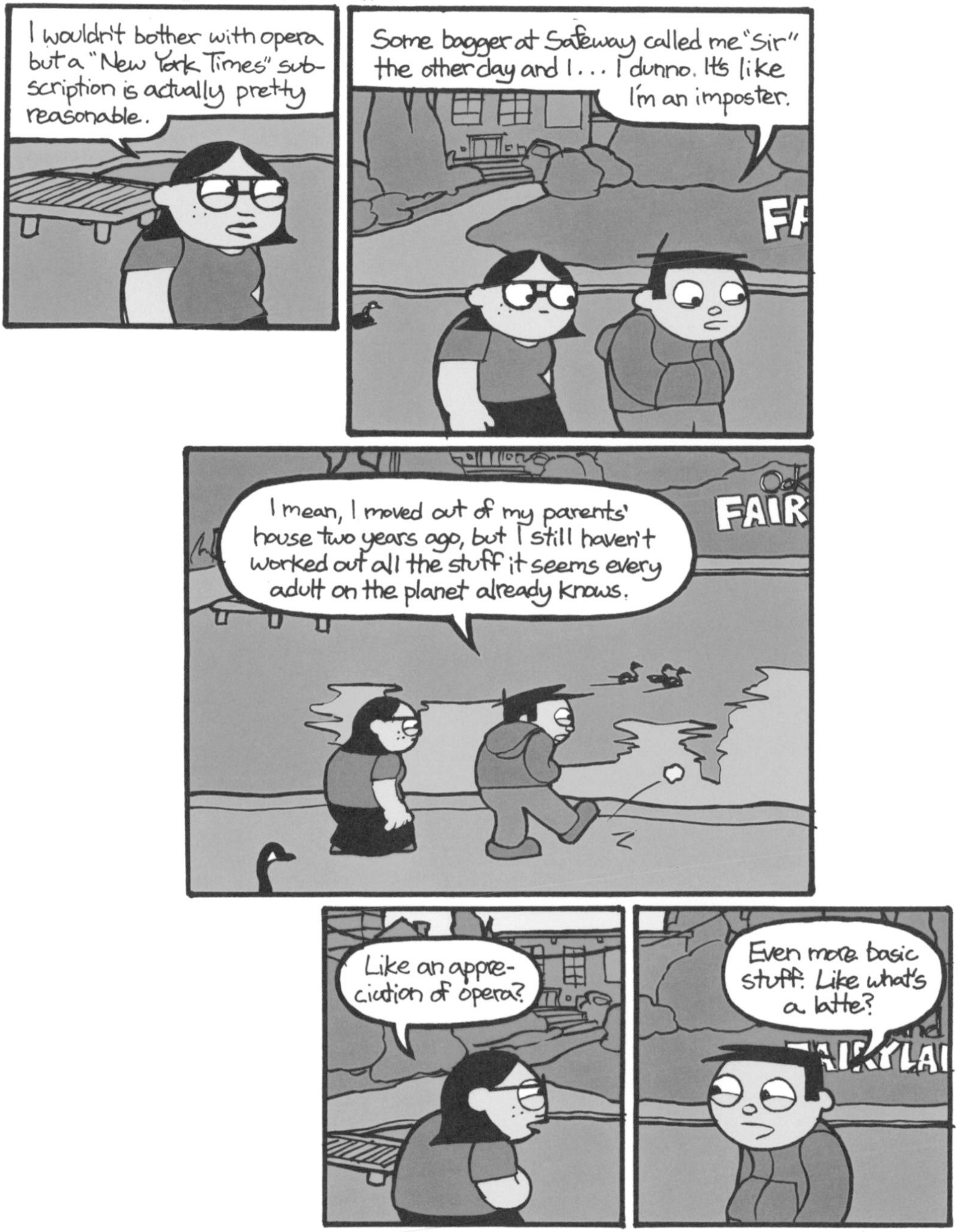
I wouldn't bother with opera but a "New York Times" subscription is actually pretty reasonable.
Some bagger at Safeway called me "Sir" the other day and I . . . I dunno. It's like I'm an imposter.
FA
I mean, I moved out of my parents' house two years ago, but I still haven't worked out all the stuff it seems every adult on the planet already knows.
FAIR
Like an appreciation of opera?
Even more basic stuff. Like what's a latte?

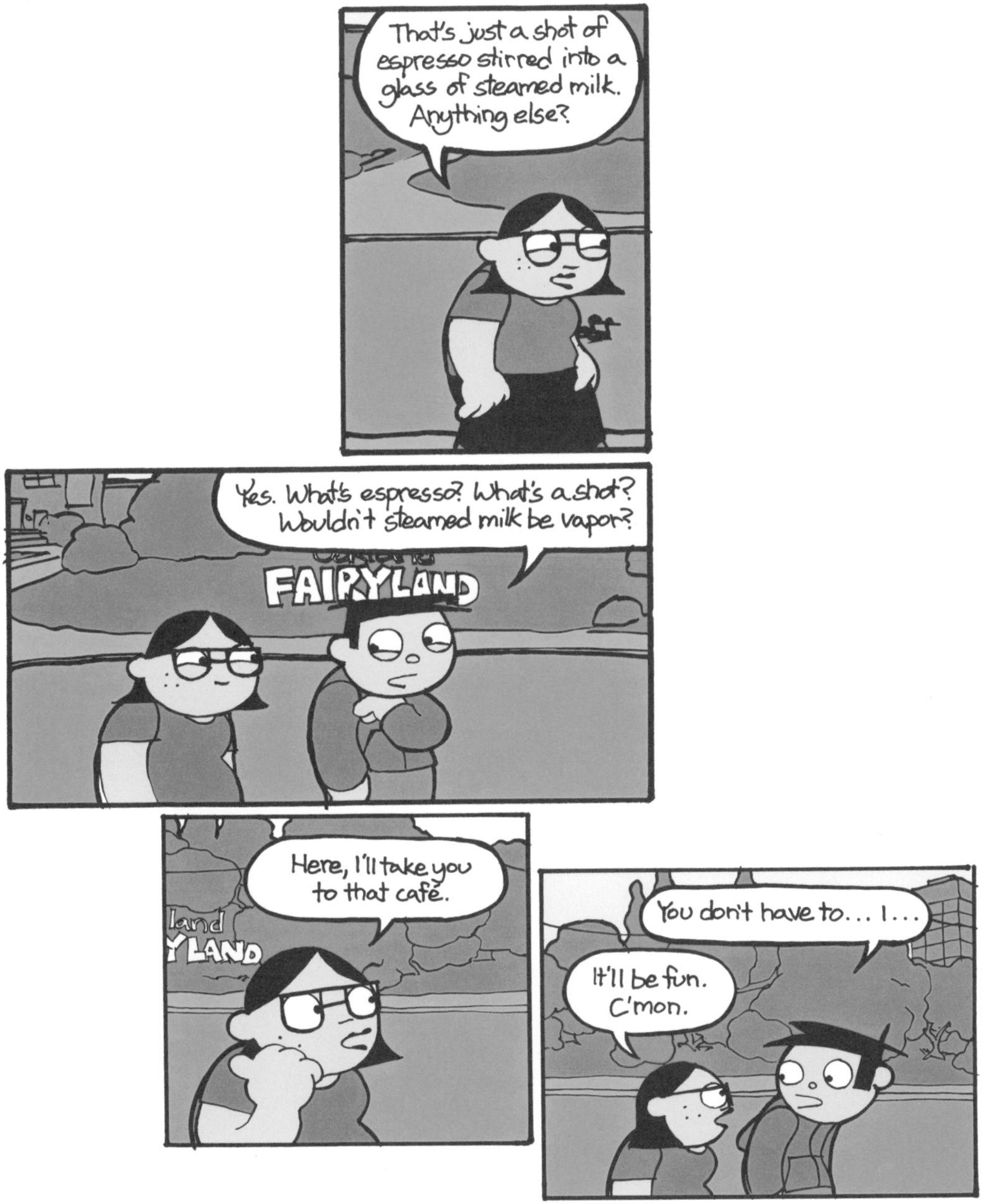
That's just a shot of espresso stirred into a glass of steamed milk. Anything else?
Yes. What's espresso? What's a shot? Wouldn't steamed milk be vapor?
FAIRYLAND
Here, I'll take you to that café.
You don't have to... I...
It'll be fun. C'mon.

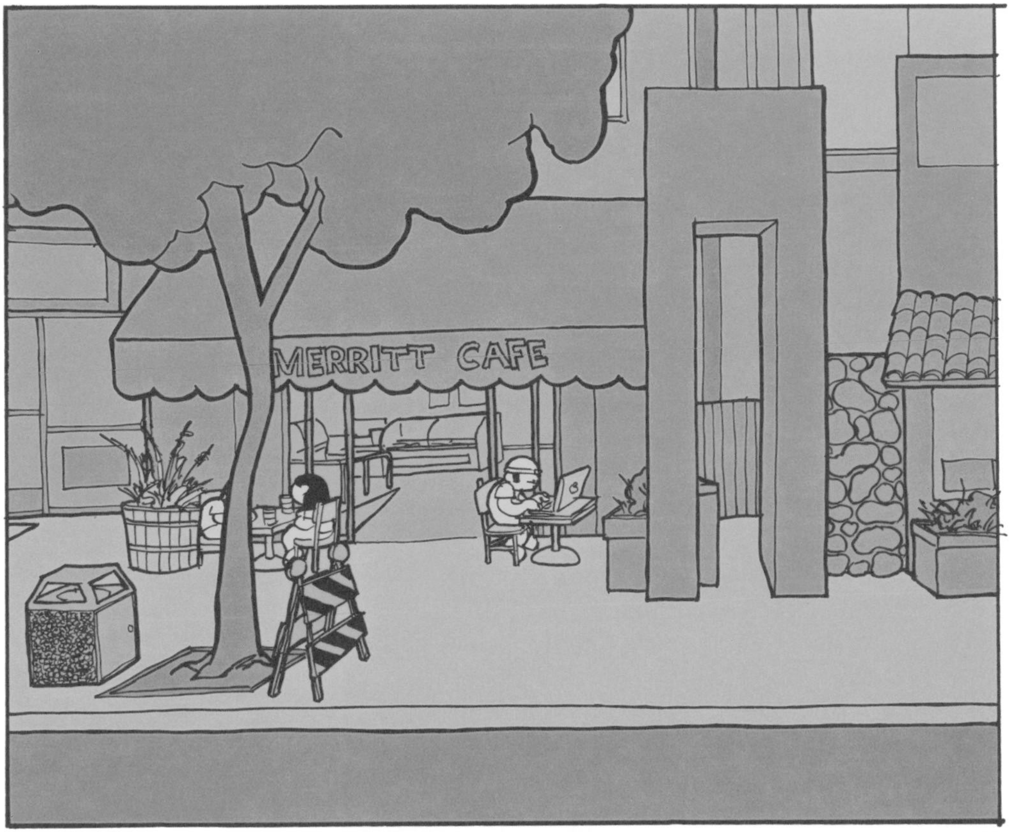
MERRITT CAFE

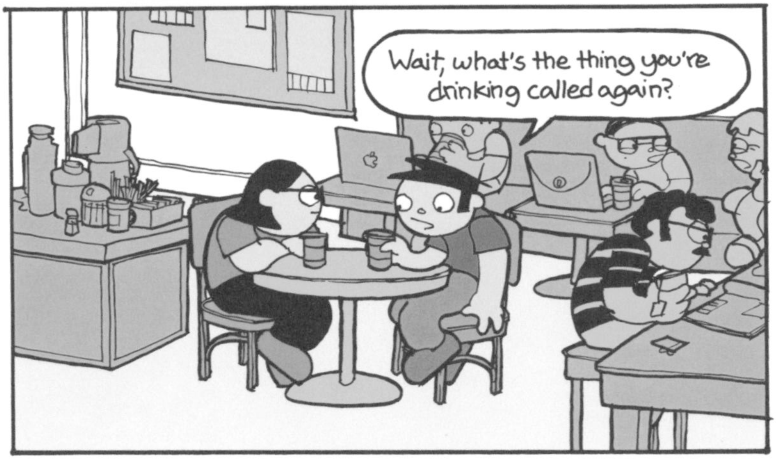
Wait, what's the thing you're drinking called again?

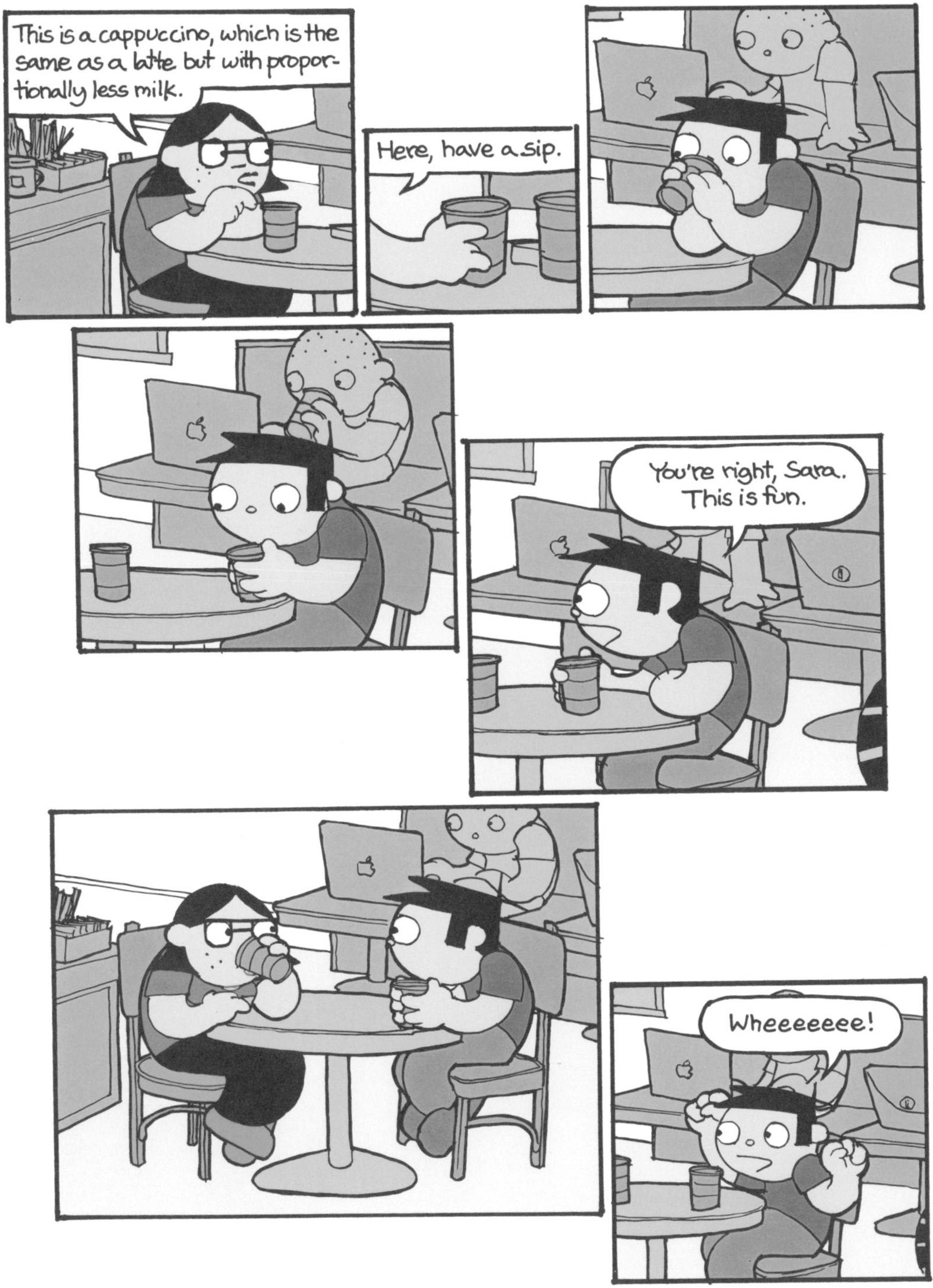
This is a cappuccino, which is the same as a latte but with proportionally less milk.
Here, have a sip.
You're right, Sara. This is fun.
Wheeeeeee!

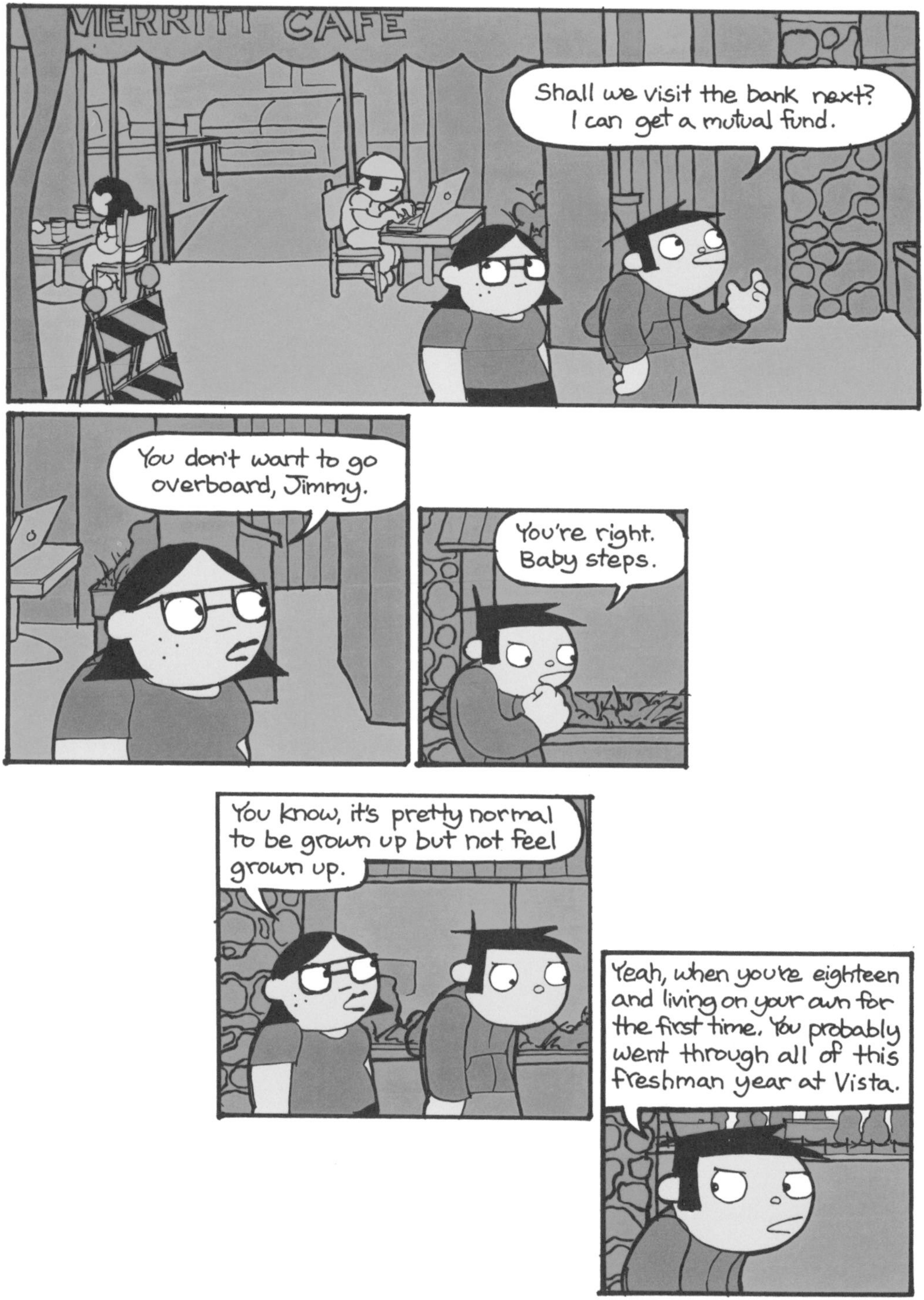
MERRITT CAFE
Shall we visit the bank next? I can get a mutual fund.
You don't want to go overboard, Jimmy.
You're right. Baby steps.
You know, it's pretty normal to be grown up but not feel grown up.
Yeah, when you're eighteen and living on your own for the first time. You probably went through all of this freshman year at Vista.

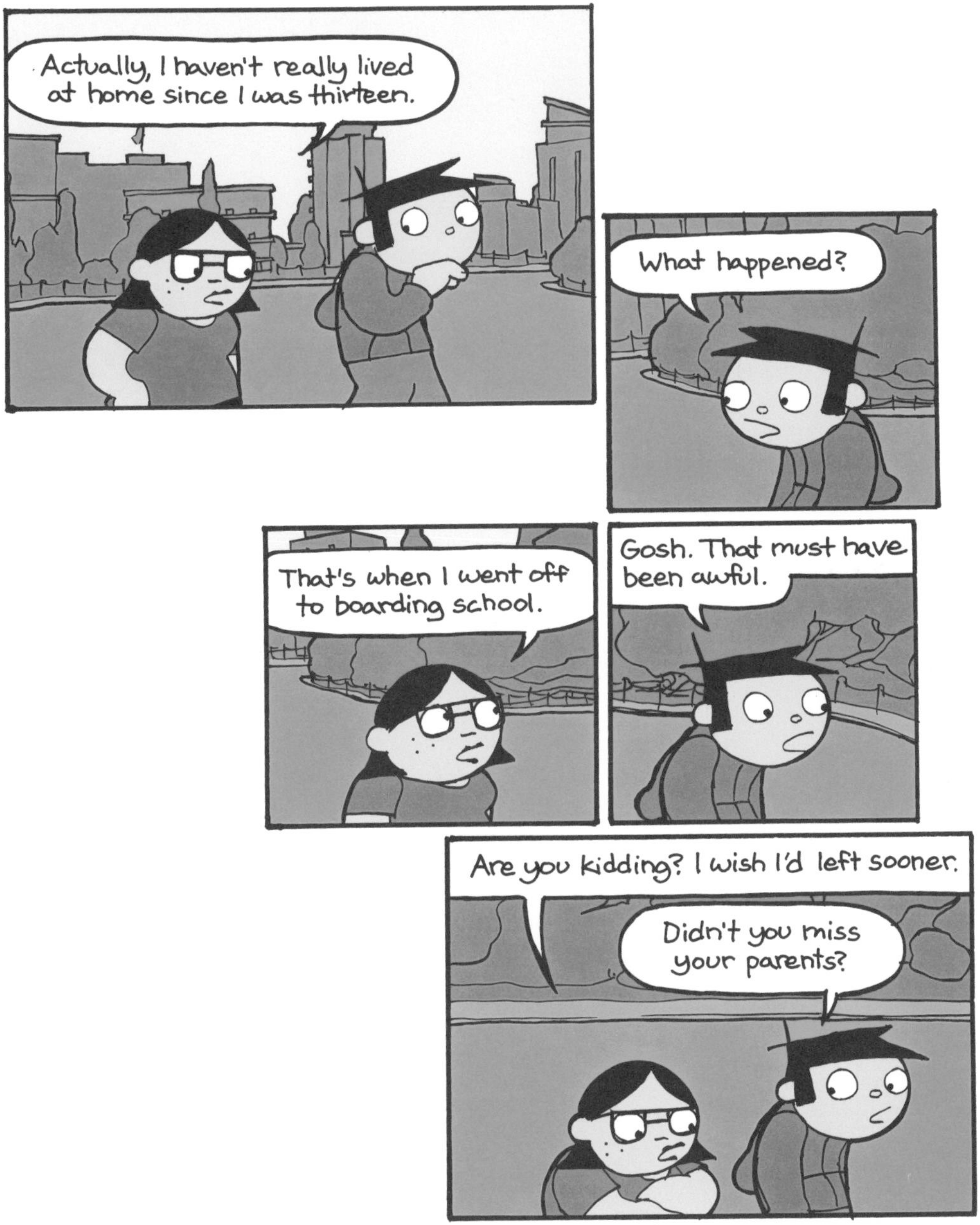
Actually, I haven't really lived at home since I was thirteen.
What happened?
That's when I went off to boarding school.
Gosh. That must have been awful.
Didn't you miss your parents?
Are you kidding? I wish I'd left sooner.

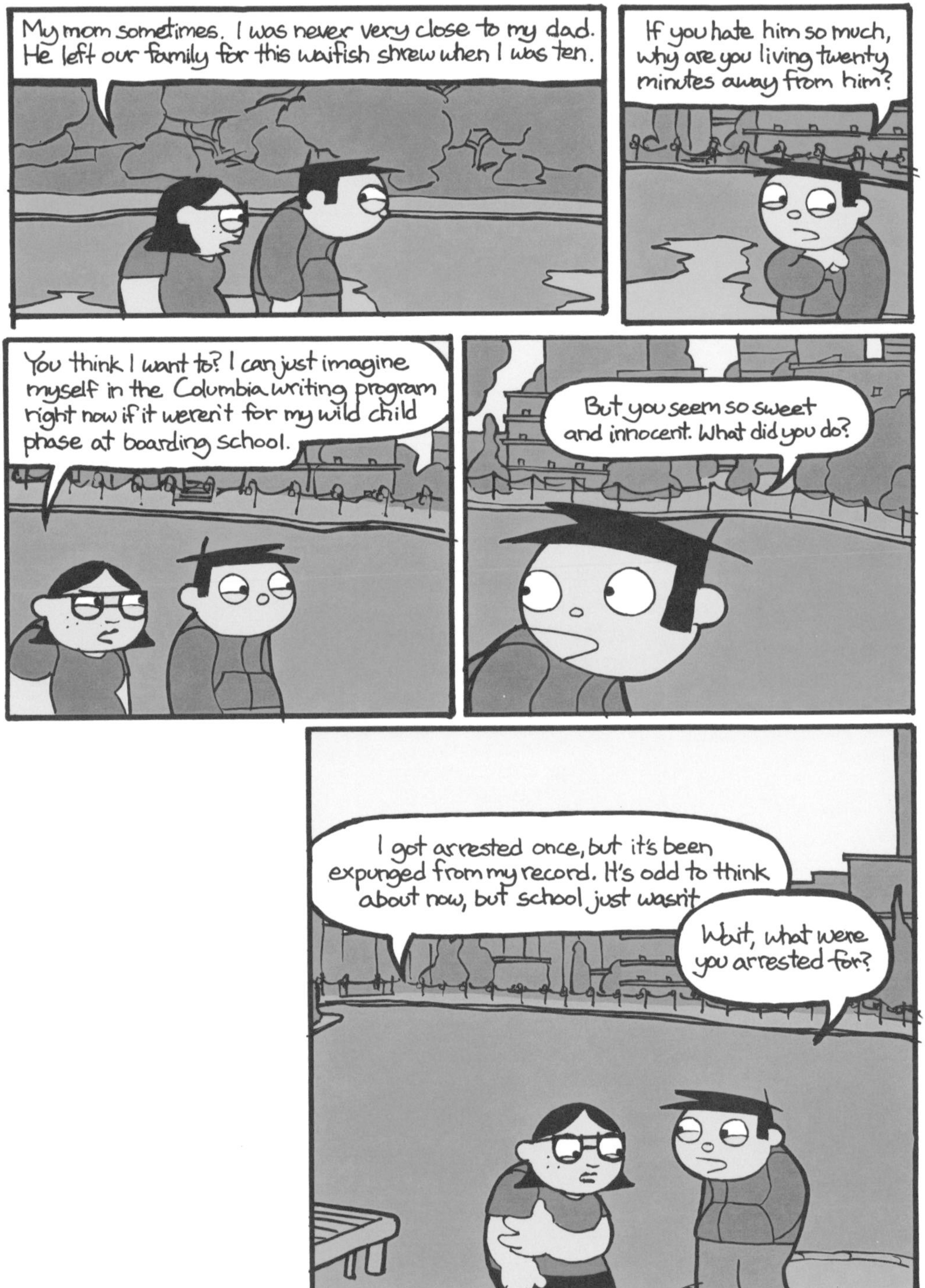
My mom sometimes. I was never very close to my dad. He left our family for this waifish shrew when I was ten.
If you hate him so much, why are you living twenty minutes away from him?
You think I want to? I can just imagine myself in the Columbia writing program right now if it weren't for my wild child phase at boarding school.
But you seem so sweet and innocent. What did you do?
I got arrested once, but it's been expunged from my record. It's odd to think about now, but school just wasn't
Wait, what were you arrested for?

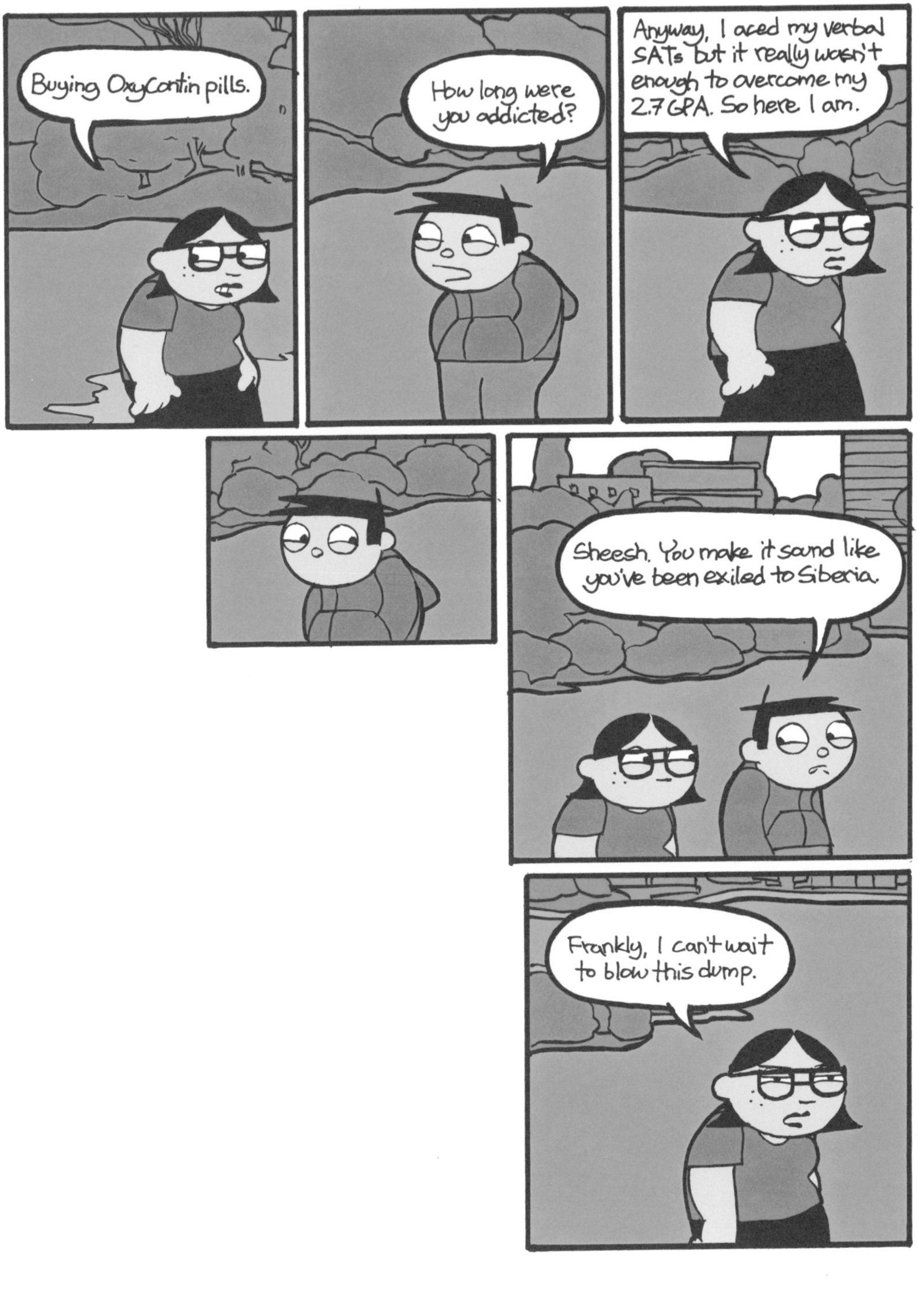
Buying OxyContin pills.
How long were you addicted?
Anyway, I aced my verbal SATs but it really wasn't enough to overcome my 2.7 GPA. So here I am.
Sheesh. You make it sound like you've been exiled to Siberia.
Frankly, I can't wait to blow this dump.

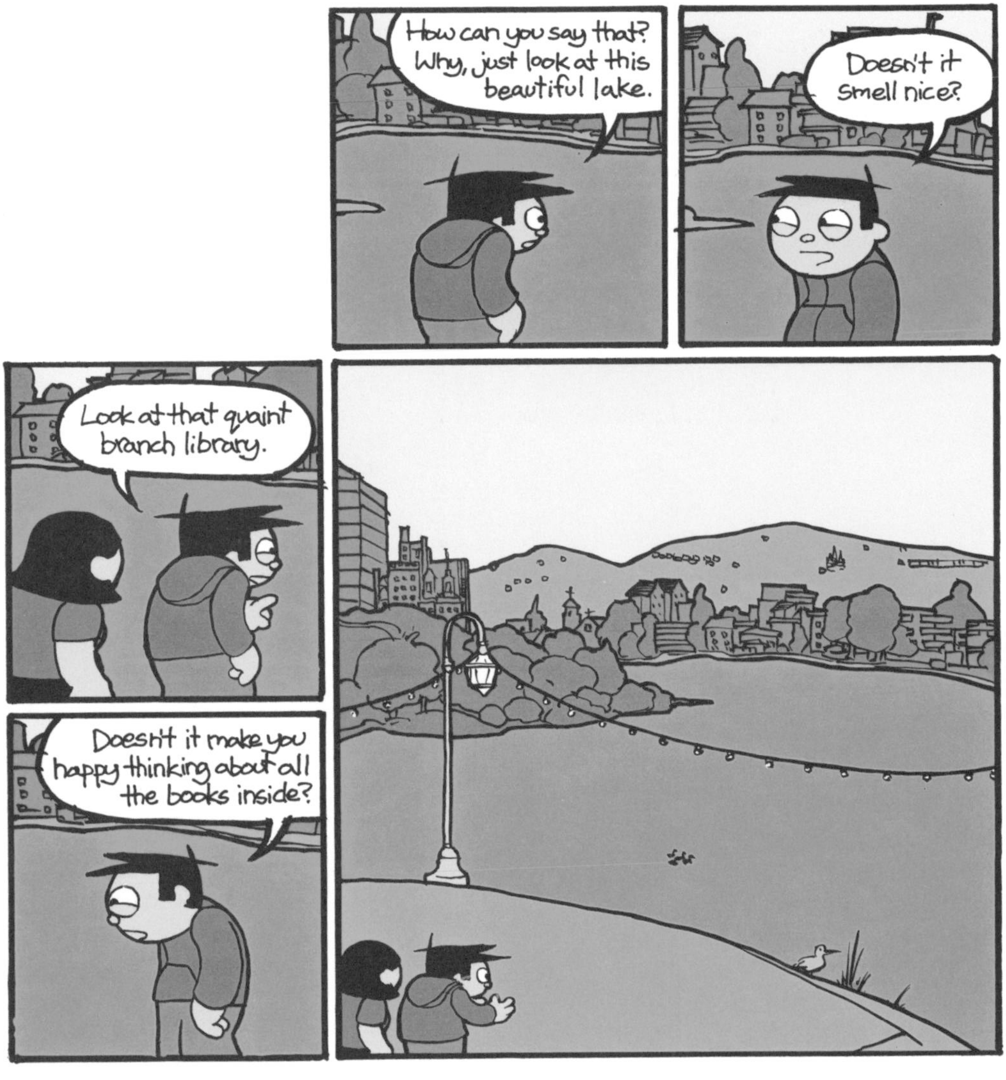
How can you say that? Why, just look at this beautiful lake.
Doesn't it smell nice?
Look at that quaint branch library.
Doesn't it make you happy thinking about all the books inside?

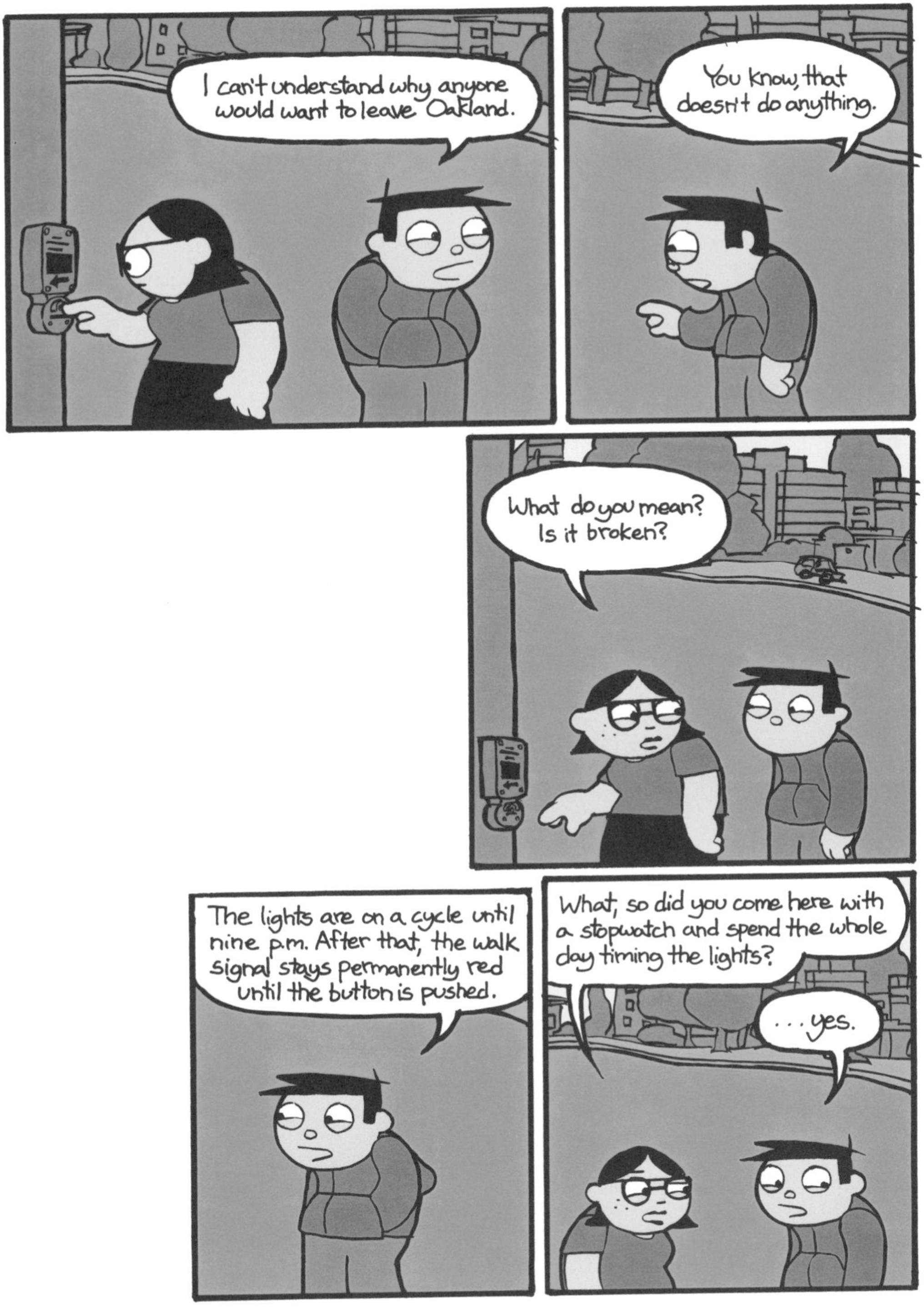
I can't understand why anyone would want to leave Oakland.
You know, that doesn't do anything.
What do you mean? Is it broken?
The lights are on a cycle until nine p.m. After that, the walk signal stays permanently red until the button is pushed.
What, so did you come here with a stopwatch and spend the whole day timing the lights?
. . . yes.

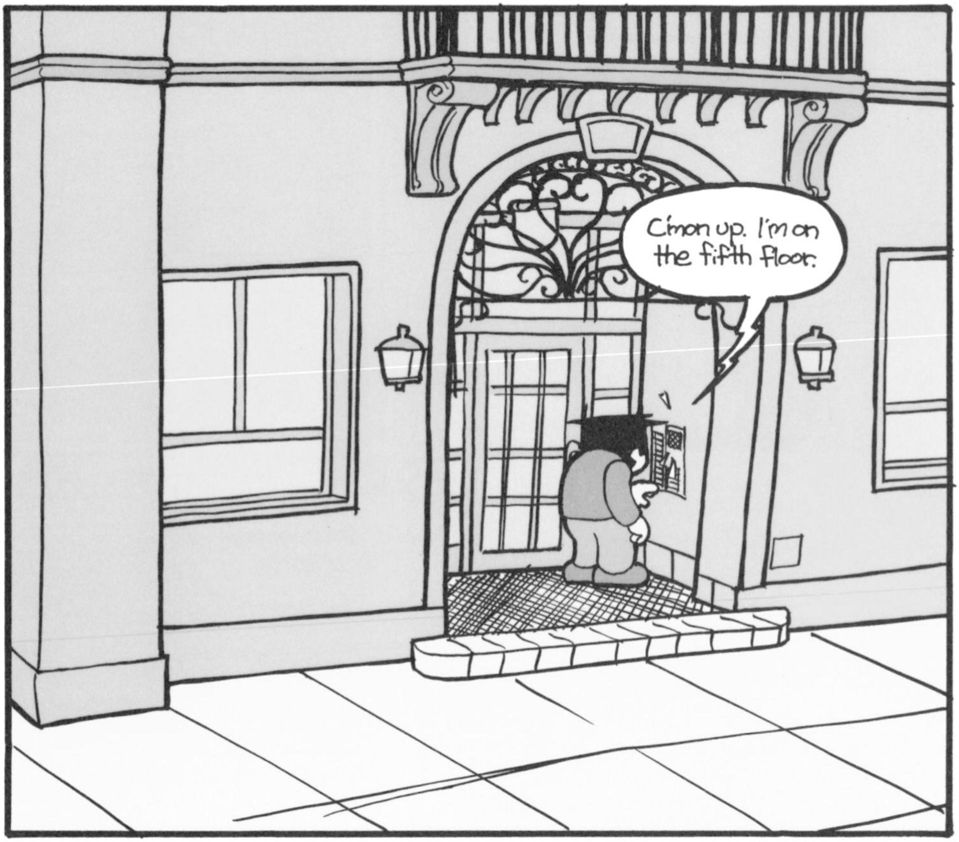
C'mon up. I'm on the fifth floor.

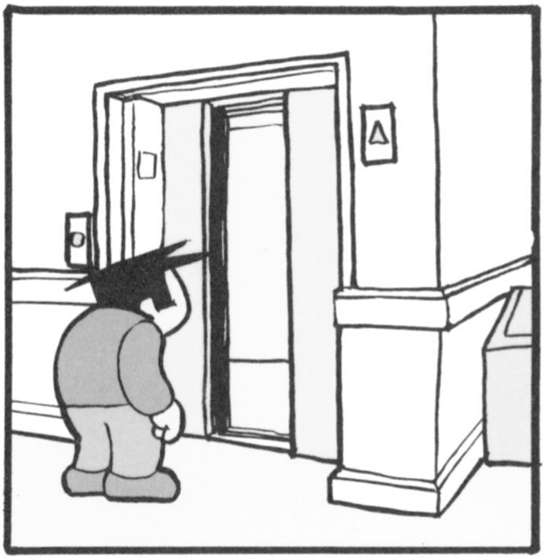

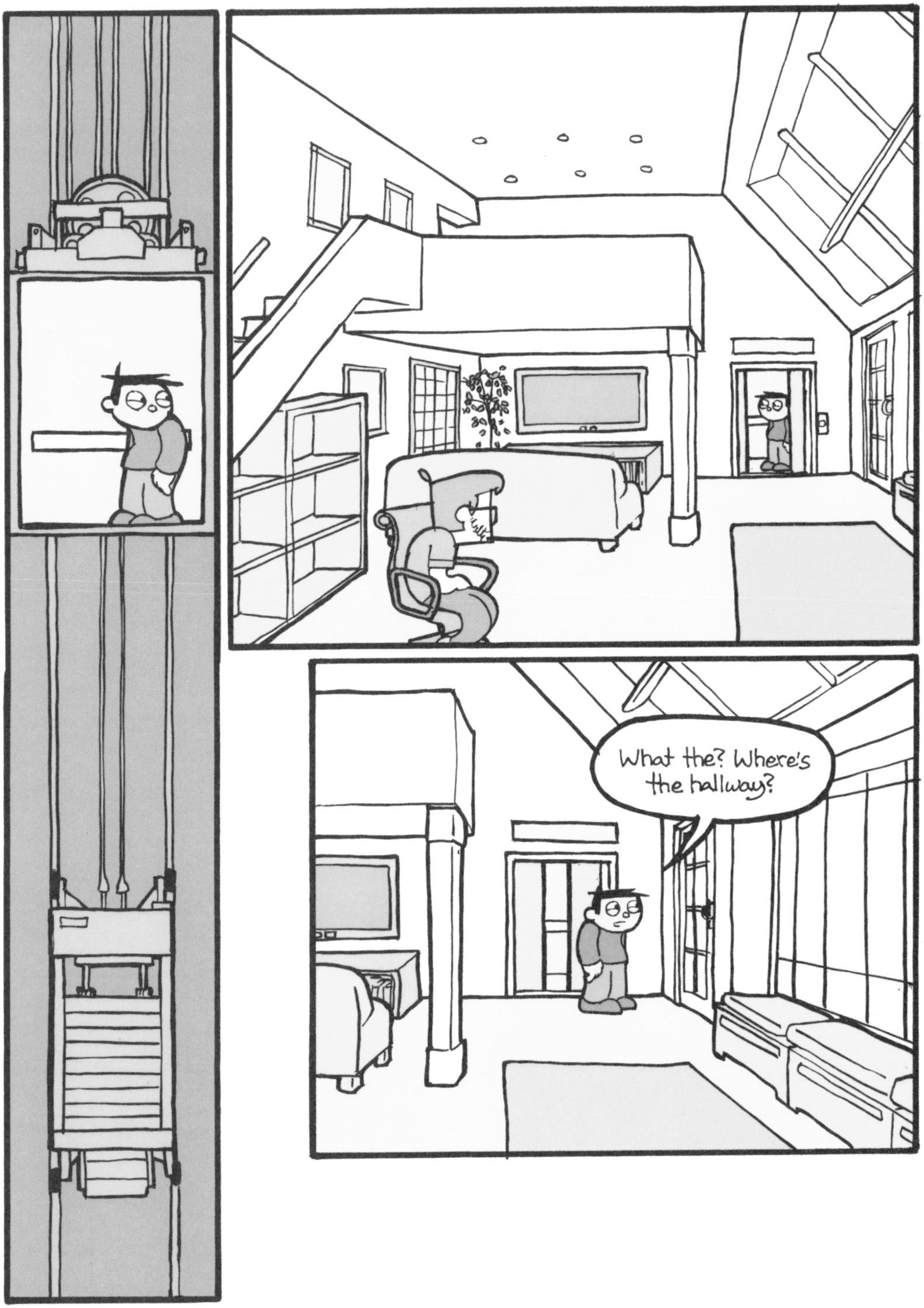
What the? Where's the hallway?

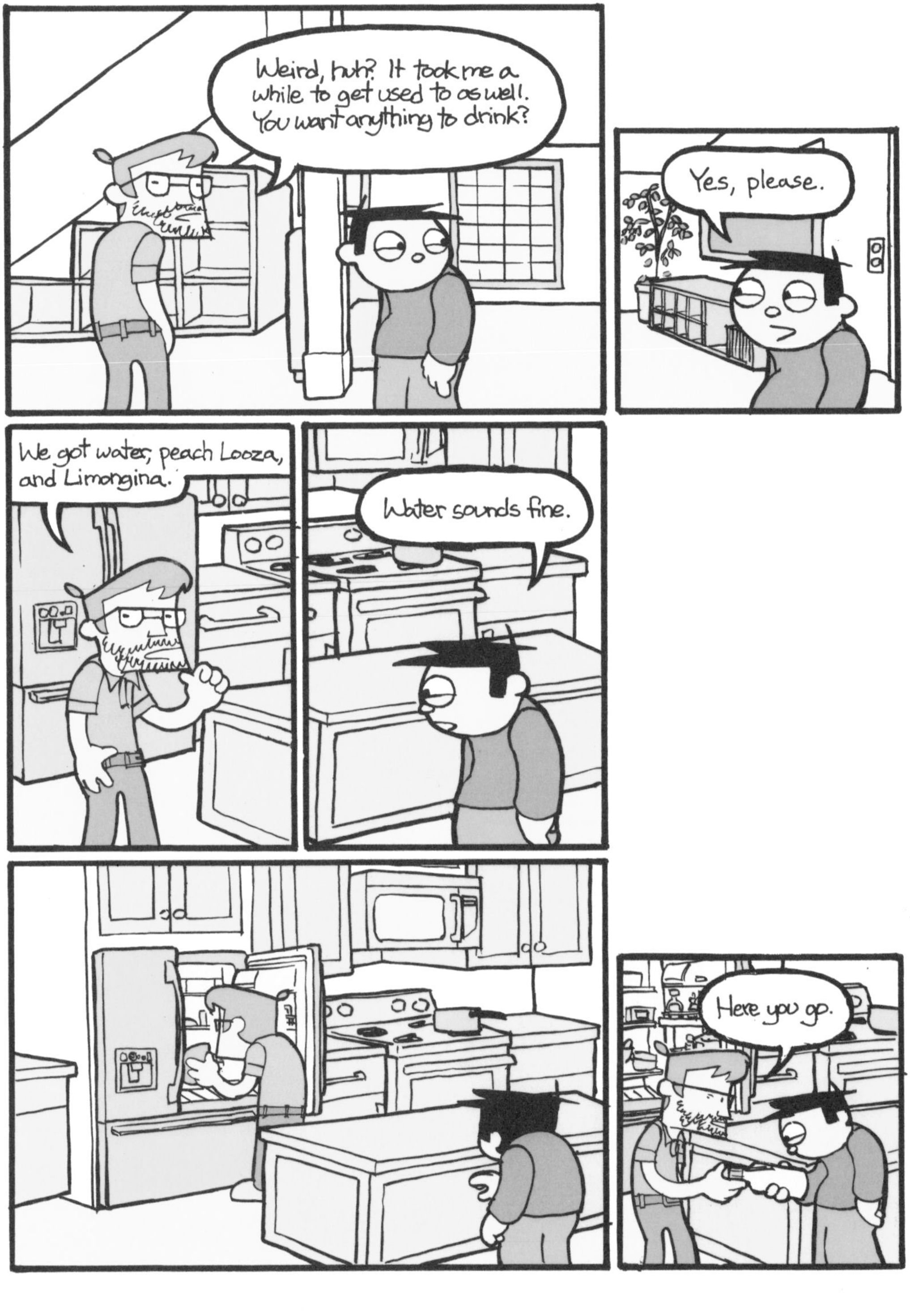
Weird, huh? It took me a while to get used to as well. You want anything to drink?
Yes, please.
We got water, peach Looza, and Limongina.
Water sounds fine.
Here you go.

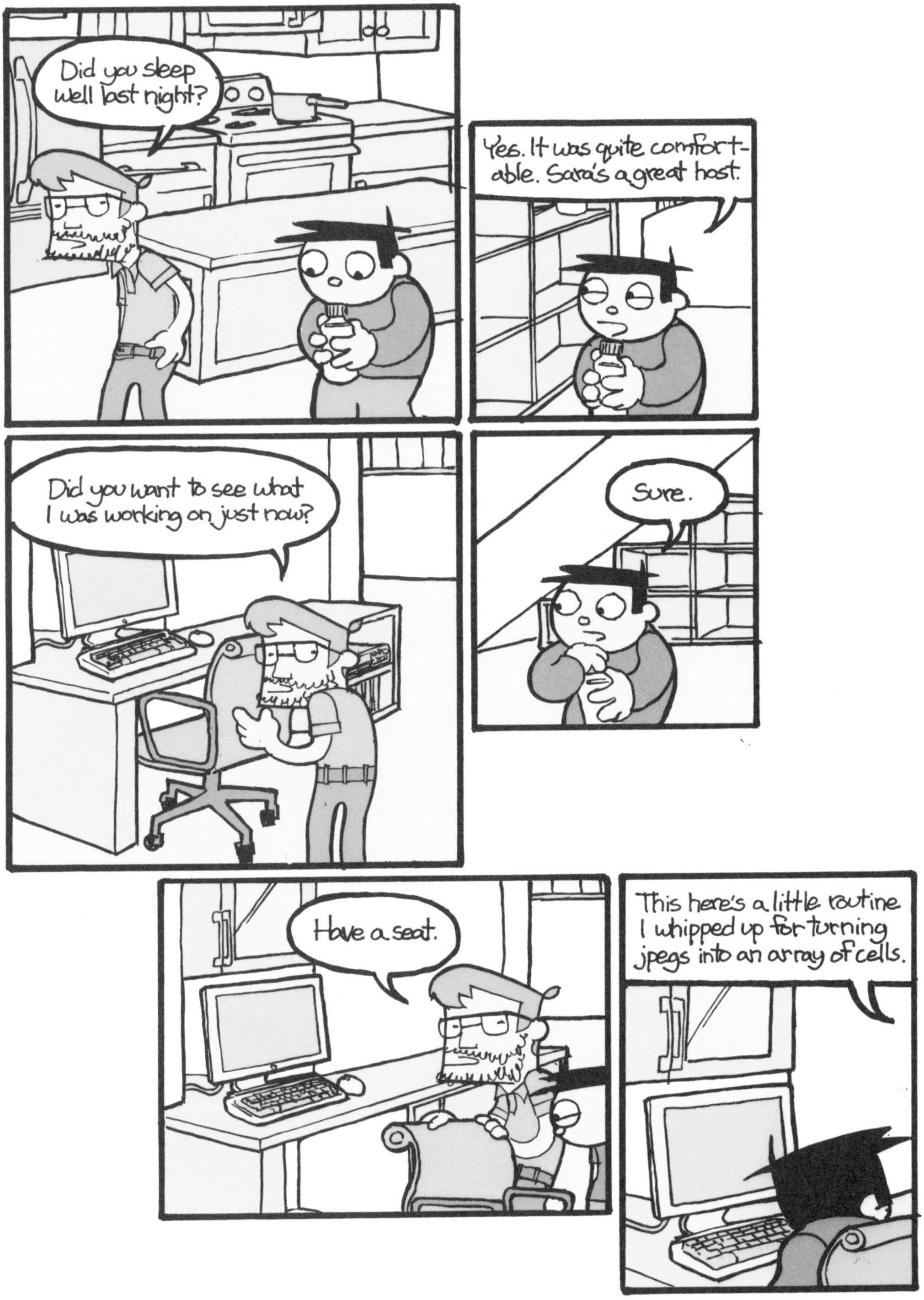
Did you sleep well last night?
Yes. It was quite comfortable. Sara's a great host.
Did you want to see what I was working on just now?
Sure.
Have a seat.
This here's a little routine I whipped up for turning jpegs into an array of cells.

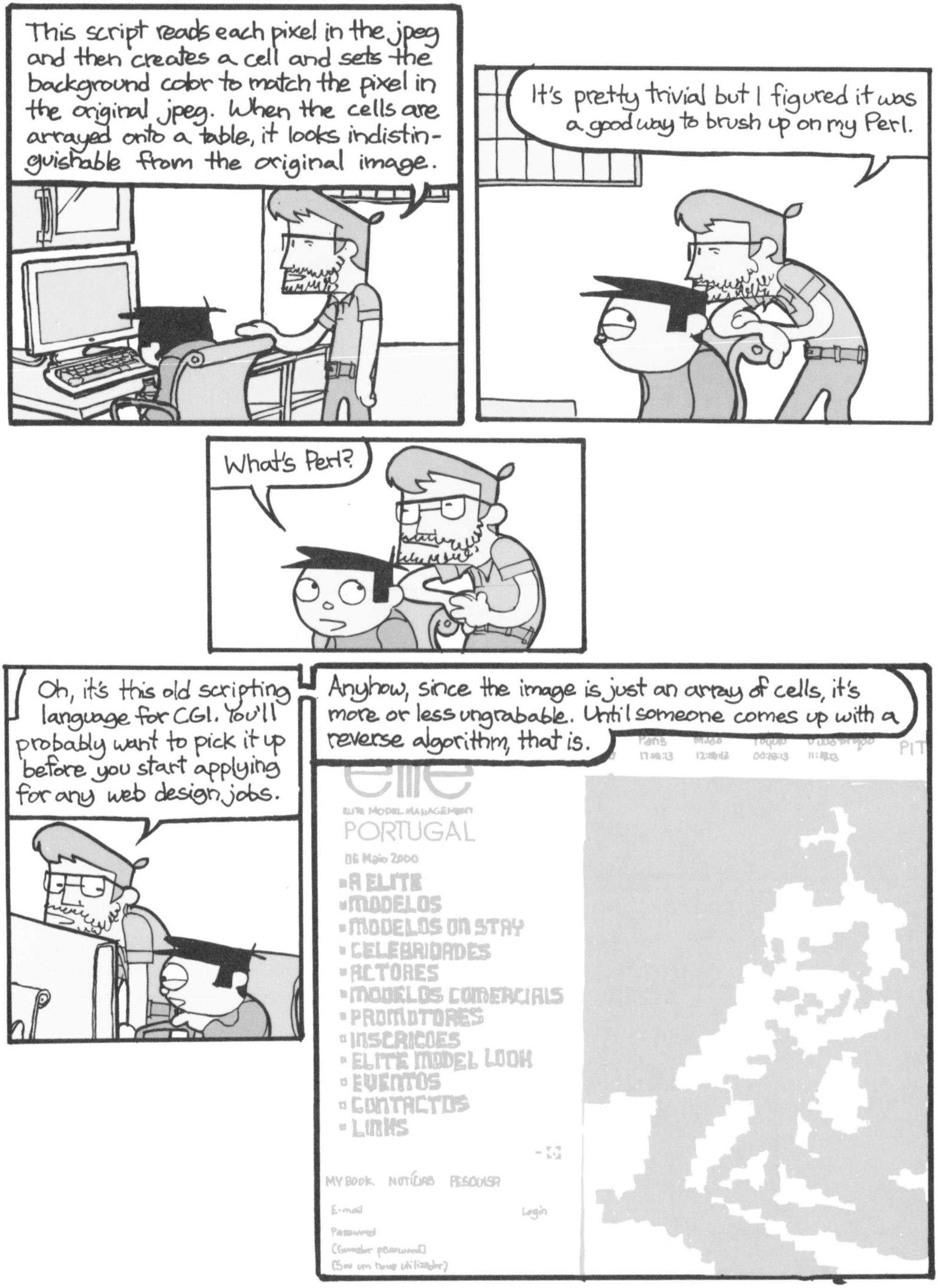
This script reads each pixel in the jpeg and then creates a cell and sets the background color to match the pixel in the original jpeg. When the cells are arrayed onto a table, it looks indistinguishable from the original image.
It's pretty trivial but I figured it was a good way to brush up on my Perl.
What's Perl?
Oh, it's this old scripting language for CGI. You'll probably want to pick it up before you start applying for any web design jobs.
Anyhow, since the image is just an array of cells, it's more or less ungrabable. Until someone comes up with a reverse algorithm, that is.
ELITE MODEL MANAGEMENT
PORTUGAL
06 Maio 2000
A ELITE
MODELOS
MODELOS ON STAY
CELEBRIDADES
ACTORES
MODELOS COMERCIAIS
PROMOTORES
INSCRICOES
ELITE MODEL LOOK
EVENTOS
CONTACTOS
LINKS
MY BOOK
NOTÍCIAS
PESQUISA
E-mail
Login
Password

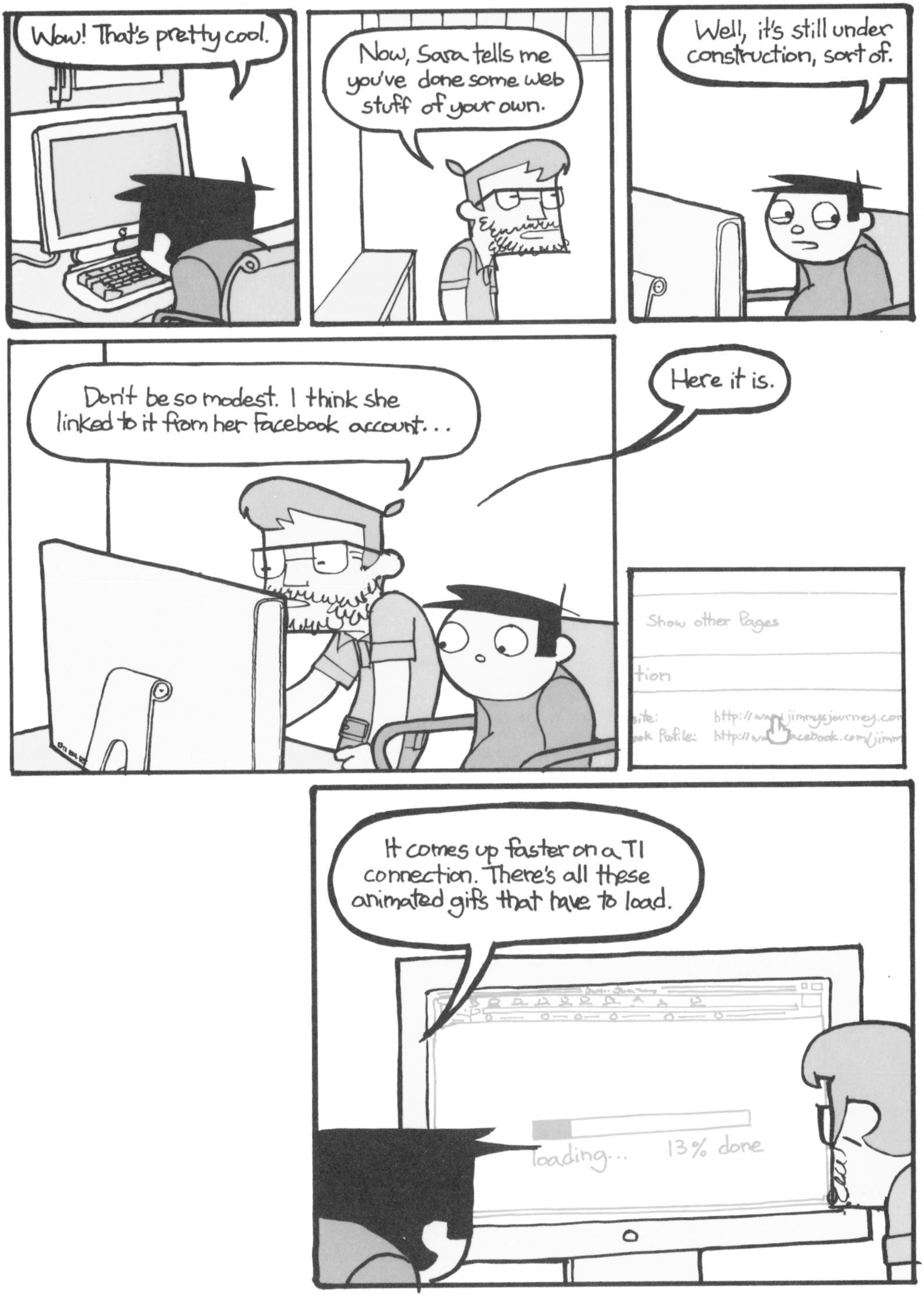
Wow! That's pretty cool.
Now, Sara tells me you've done some web stuff of your own.
Well, it's still under construction, sort of.
Don't be so modest. I think she linked to it from her Facebook account...
Here it is.
Show other Pages
It comes up faster on a T1 connection. There's all these animated gifs that have to load.
loading... 13% done

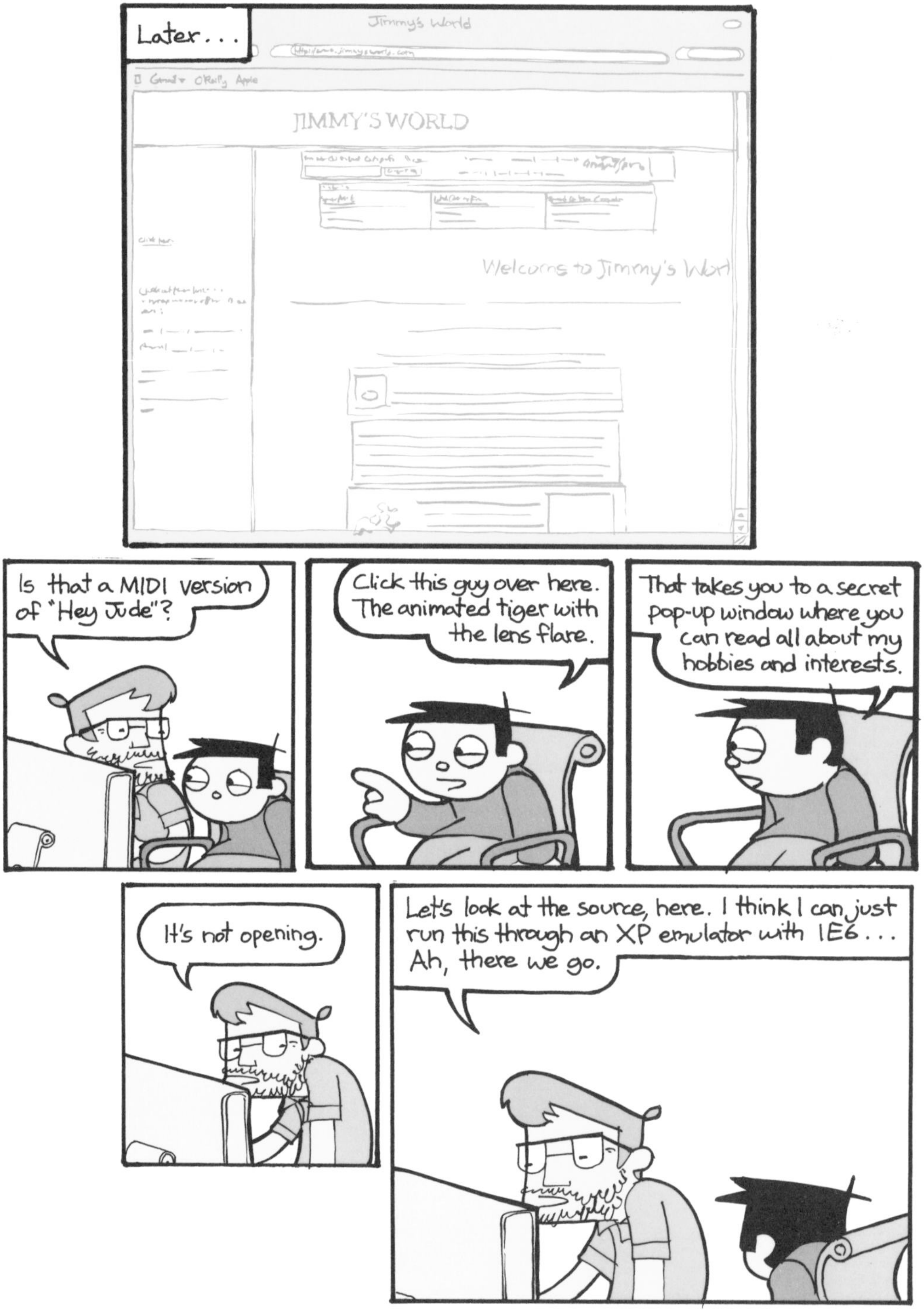

Later . . .
Jimmy's World
JIMMY'S WORLD
Is that a MIDI version of "Hey Jude"?
Click this guy over here. The animated tiger with the lens flare.
That takes you to a secret pop-up window where you can read all about my hobbies and interests.
It's not opening.
Let's look at the source, here. I think I can just run this through an XP emulator with IE6 . . . Ah, there we go.

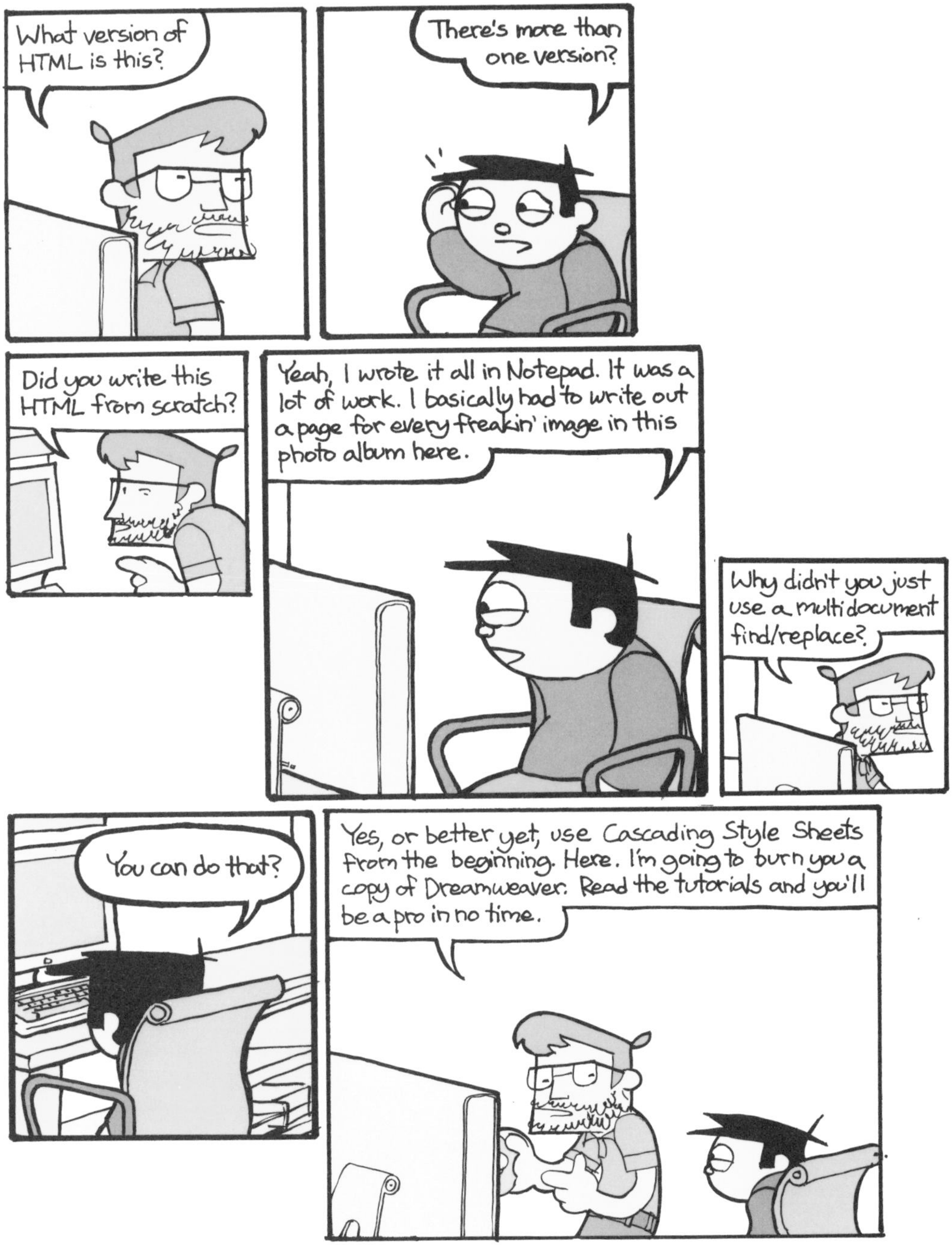
What version of HTML is this?
There's more than one version?
Did you write this HTML from scratch?
Yeah, I wrote it all in Notepad. It was a lot of work. I basically had to write out a page for every freakin' image in this photo album here.
Why didn't you just use a multidocument find/replace?
You can do that?
Yes, or better yet, use Cascading Style Sheets from the beginning. Here. I'm going to burn you a copy of Dreamweaver. Read the tutorials and you'll be a pro in no time.

So, on Thursdays Caroline and I like to go to the Red Star Bar after work.

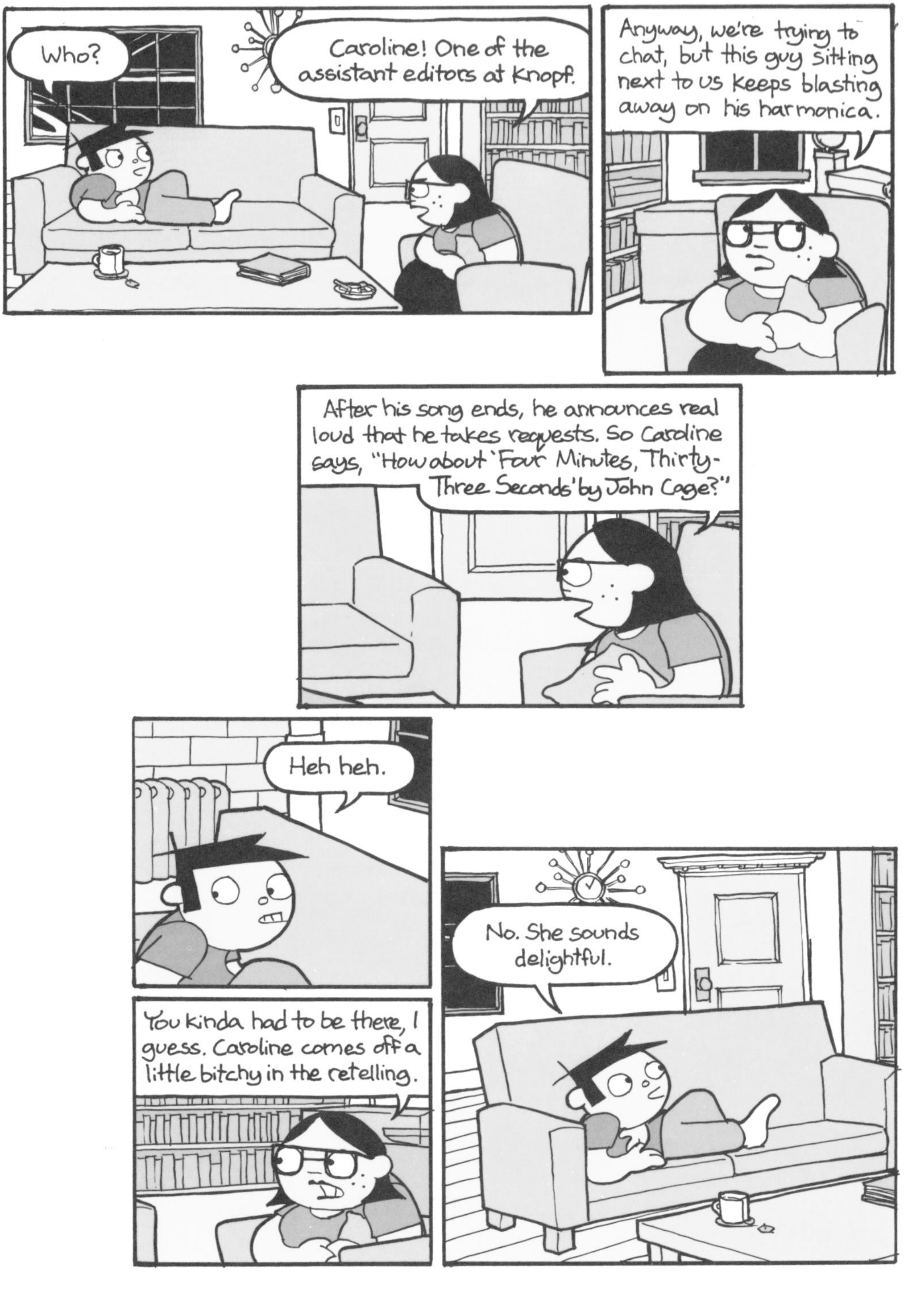
Who?
Caroline! One of the assistant editors at Knopf.
Anyway, we're trying to chat, but this guy sitting next to us keeps blasting away on his harmonica.
After his song ends, he announces real loud that he takes requests. So Caroline says, "How about 'Four Minutes, Thirty-Three Seconds' by John Cage?"
Heh heh.
You kinda had to be there, I guess. Caroline comes off a little bitchy in the retelling.
No. She sounds delightful.

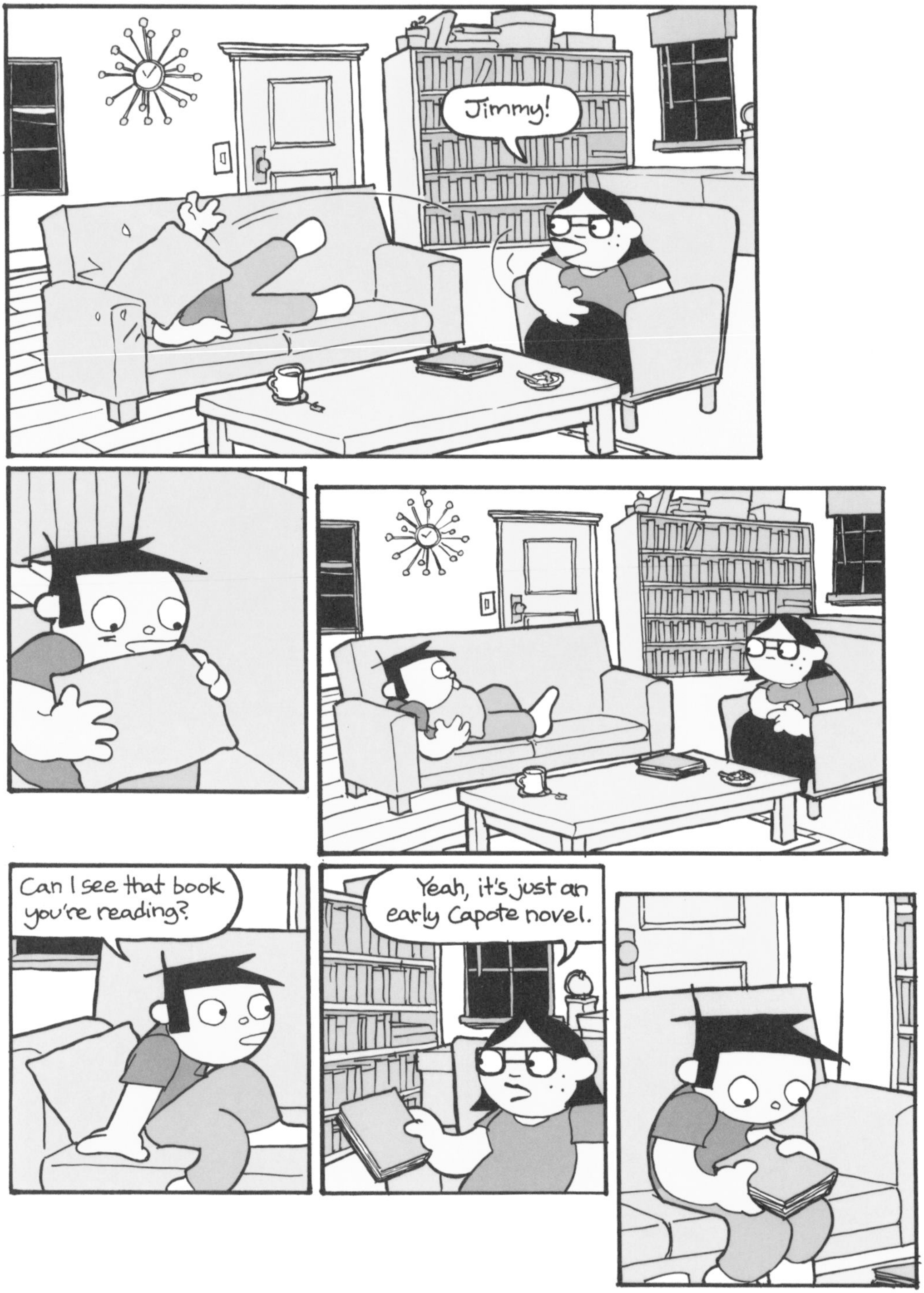
Jimmy!
Can I see that book you're reading?
Yeah, it's just an early Capote novel.

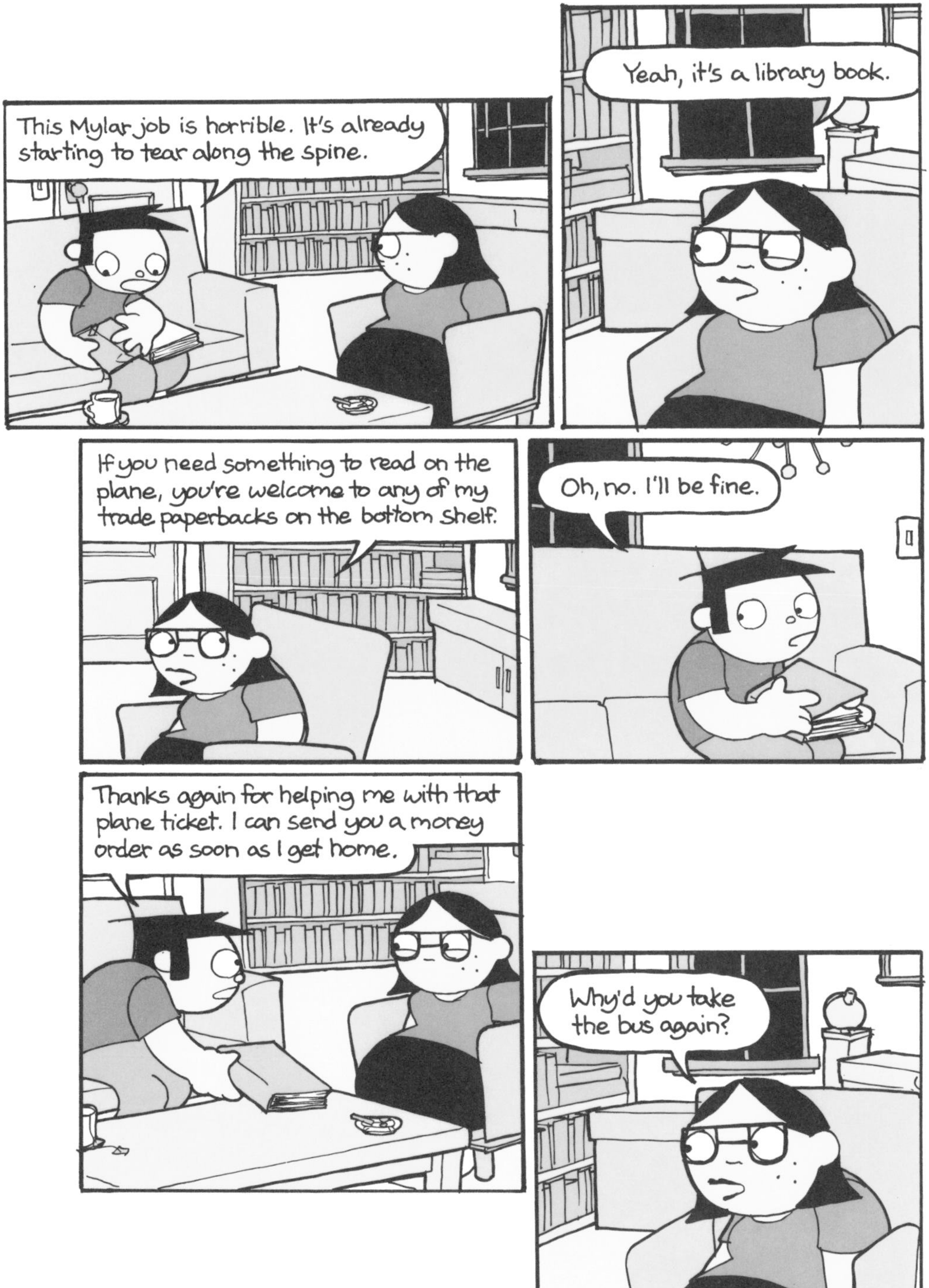
This Mylar job is horrible. It's already starting to tear along the spine.
Yeah, it's a library book.
If you need something to read on the plane, you're welcome to any of my trade paperbacks on the bottom shelf.
Oh, no. I'll be fine.
Thanks again for helping me with that plane ticket. I can send you a money order as soon as I get home.
Why'd you take the bus again?

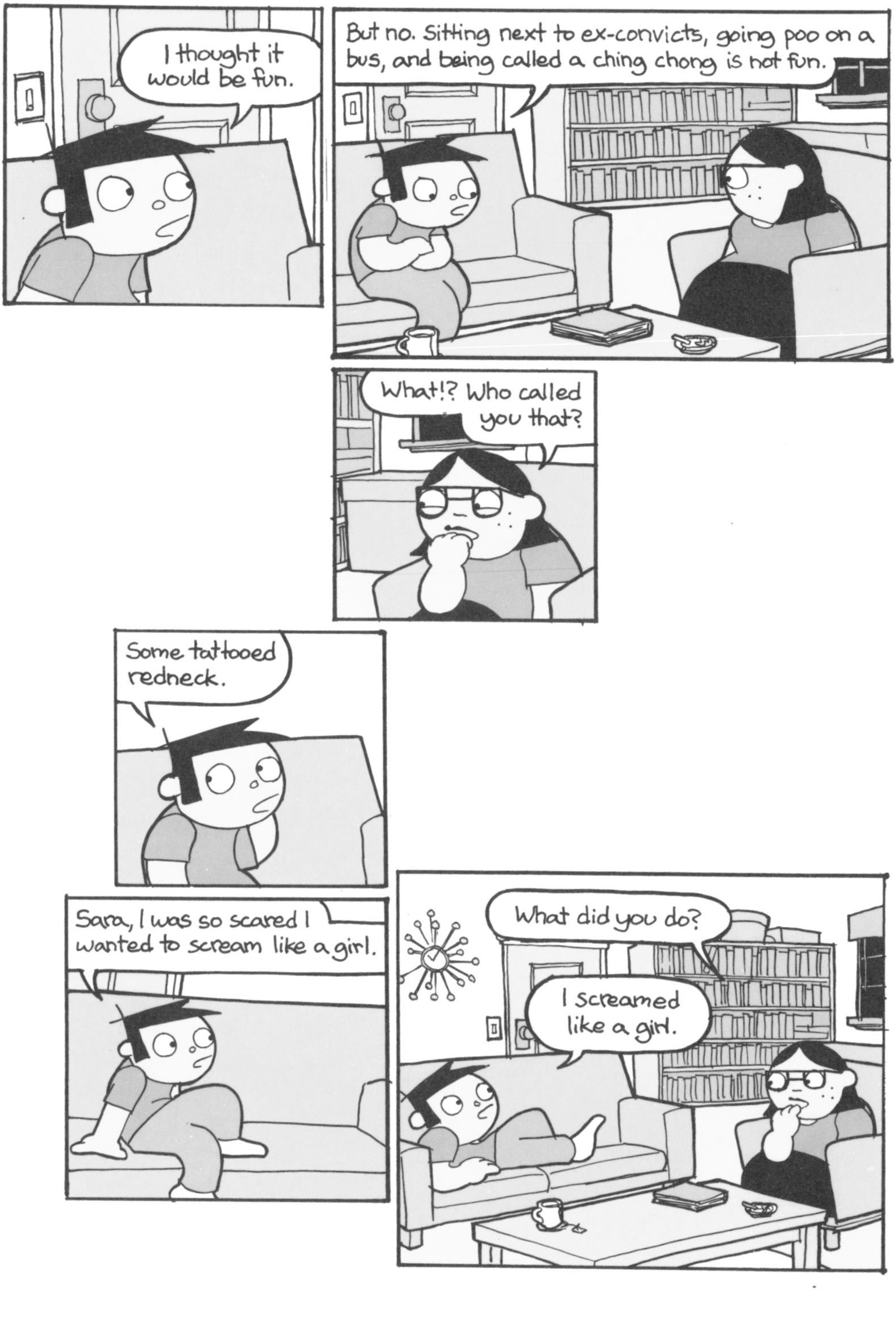
I thought it would be fun.
But no. Sitting next to ex-convicts, going poo on a bus, and being called a ching chong is not fun.
What!? Who called you that?
Some tattooed redneck.
Sara, I was so scared I wanted to scream like a girl.
What did you do?
I screamed like a girl.

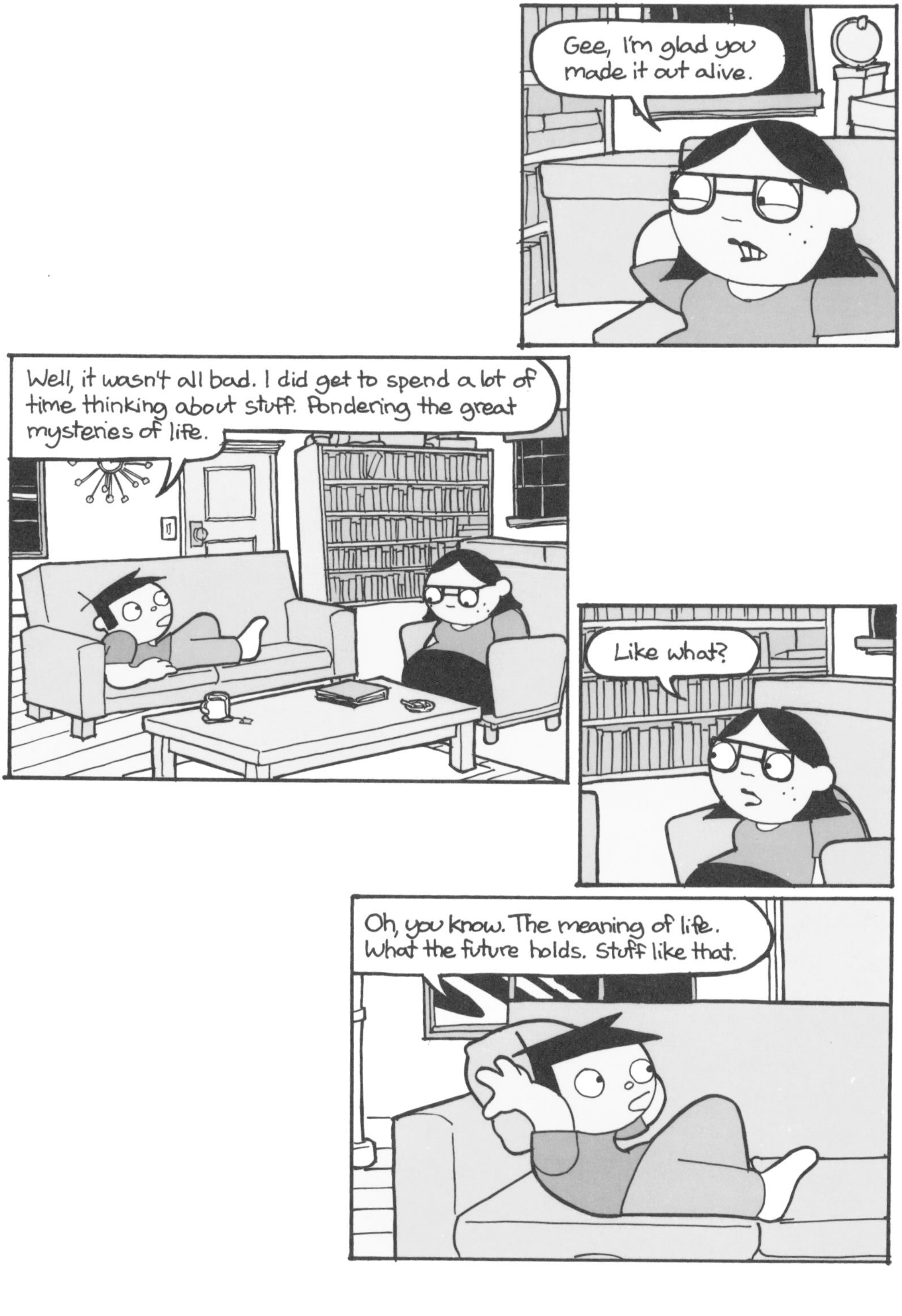
Gee, I'm glad you made it out alive.
Well, it wasn't all bad. I did get to spend a lot of time thinking about stuff. Pondering the great mysteries of life.
Like what?
Oh, you know. The meaning of life. What the future holds. Stuff like that.

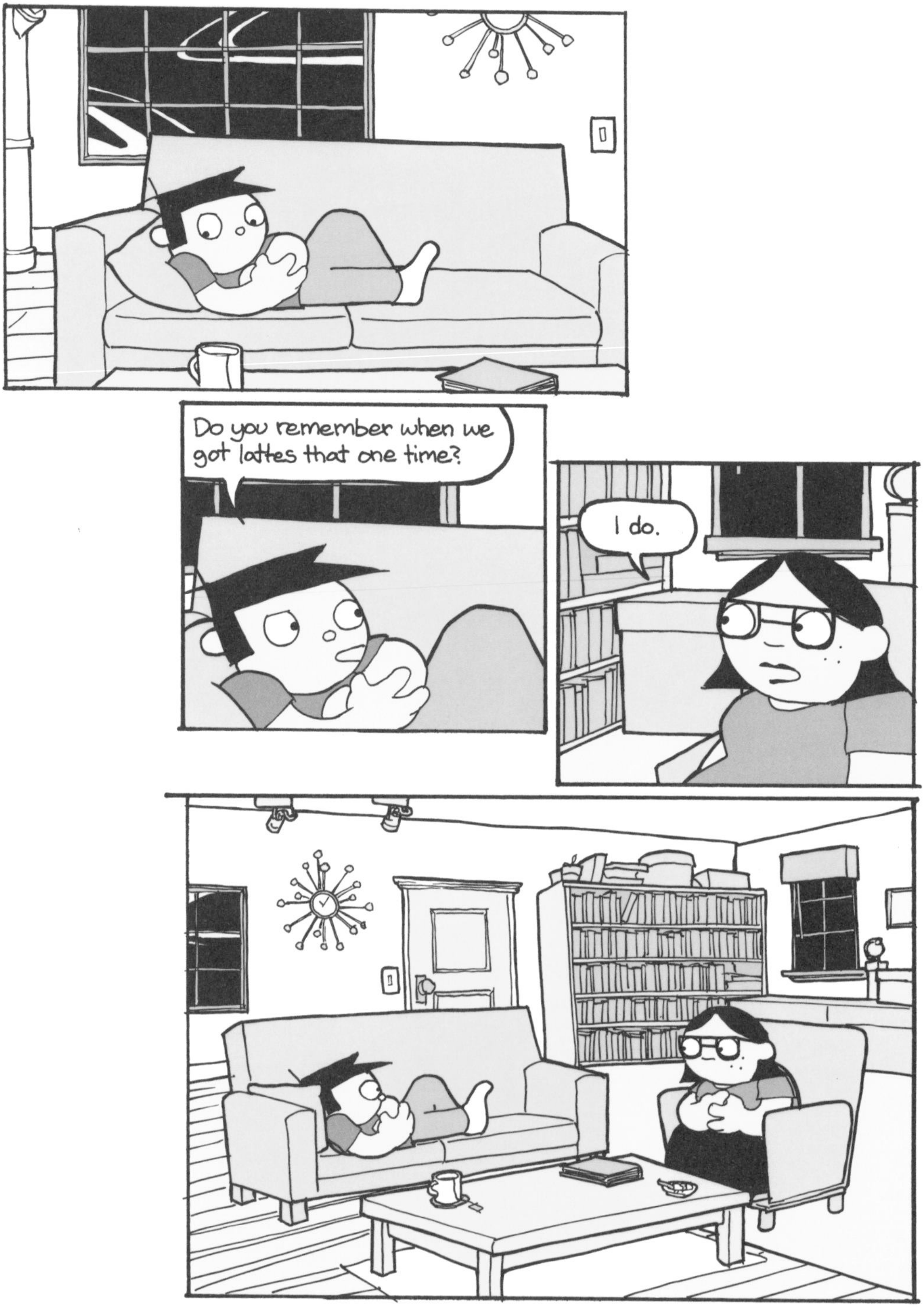
Do you remember when we got lattes that one time?
I do.

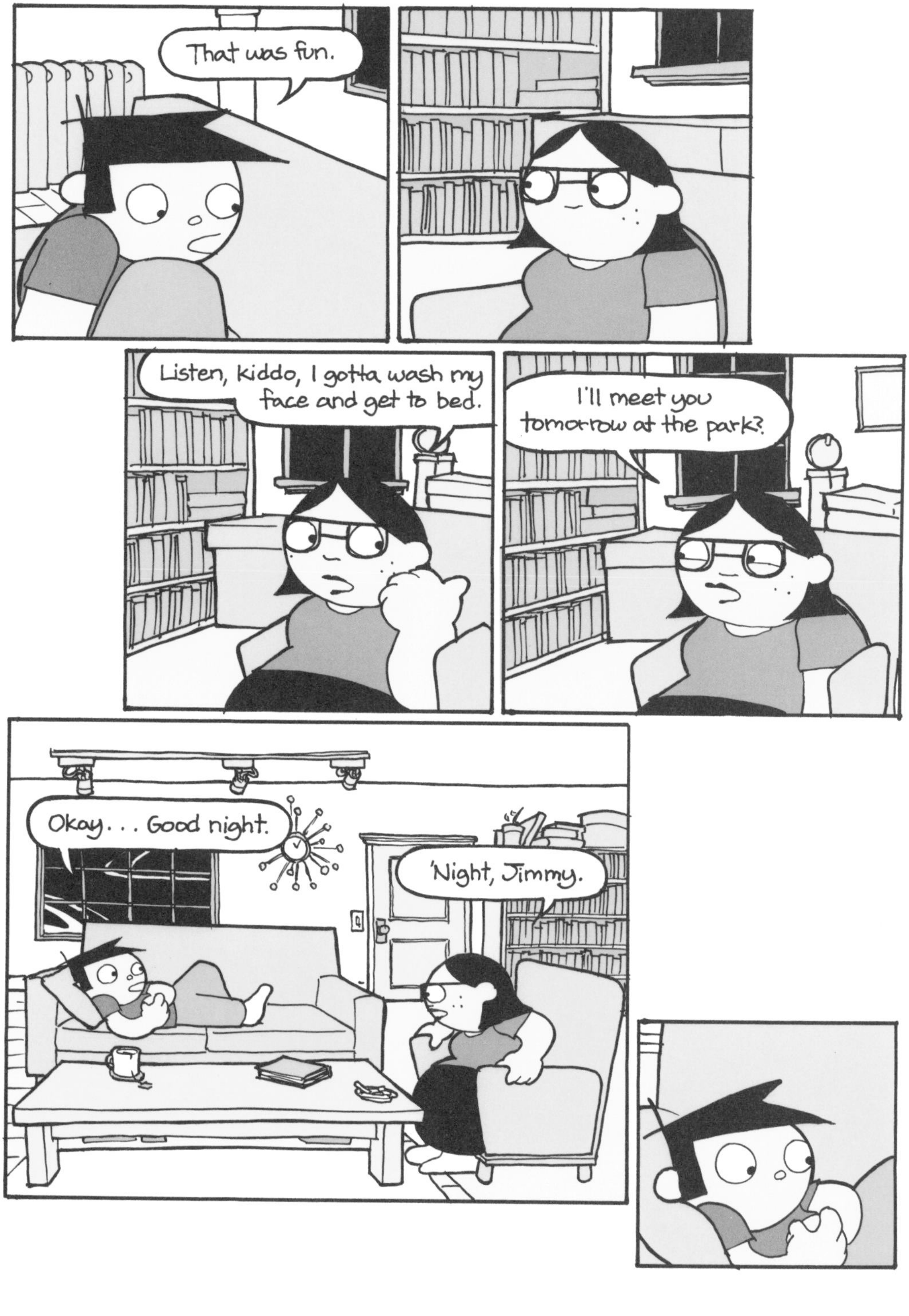
That was fun.
Listen, kiddo, I gotta wash my face and get to bed.
I'll meet you tomorrow at the park?
Okay. . . Good night.
'Night, Jimmy.

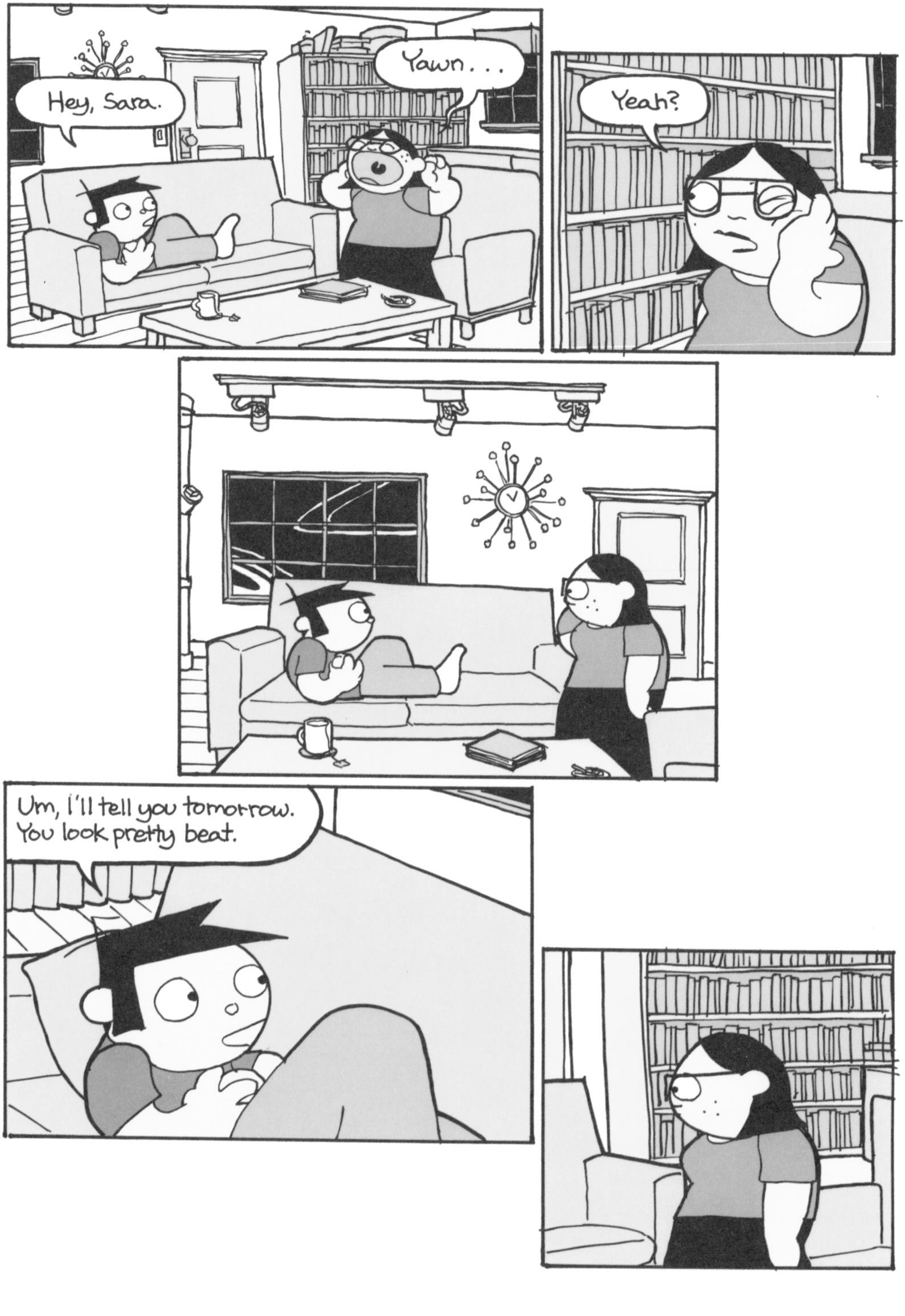
Hey, Sara.
Yawn...
Yeah?
Um, I'll tell you tomorrow. You look pretty beat.

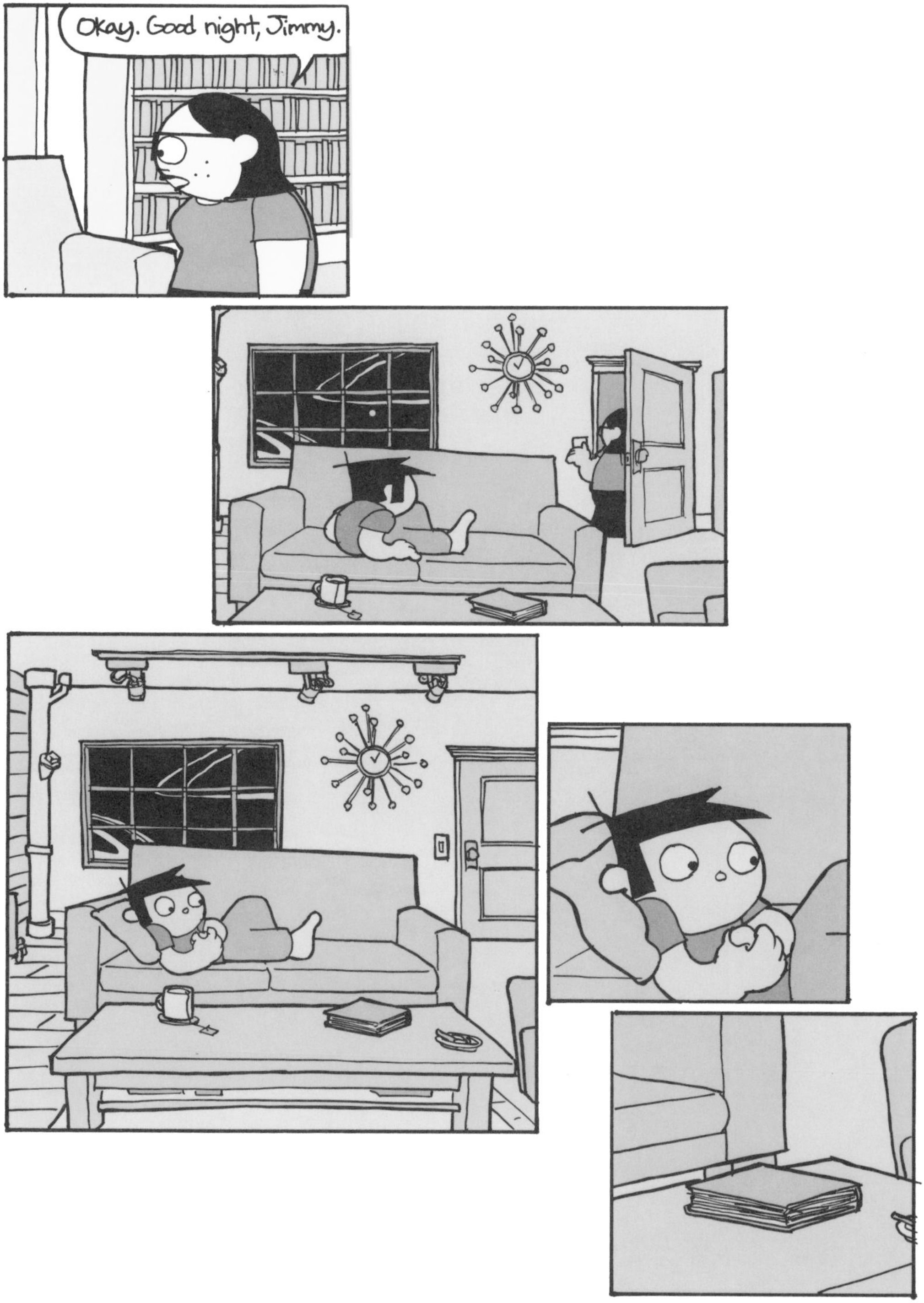
Okay. Good night, Jimmy.

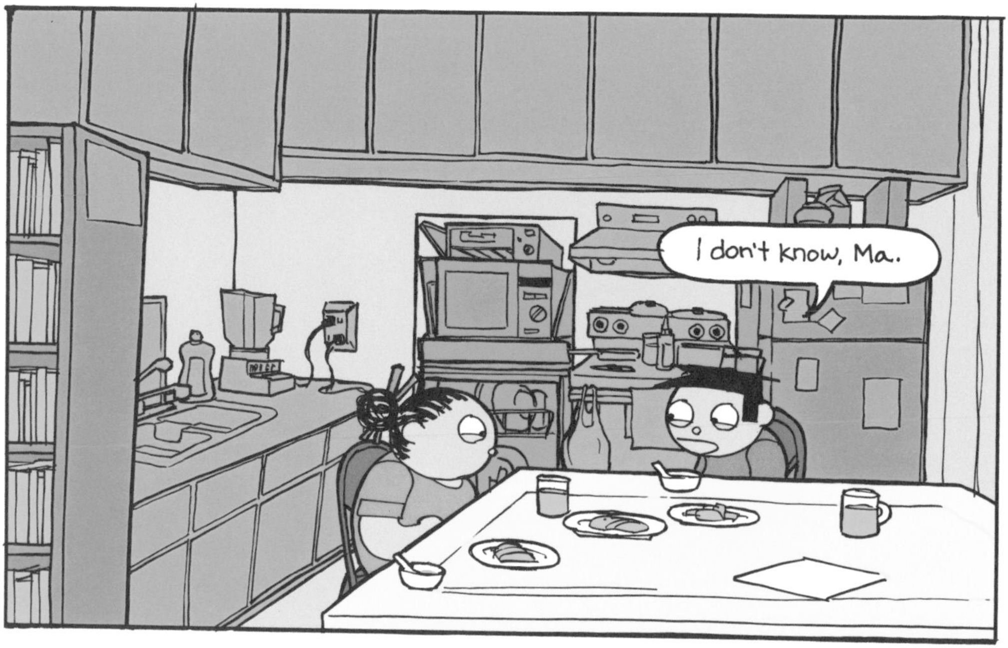
I don't know, Ma.

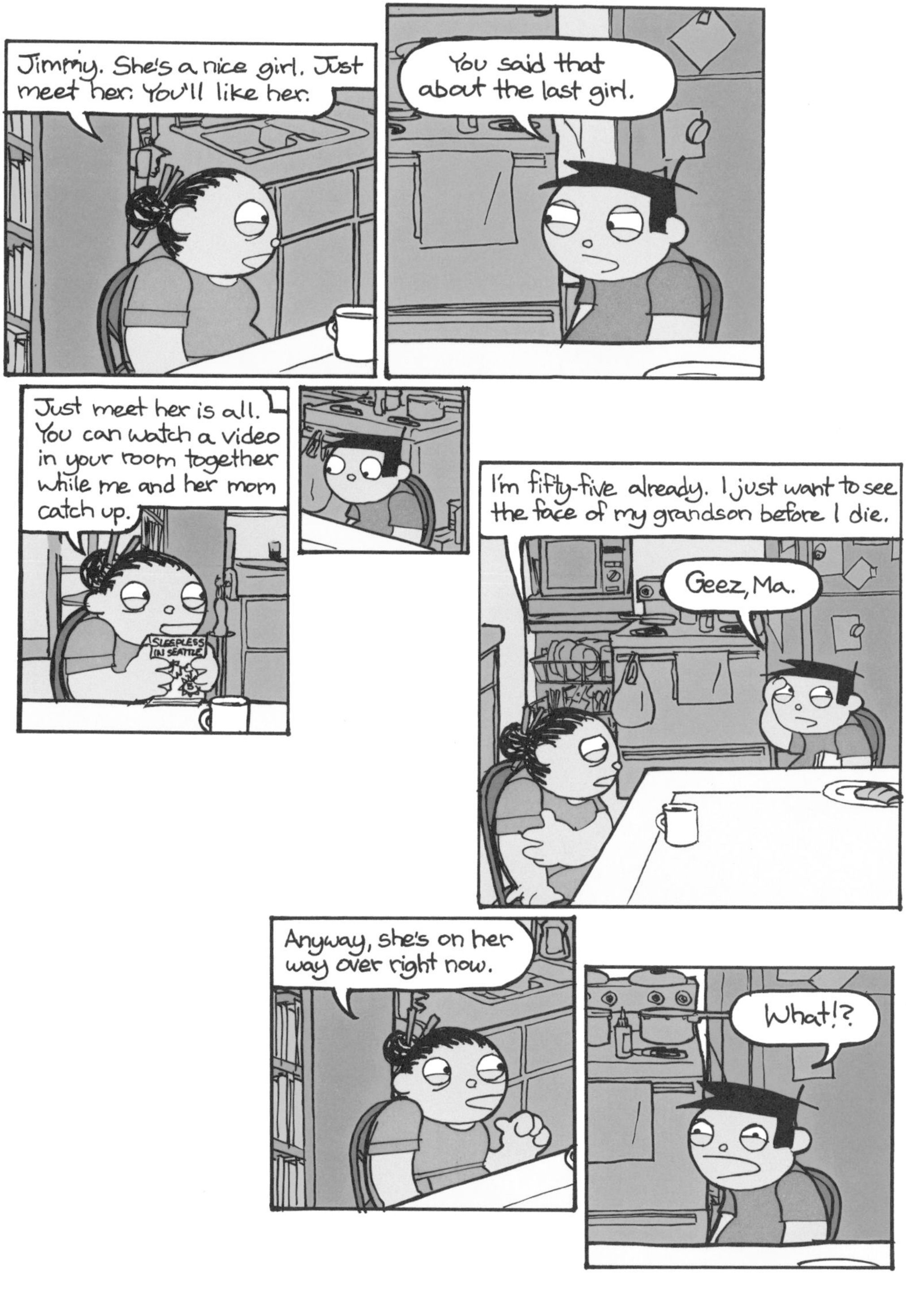
Jimmy. She's a nice girl. Just meet her. You'll like her.
You said that about the last girl.
Just meet her is all. You can watch a video in your room together while me and her mom catch up.
SLEEPLESS IN SEATTLE
I'm fifty-five already. I just want to see the face of my grandson before I die.
Geez, Ma.
Anyway, she's on her way over right now.
What!?

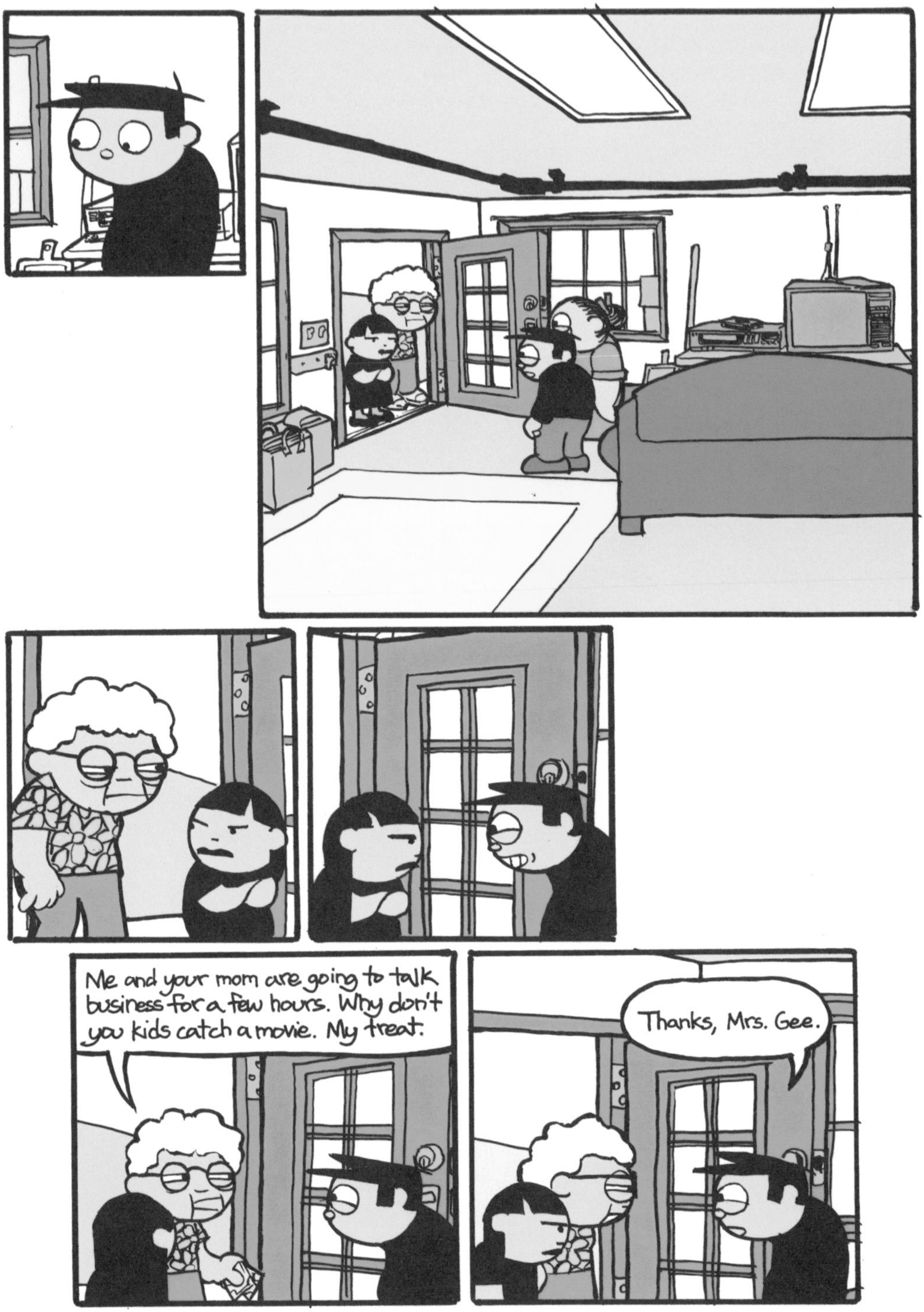
Me and your mom are going to talk business for a few hours. Why don't you kids catch a movie. My treat.
Thanks, Mrs. Gee.

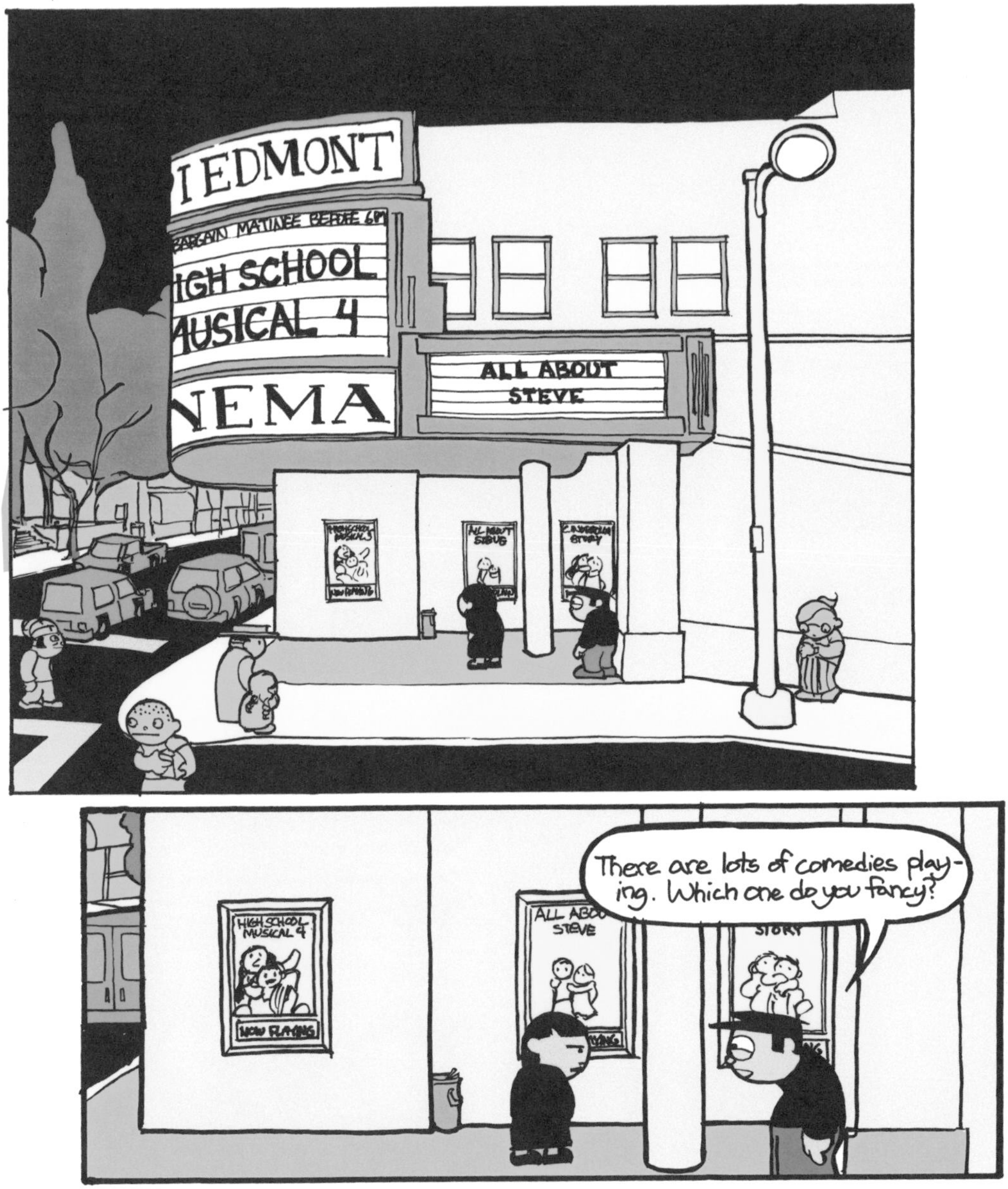

IEDMONT
BARGAIN MATINEE BEFORE 6PM
IGH SCHOOL
USICAL 4
NEMA
ALL ABOUT
STEVE
HIGH SCHOOL
MUSICAL 4
NOW PLAYING
ALL ABOU
STEVE
STORY
There are lots of comedies play-ing. Which one do you fancy?

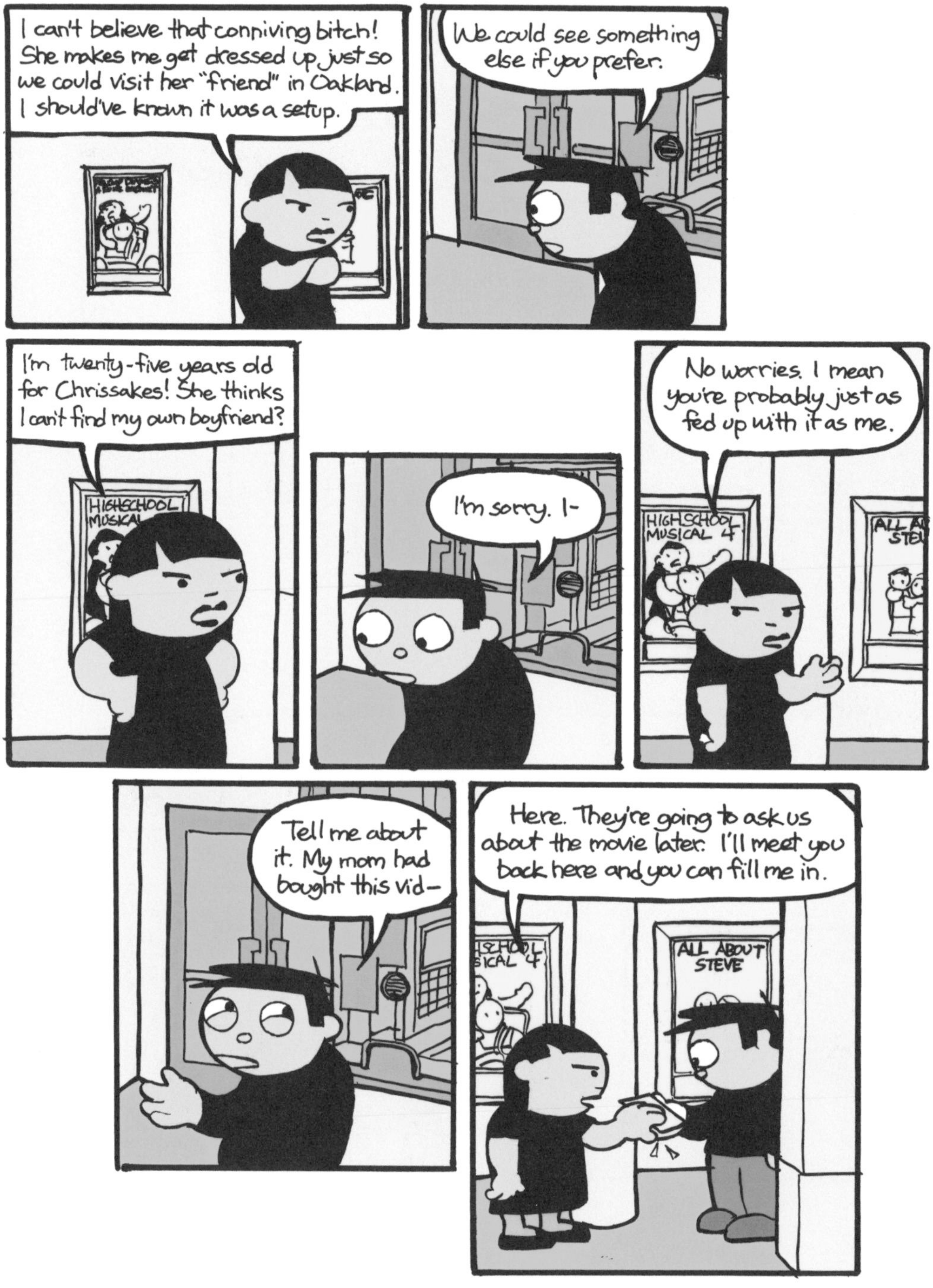
I can't believe that conniving bitch! She makes me get dressed up just so we could visit her "friend" in Oakland. I should've known it was a setup.
We could see something else if you prefer.
I'm twenty-five years old for Chrissakes! She thinks I can't find my own boyfriend?
HIGHSCHOOL MUSICAL
I'm sorry. I-
No worries. I mean you're probably just as fed up with it as me.
HIGHSCHOOL MUSICAL 4
Tell me about it. My mom had bought this vid-
Here. They're going to ask us about the movie later. I'll meet you back here and you can fill me in.
ALL ABOUT STEVE

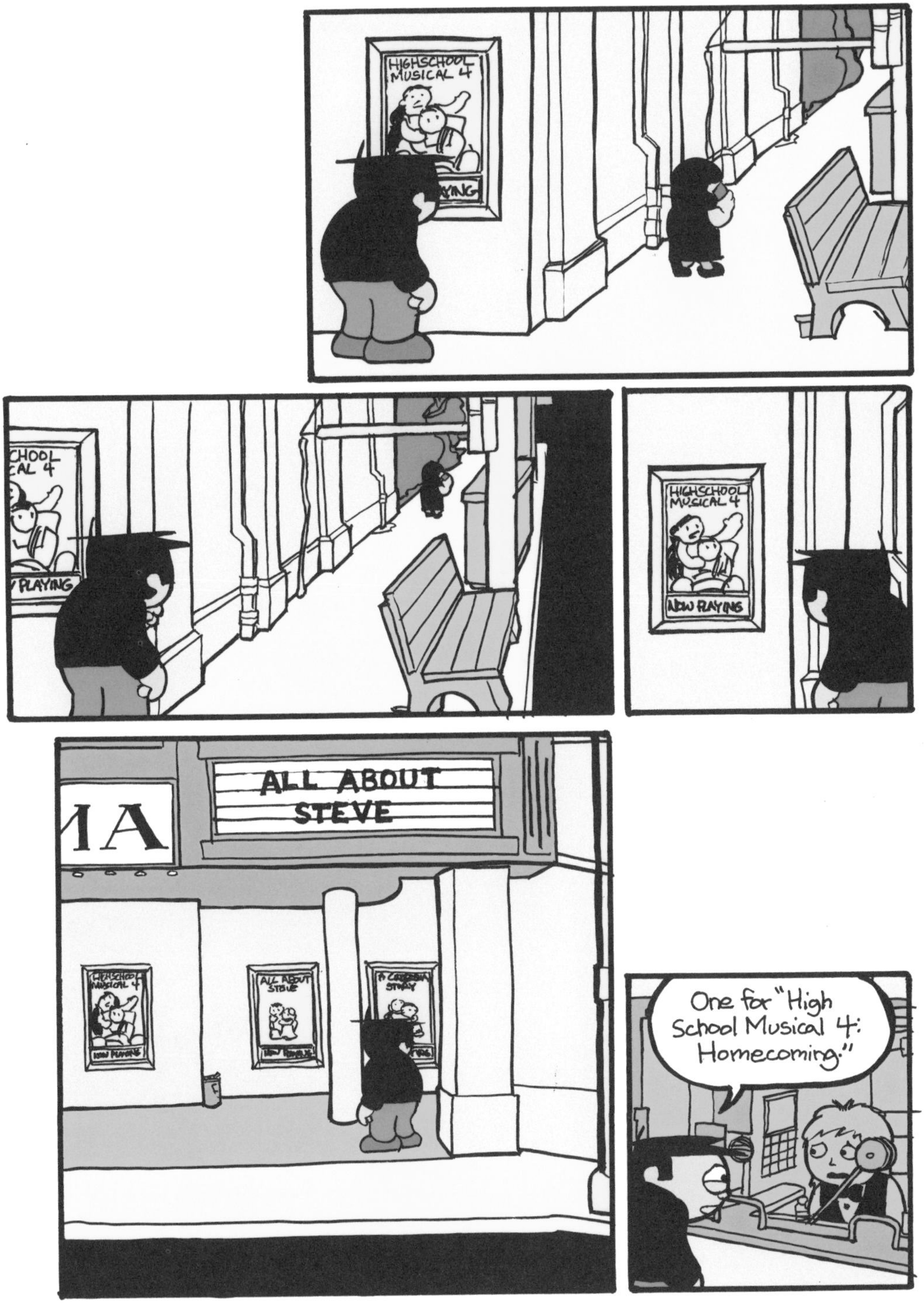
HIGHSCHOOL MUSICAL 4
NOW PLAYING
ALL ABOUT STEVE
MA
One for "High School Musical 4: Homecoming."

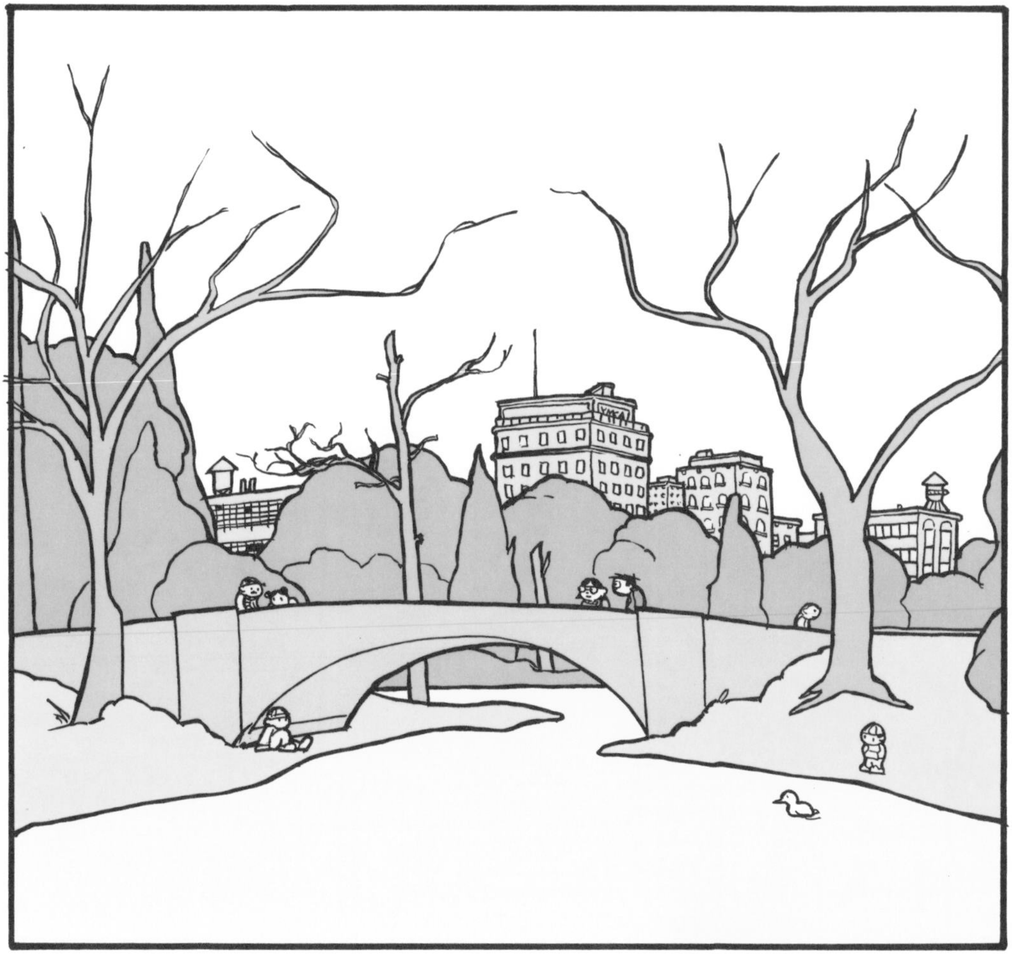

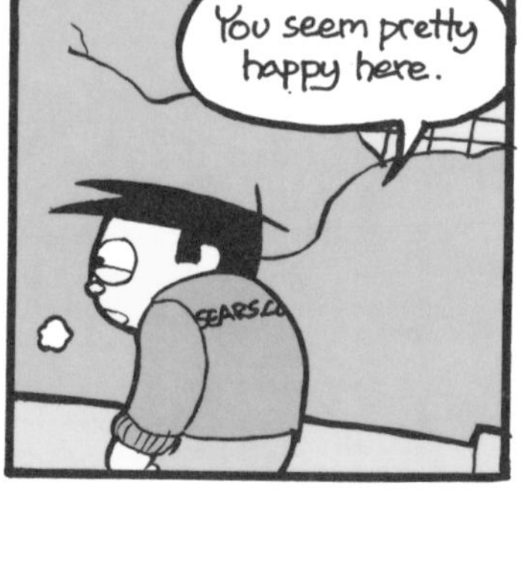
You seem pretty happy here.
SEARS CO

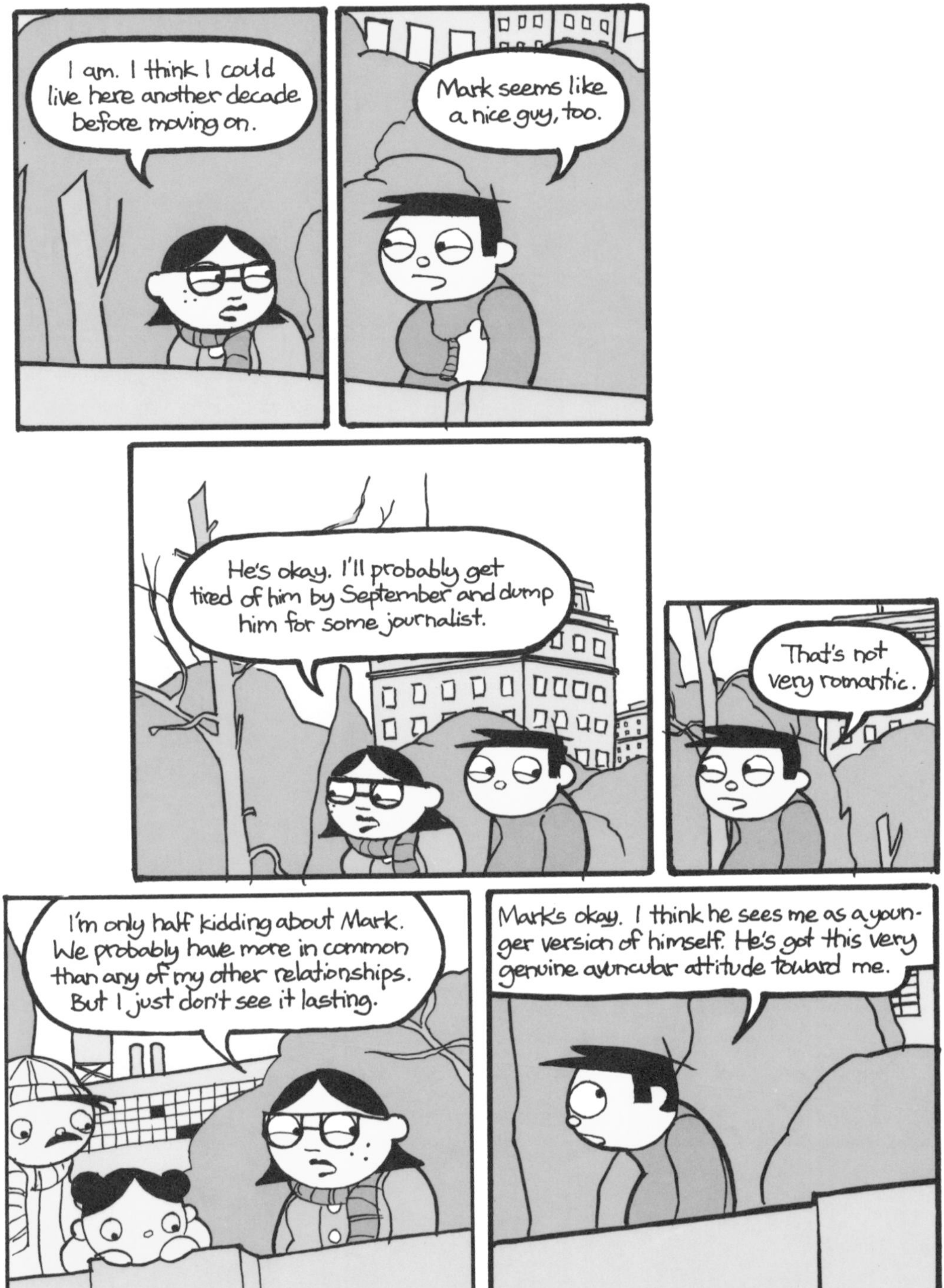
I am. I think I could live here another decade before moving on.
Mark seems like a nice guy, too.
He's okay. I'll probably get tired of him by September and dump him for some journalist.
That's not very romantic.
I'm only half kidding about Mark. We probably have more in common than any of my other relationships. But I just don't see it lasting.
Mark's okay. I think he sees me as a younger version of himself. He's got this very genuine avuncular attitude toward me.

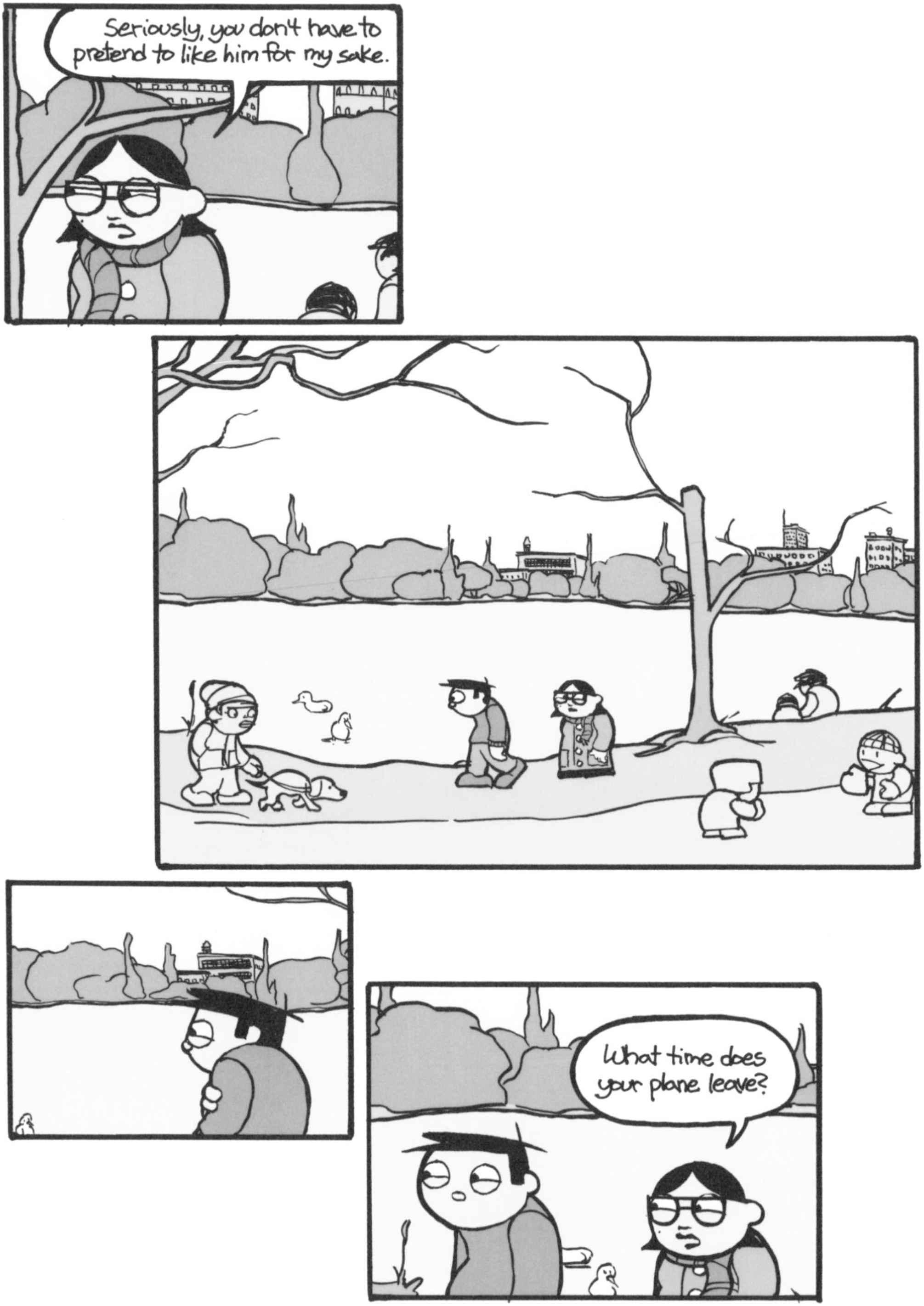
Seriously, you don't have to pretend to like him for my sake.
What time does your plane leave?

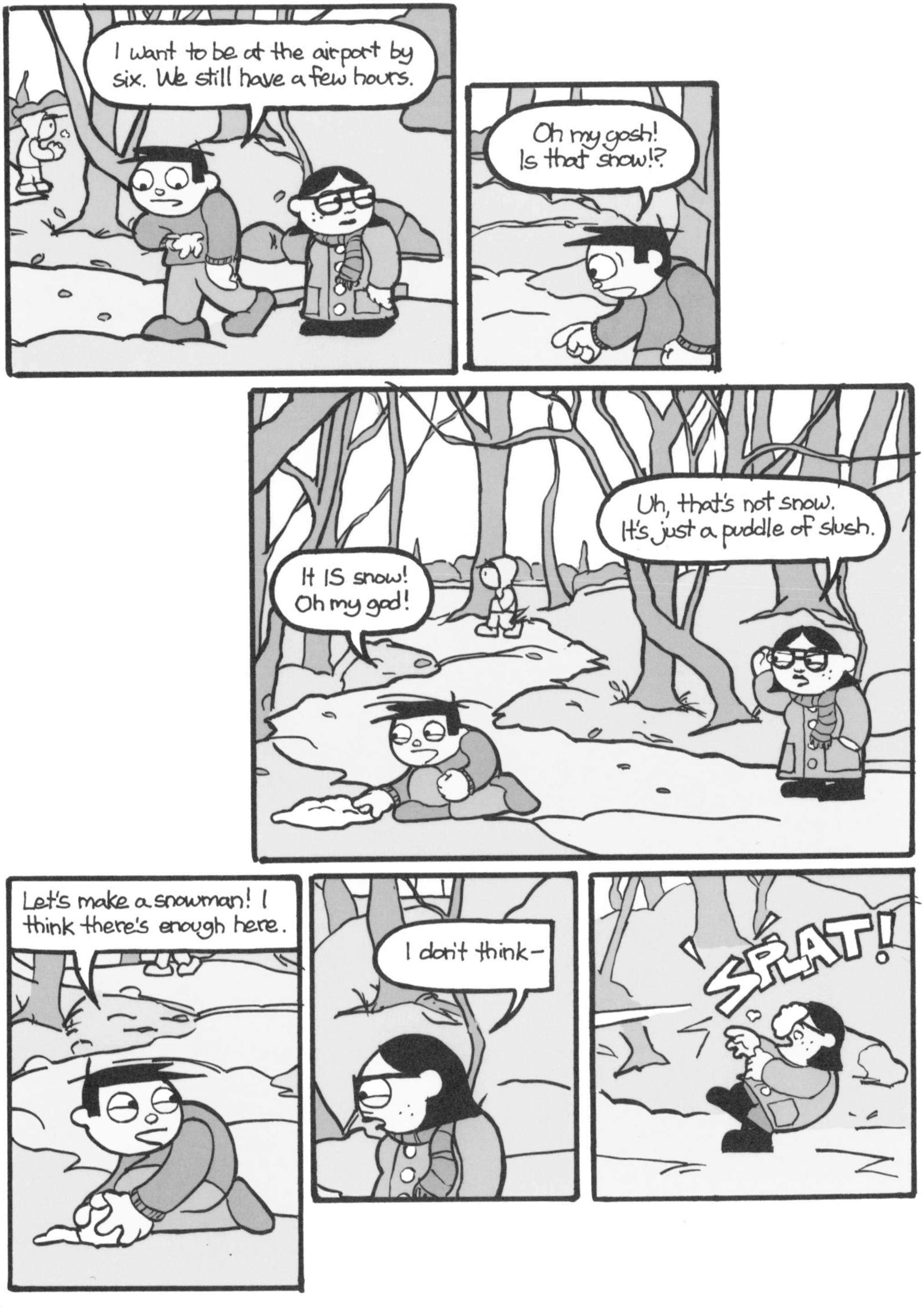
I want to be at the airport by six. We still have a few hours.
Oh my gosh! Is that snow!?
Uh, that's not snow. It's just a puddle of slush.
It IS snow! Oh my god!
Let's make a snowman! I think there's enough here.
I don't think-
SPLAT!

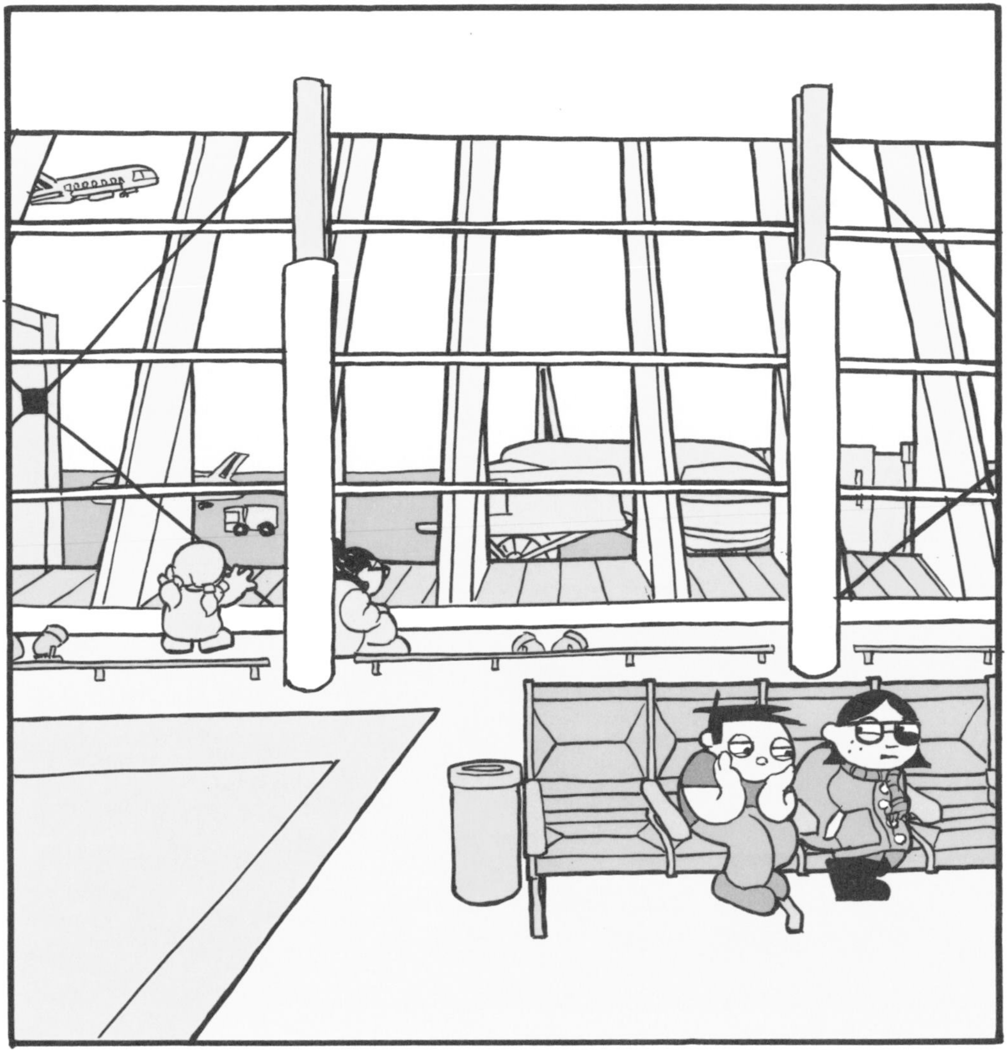

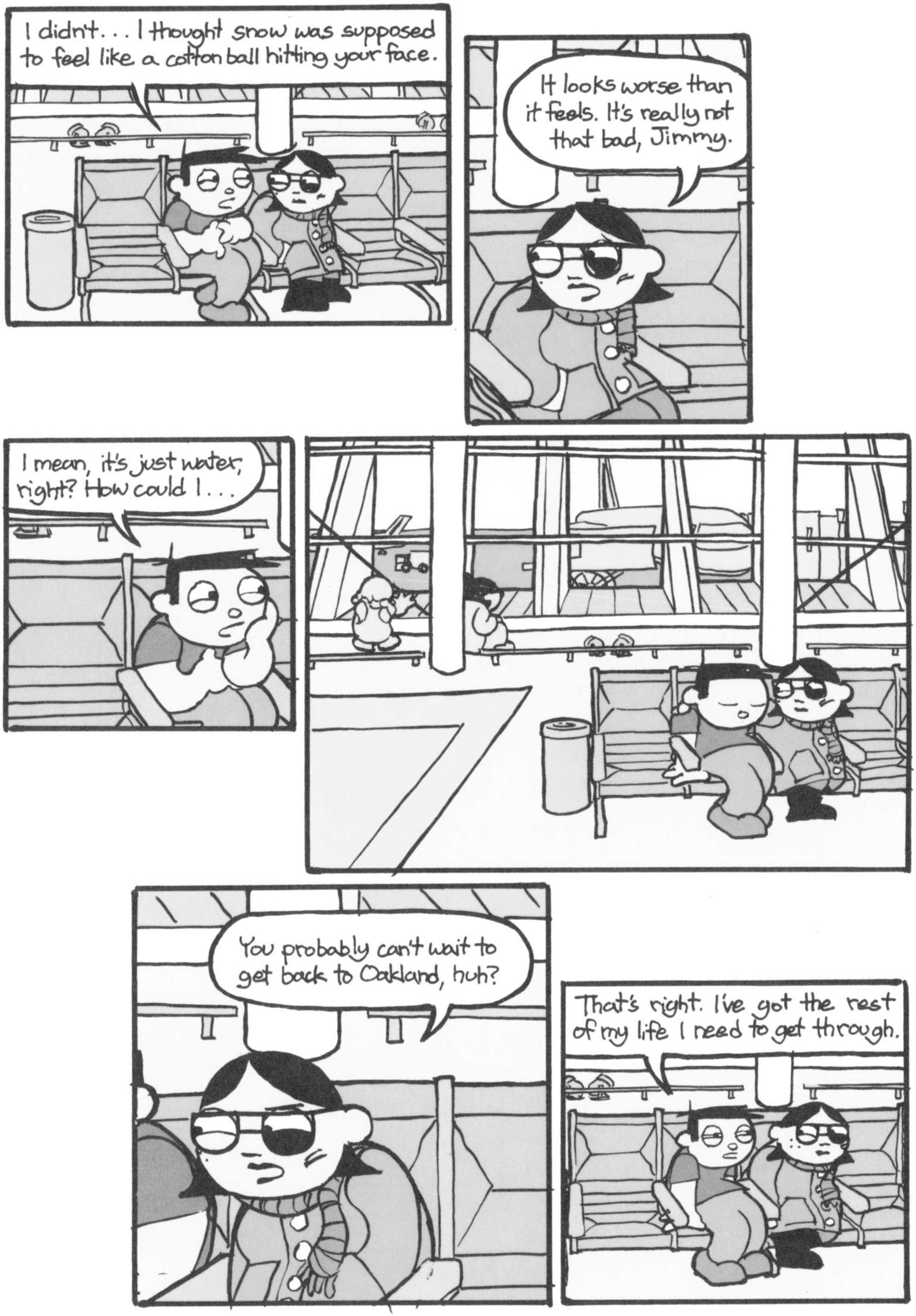
I didn't... I thought snow was supposed to feel like a cotton ball hitting your face.
It looks worse than it feels. It's really not that bad, Jimmy.
I mean, it's just water, right? How could I...
You probably can't wait to get back to Oakland, huh?
That's right. I've got the rest of my life I need to get through.

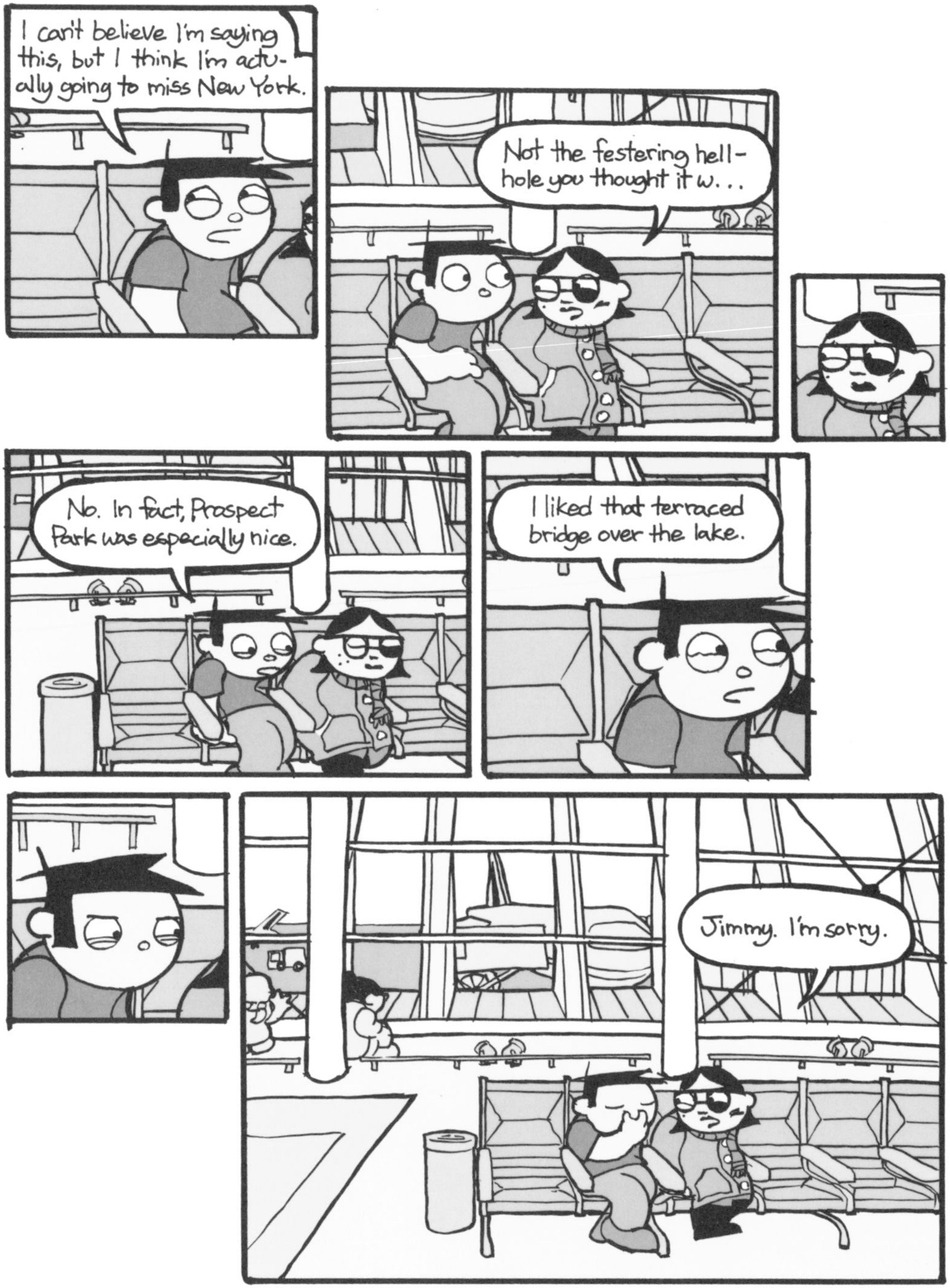
I can't believe I'm saying this, but I think I'm actu-ally going to miss New York.
Not the festering hell-hole you thought it w. . .
No. In fact, Prospect Park was especially nice.
I liked that terraced bridge over the lake.
Jimmy. I'm sorry.

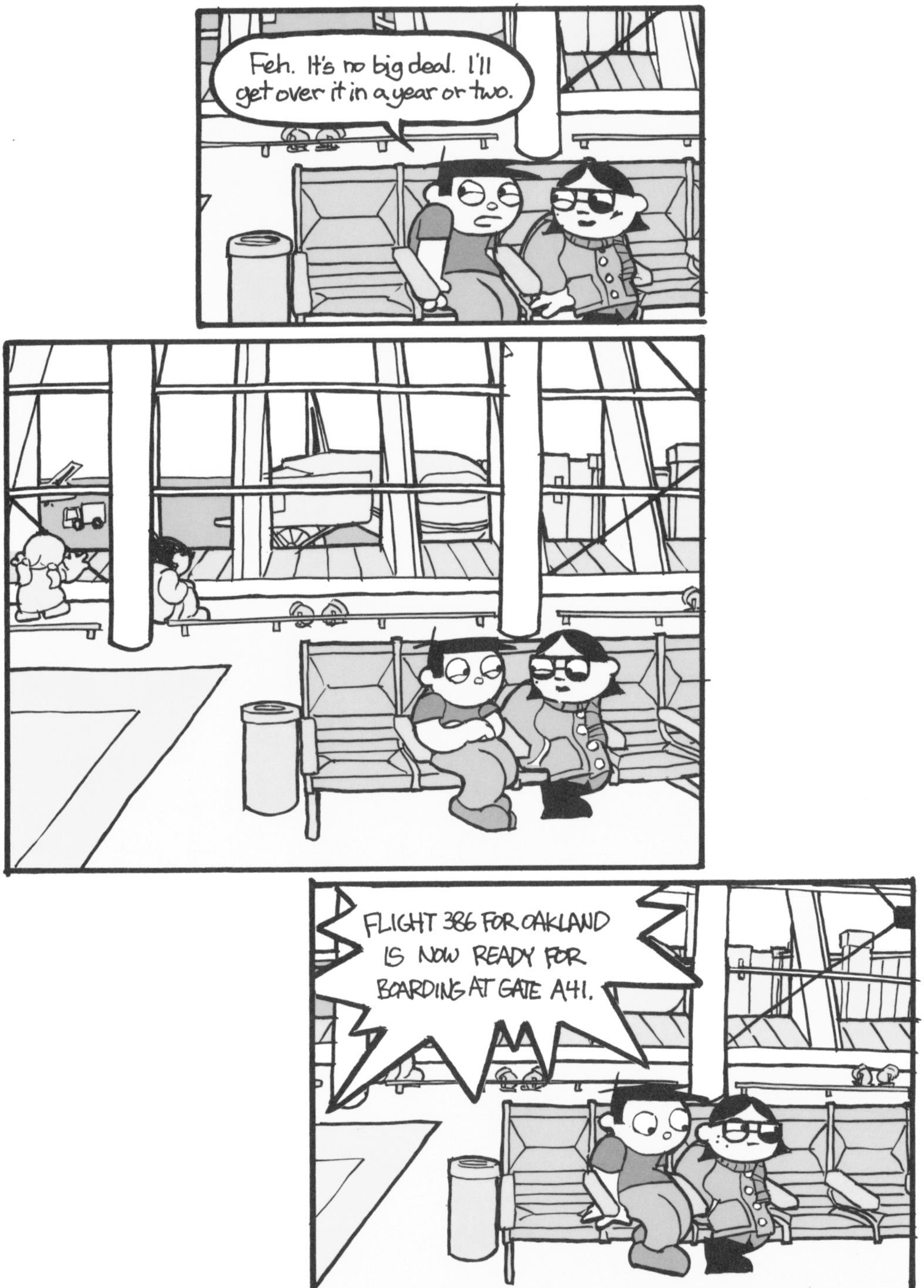
Feh. It's no big deal. I'll get over it in a year or two.
FLIGHT 386 FOR OAKLAND IS NOW READY FOR BOARDING AT GATE A41.

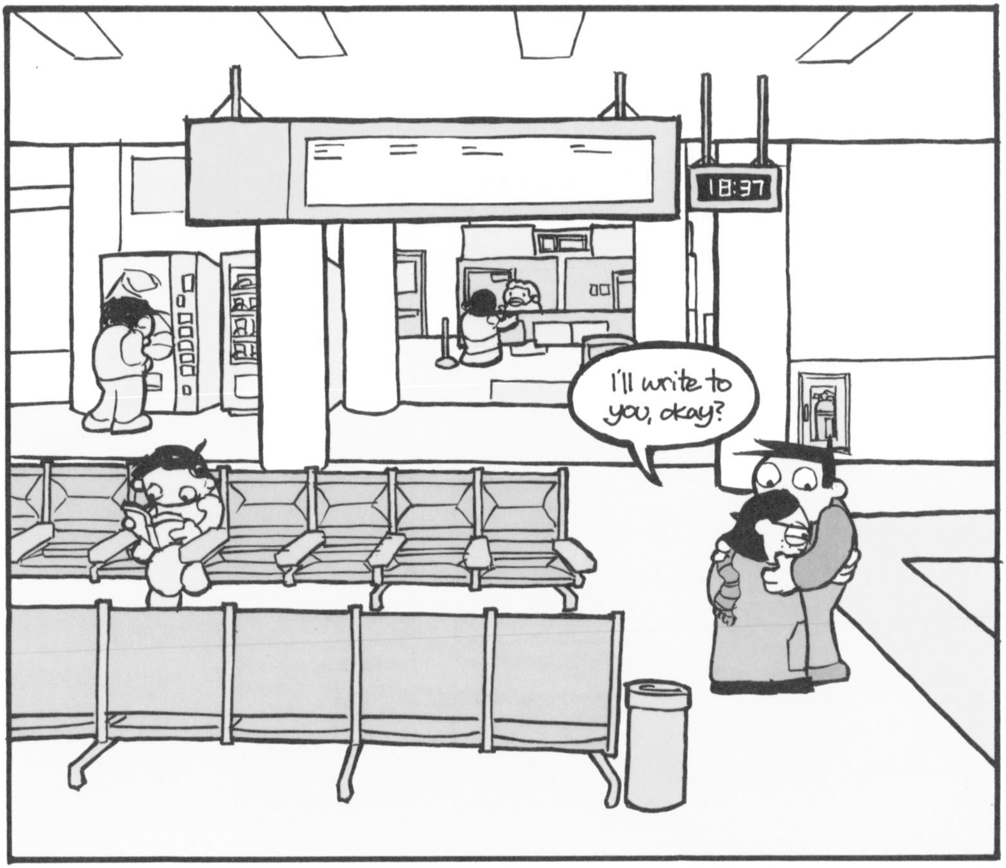
18:37
I'll write to you, okay?

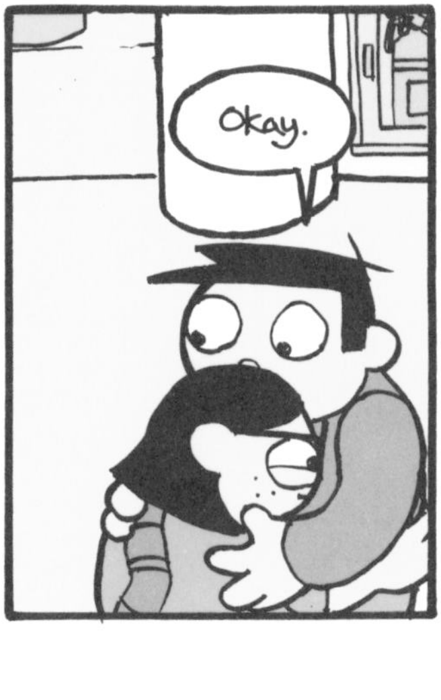
Okay.

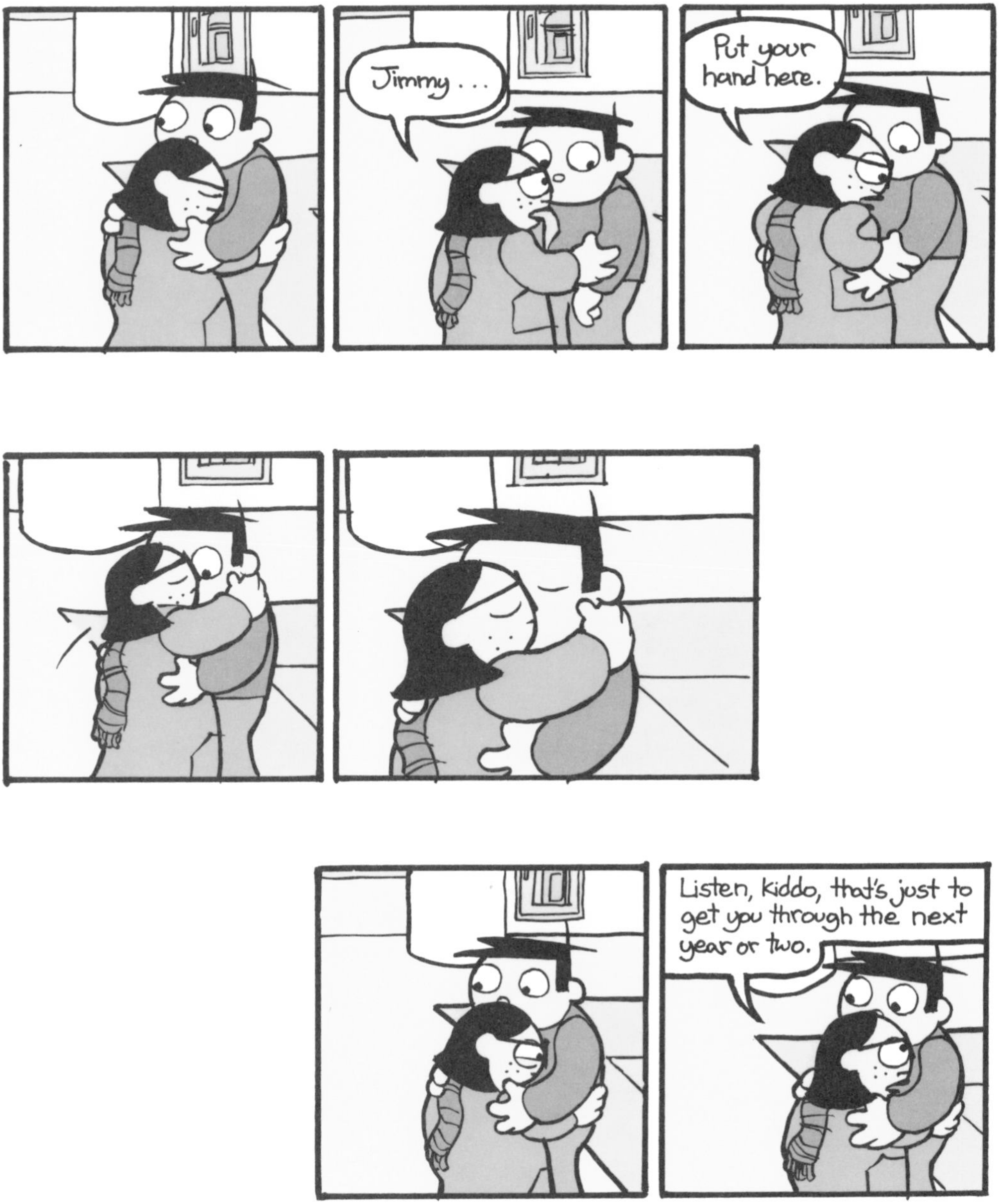
Jimmy . . .
Put your hand here.
Listen, kiddo, that's just to get you through the next year or two.

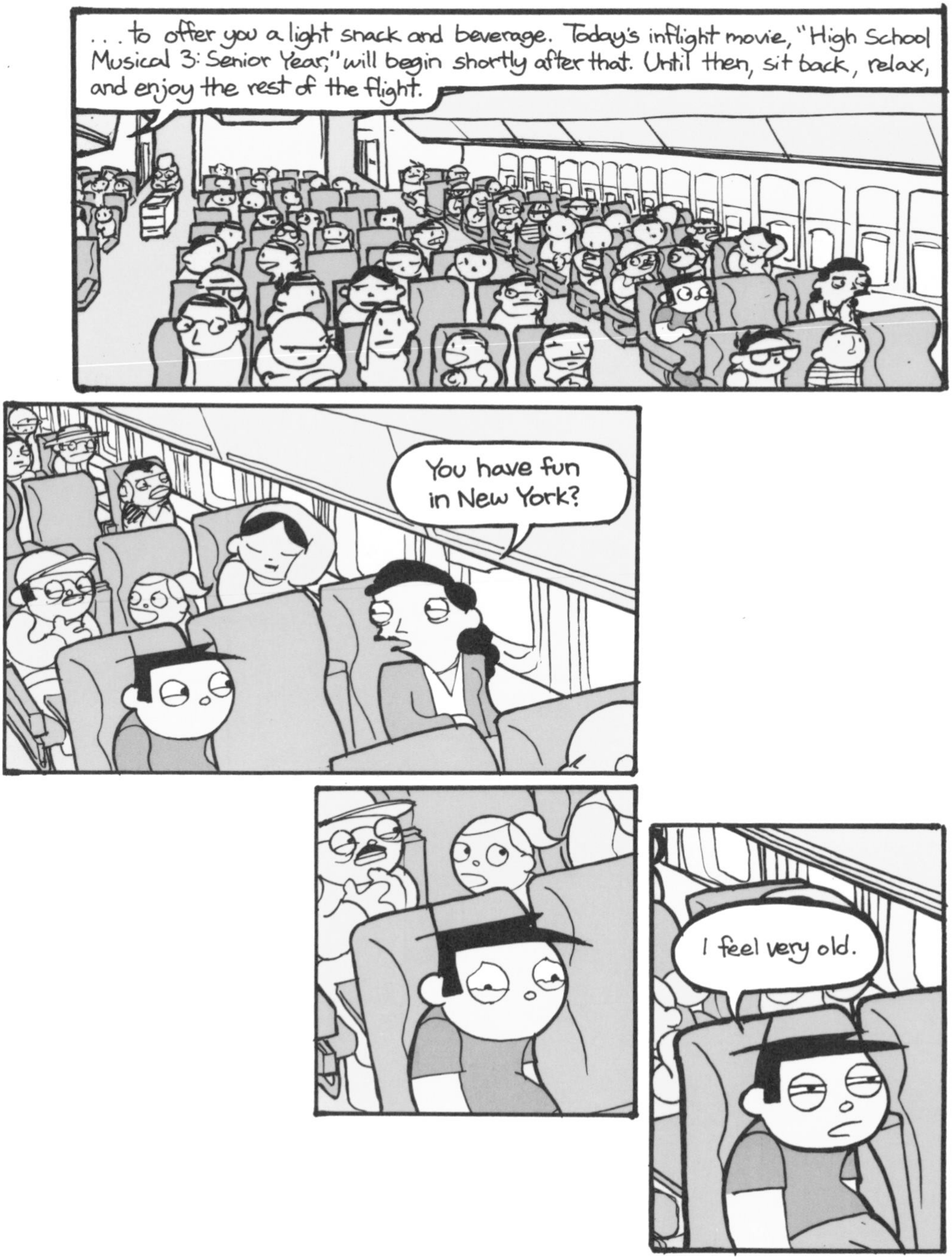
. . . to offer you a light snack and beverage. Today's inflight movie, "High School Musical 3: Senior Year," will begin shortly after that. Until then, sit back, relax, and enjoy the rest of the flight.
You have fun in New York?
I feel very old.

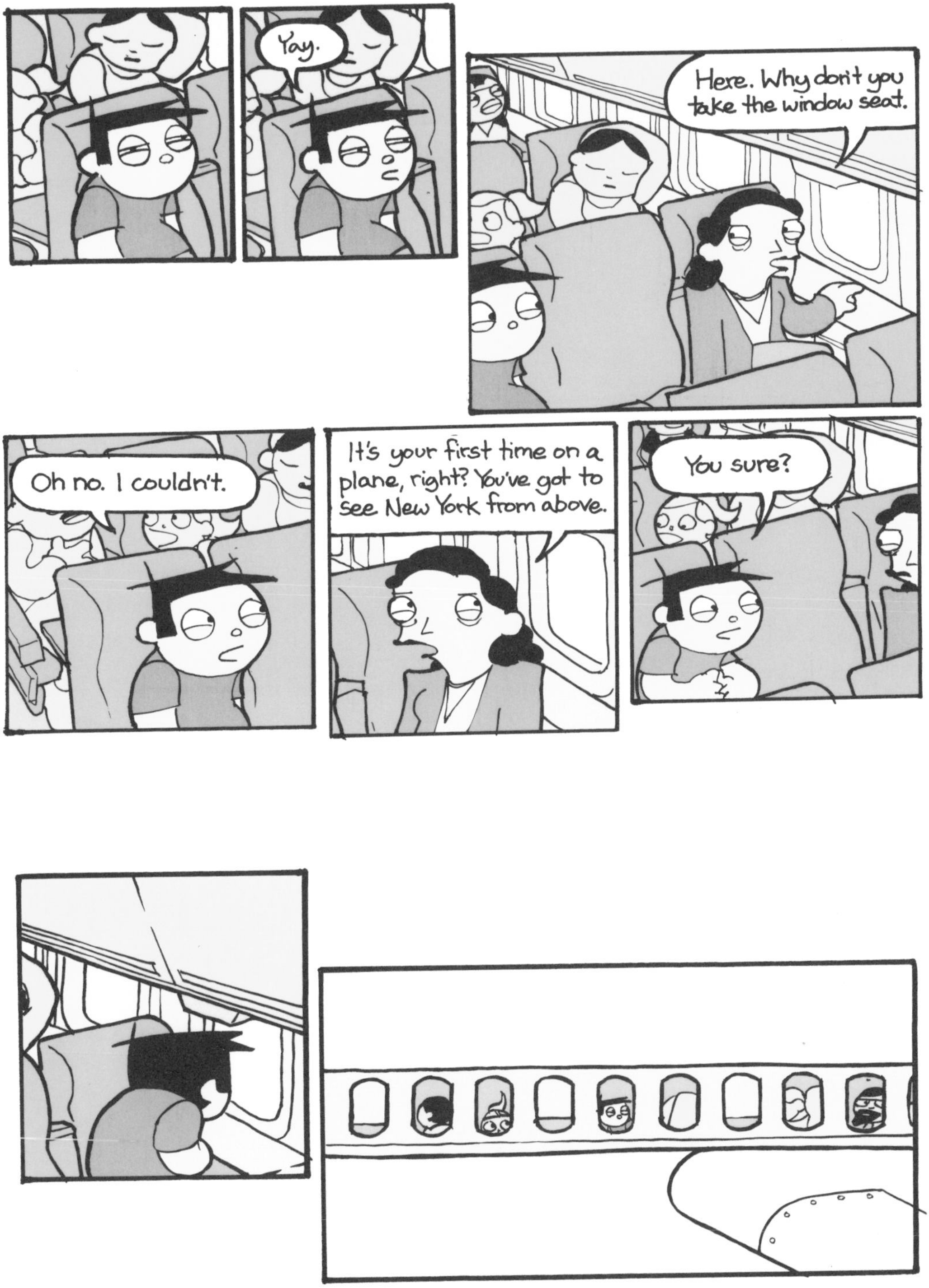
Yay.
Here. Why don't you take the window seat.
Oh no. I couldn't.
It's your first time on a plane, right? You've got to see New York from above.
You sure?

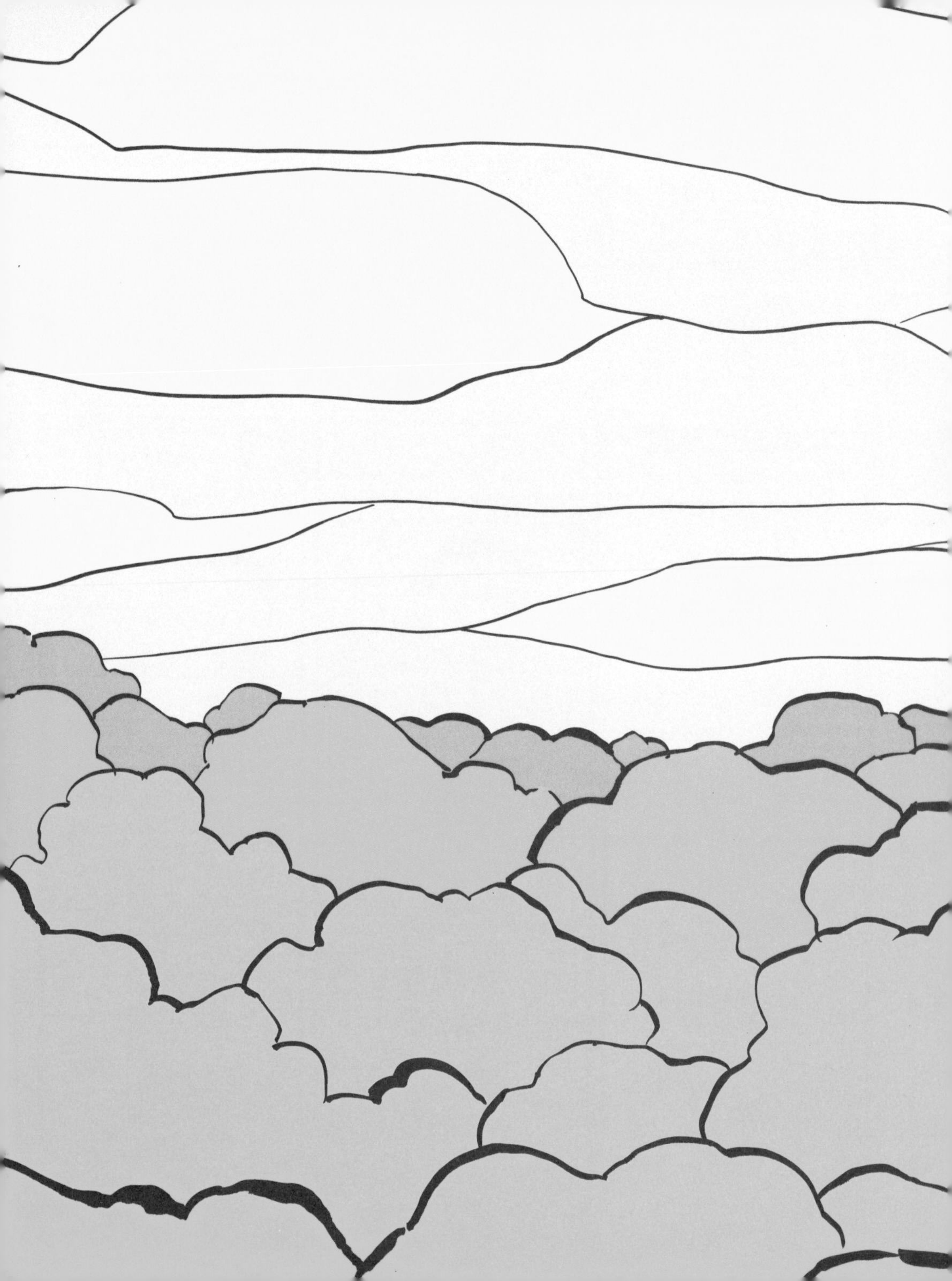

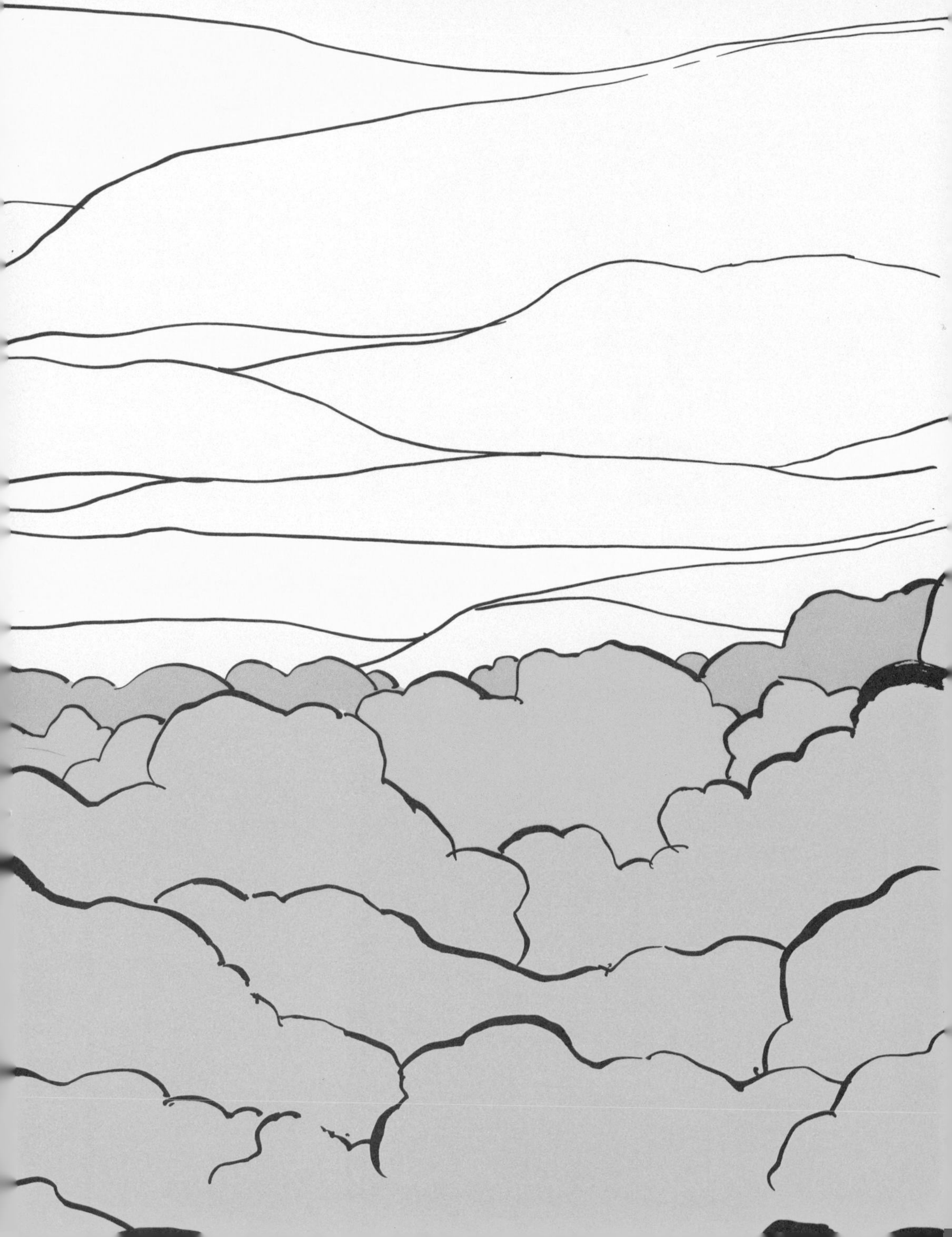

ABOUT THE AUTHOR

Jason Shiga was born and raised in Oakland, California, where he now lives. He graduated from the University of California at Berkeley in 1998, where he majored in pure mathematics. He is the author of more than twenty comic books and graphic novels, including *Fleep*, *Bookhunter*, and *Meanwhile*. He is also the inventor of the greedy mug, the bus clock, three board games, two card tricks, and the world's second-largest interactive comic, which spans twenty-five square feet. His puzzles and mazes have appeared in *McSweeney's* and *Nickelodeon Magazine*.

Empire State was inspired by a real-life Greyhound bus trip from Oakland to New York. The art was drawn on copy paper with a yellow No. 2 pencil. It was then inked over a lightbox with a series 222 size 2 Winsor & Newton brush and lettered with a Micron 08 felt-tip pen. The colors were then applied digitally by artist John Pham.

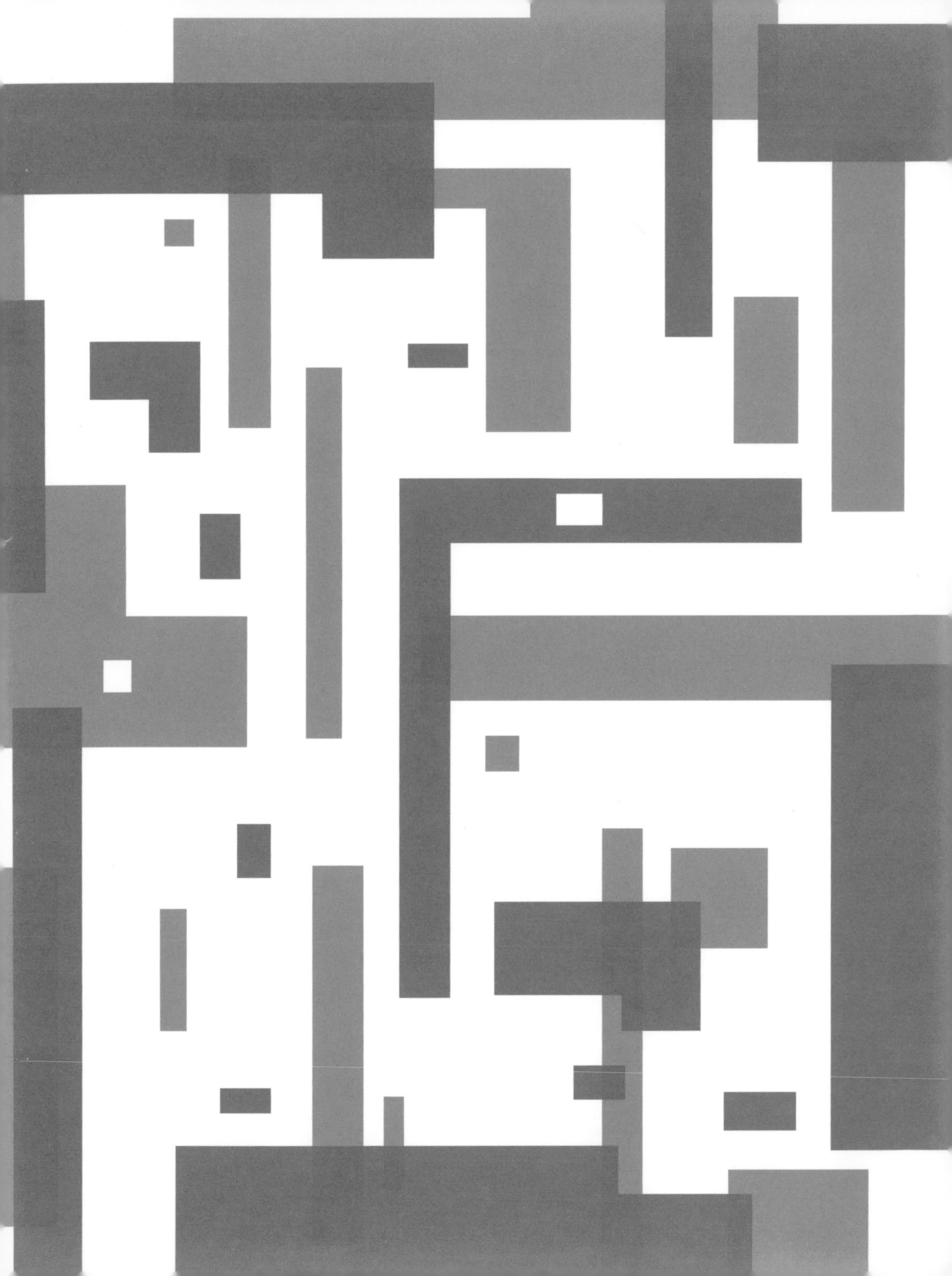

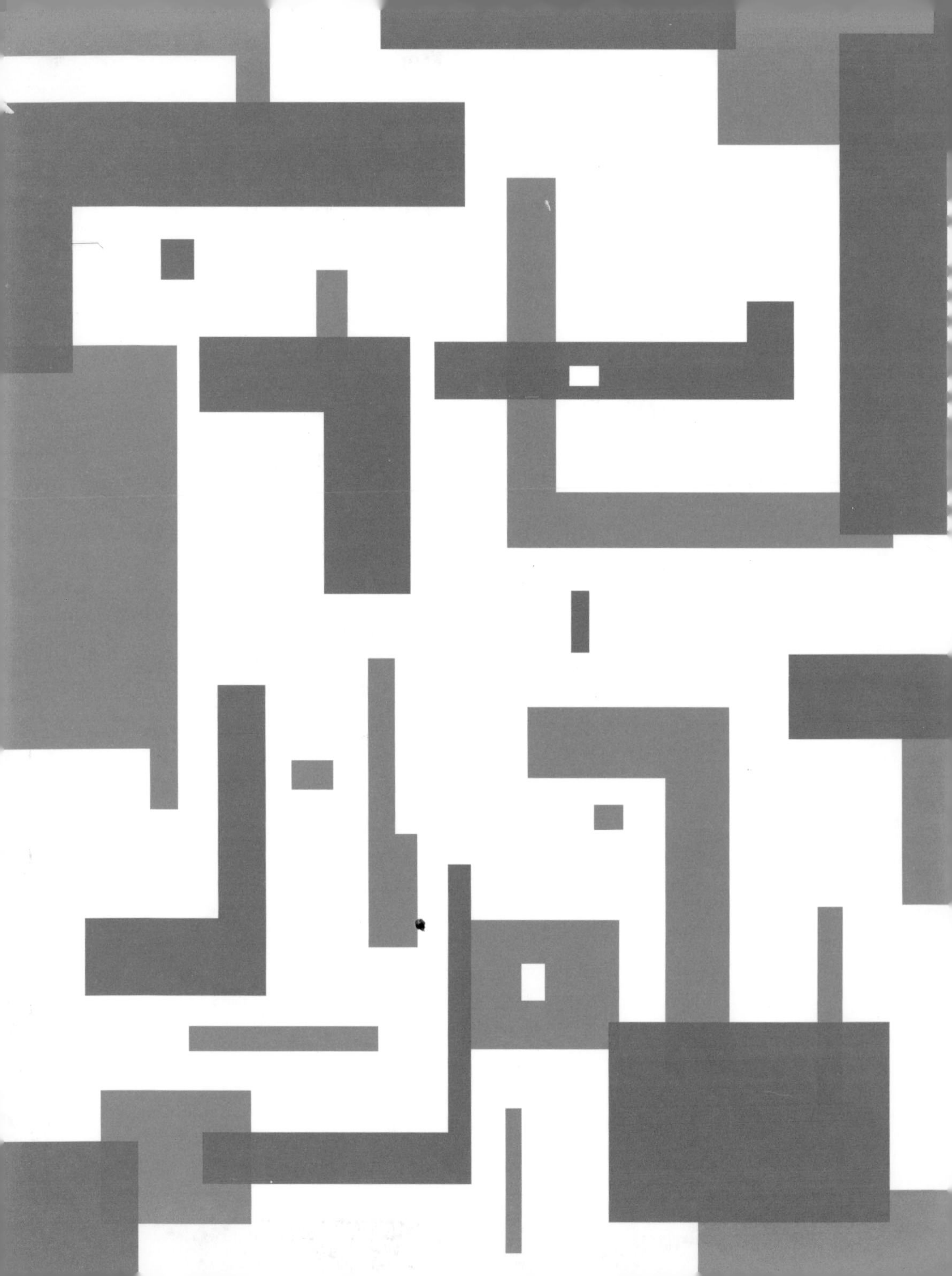